# LIVING
## IN THE
# CROSSHAIRS

# LIVING
## IN THE
# CROSSHAIRS

*THE UNTOLD STORIES OF*
*ANTI-ABORTION TERRORISM*

DAVID S. COHEN
AND
KRYSTEN CONNON

OXFORD
UNIVERSITY PRESS

# OXFORD
UNIVERSITY PRESS

Oxford University Press is a department of the University of
Oxford. It furthers the University's objective of excellence in research,
scholarship, and education by publishing worldwide.

Oxford   New York

Auckland   Cape Town   Dar es Salaam   Hong Kong   Karachi
Kuala Lumpur   Madrid   Melbourne   Mexico City   Nairobi
New Delhi   Shanghai   Taipei   Toronto

With offices in

Argentina   Austria   Brazil   Chile   Czech Republic   France   Greece
Guatemala   Hungary   Italy   Japan   Poland   Portugal   Singapore
South Korea   Switzerland   Thailand   Turkey   Ukraine   Vietnam

Oxford is a registered trademark of Oxford University Press
in the UK and certain other countries.

Published in the United States of America by
Oxford University Press
198 Madison Avenue, New York, NY 10016

© Oxford University Press 2015

First issued as an Oxford University Press paperback, 2016

Library of Congress Cataloging-in-Publication Data
ISBN 978–0–19–937755–8 (hardcover); 978–0–19–062337–1 (pbk.)

1 3 5 7 9 8 6 4 2
Printed in Canada

*To Jennifer Boulanger*

# CONTENTS

# PREFACE

———— ⊰⊱ ————

Abortion is one of the most common medical procedures in the United States, as three in ten women will have the procedure in their lifetime. Every year, over one million women have an abortion. Since the US Supreme Court decided *Roe v. Wade* in 1973 and decriminalized abortion, there have been over fifty million abortions performed in the United States. Although there is variation, women of all ages, religions, races, socioeconomic groups, and family statuses have abortions.[1]

Not only is abortion one of the most common medical procedures, but it is also an incredibly safe procedure in the United States. In fact, abortion is much safer than childbirth. From 1998 to 2005, sixty-four women died from a legal abortion out of over ten million abortions performed; in contrast, over 2,800 women died from childbirth out of thirty-two million pregnancies that resulted in live birth. The rate of death of women undergoing legal abortion is fourteen times lower than the rate of death from childbirth. Moreover, every significant complication associated with pregnancy is more common with childbirth than with abortion.[2]

However, despite abortion being such a common and safe medical procedure, individuals who provide abortion care cannot count on their own personal safety, and partly because abortion providers are not safe, there are very few abortion providers in the United States. Because of their work, abortion providers have been murdered, shot, kidnapped, assaulted, stalked, and subjected to death threats. Their clinics have been bombed, attacked with noxious chemicals, invaded, vandalized, burglarized, and set ablaze. Individual abortion providers have been picketed at home and have received harassing mail and phone calls. Their family members have been followed where they work, their children have been protested at school, and their neighbors' privacy has been invaded. Partly as a result of this terrorism, medical facilities providing abortion services have decreased by almost 40% since 1982, 89% of counties in the United States have no abortion provider, and only 14% of obstetrician-gynecologists perform the procedure.[3]

This book tells the stories of abortion providers targeted by anti-abortion harassment in these extreme ways, explores how this harassment seriously affects their lives, and offers suggestions as to what the legal system can do about it.

# Introduction

ON SUNDAY, MAY 31, 2009, in Wichita, Kansas, anti-abortion extremist Scott Roeder assassinated Dr. George Tiller. That morning, Dr. Tiller was in his church foyer awaiting the beginning of services, having completed his duties as an usher. As the pastor began the music signaling the start of services, Roeder, who had been sitting in the adjacent sanctuary waiting for Dr. Tiller, walked through the doors into the foyer. He walked straight to Dr. Tiller, pulled a gun from his pocket, pressed the barrel against Dr. Tiller's forehead just above his right eye, and pulled the trigger. Dr. Tiller dropped to the floor, dead from the single gunshot.[1]

George Tiller was not the victim of a random act of violence; instead, he was murdered because he had become one of the most prominent abortion providers in the country. His medical practice started in 1970 when he took over his father's family medicine clinic. Over the years, Dr. Tiller's practice grew to include abortion care, and he eventually converted the general family medicine practice into a clinic that provided only abortion care.[2]

Dr. Tiller was at the center of the national controversy over abortion because of the particular nature of his clinic. As a result of both Kansas law and Dr. Tiller's compassion for patients in difficult situations, Dr. Tiller became an expert in late abortion. Like doctors in other clinics, Dr. Tiller performed routine and less controversial abortions in the first and second trimesters of pregnancy; however, unlike most other physicians, Dr. Tiller was both willing and able to perform abortions later in pregnancy. Women came to Dr. Tiller from around the country for abortions because of extreme fetal anomalies and severe maternal health complications that developed after the sixth month of pregnancy. For these women, Dr. Tiller was both a compassionate physician and one of their only options.[3]

However, to those who opposed abortion, Dr. Tiller became a national symbol of everything wrong with a country that permitted abortion. For instance, in the years preceding Dr. Tiller's murder, Bill O'Reilly, the nationally syndicated talk show personality and *Fox News* prime-time host, railed against Dr. Tiller. O'Reilly mentioned Dr. Tiller on his program twenty-nine times between 2005 and the month before Dr. Tiller's murder, repeatedly referring to Dr. Tiller as "Tiller the Baby Killer." O'Reilly accused Dr. Tiller of "operating a death mill," "executing babies about to be born," and "destroy[ing] fetuses for just about any reason right up until the birth date." In one particularly noteworthy rant, O'Reilly proclaimed, "If I could get my hands on Tiller—well, you know. Can't be vigilantes. Can't do that. It's just a figure of speech. But despicable? Oh, my God. Oh, it doesn't get worse. Does it get worse? No."[4]

As Dr. Tiller's abortion practice gained prominence, both Dr. Tiller and his clinic were the victims of many serious attacks and threats at the hands of anti-abortion[5] protesters. In 1986, Dr. Tiller's clinic was bombed, affecting two-thirds of the clinic structure and causing $100,000 in damage. In the summer of 1991, Operation Rescue, a New York-based anti-abortion group launched in 1986,[6] descended on Dr. Tiller's clinic and staged its largest protest ever. For six weeks, in what Operation Rescue called its "Summer of Mercy," hundreds of protesters repeatedly blocked the entrance to Dr. Tiller's clinic. The massive demonstration resulted in 2,700 arrests and culminated in a gathering of 25,000 anti-abortion activists at the Wichita State University football stadium.[7]

After the "Summer of Mercy," the attacks on Dr. Tiller became even more extreme. In 1993, Dr. Tiller was shot at point-blank range in both arms while leaving his clinic for the evening. In 1998, Dr. Tiller's clinic received a letter warning that it would be the target of an anthrax attack.[8] In 2006, Operation Rescue used an obscure provision of Kansas law to convene a citizen grand jury and investigate Dr. Tiller for the death of one of his patients; the grand jury investigation was short-lived and did not issue an indictment against Dr. Tiller. Throughout the early 2000s, avowedly anti-abortion Kansas Attorney General Phill Kline led multiple investigations into Dr. Tiller, his patients, and his clinic, none of which resulted in any legal action against Dr. Tiller.[9] Kline's successor, Paul Morrison, filed nineteen misdemeanor charges against Dr. Tiller in 2007, alleging that Dr. Tiller sought legally mandated second opinions from a physician with whom he had a financial relationship. After a widely publicized trial in early 2009, Dr. Tiller was acquitted of all wrongdoing.[10]

Dr. Tiller also experienced attacks and threats that, although they garnered less attention, nonetheless affected his day-to-day life. He was the subject of repeated death threats, as were members of his family and clinic staff. Old West-style "Wanted" posters with Dr. Tiller's name, picture, and personal information appeared throughout Wichita. The signs offered a vague "reward" for Dr. Tiller. Anti-abortion demonstrators picketed Dr. Tiller's home and stalked his wife. They also repeatedly showed up at Dr. Tiller's church, harassing the congregants and interrupting services.[11]

Dr. Tiller significantly altered his life to deal with the constant harassment and threats. He outfitted his vehicles with armored protection, hired lawyers to protect him, and bought expensive bulletproof glass and security systems. As a result of the threats, Dr. Tiller lived with US Marshal protection at various times in his life. In addition, Dr. Tiller wore a bulletproof vest to work, strategically took different routes on his way to the clinic, and usually drove in the right-hand lane because a security expert had told him this technique gave potential attackers fewer angles of approach.[12]

Dr. Tiller's experiences with these constant threats, harassment, and attacks took place against a backdrop of increasing violence against abortion providers in the United States. Starting in the 1970s and escalating through the 1980s, abortion clinics regularly suffered bombings, arsons, and chemical weapon attacks committed by anti-abortion protesters. Protesters also developed intricate methods to physically blockade entrances to clinics, including chaining themselves underneath cars and placing their heads in cement blocks deposited in front of clinic doorways. Throughout the 1980s, anti-abortion protesters also targeted individual abortion providers by, for example, making death threats against doctors and clinic workers.[13]

In the early 1990s, anti-abortion harassment escalated. In 1993, Dr. David Gunn became the first abortion provider to be murdered by an anti-abortion extremist. Dr. Gunn provided abortions in Pensacola, Florida, and was murdered after anti-abortion protestors hanged an effigy of him and posted "Wanted" flyers of him around town. In mid-1994, Dr. John Britton and retired Air Force Lieutenant Colonel James Barrett, who worked as a volunteer escort for the clinic where Dr. Britton performed abortions, were murdered in front of the same clinic in Pensacola where Dr. Gunn was murdered. At the end of 1994, two receptionists at different clinics in the Boston area, Shannon Lowney and Leanne Nichols, were shot and killed in an attack that concluded with the murderer driving to Norfolk, Virginia, and firing shots at a clinic there. In 1998, a clinic in Birmingham, Alabama, was bombed, killing Robert Sanderson, the clinic's part-time security guard. Later in 1998, a sniper murdered Dr. Barnett Slepian by shooting him through his kitchen window while he was preparing dinner. With Dr. Tiller's murder in 2009, the total number of confirmed abortion-related murders in the United States stood at eight.[14]

That total changed on November 27, 2015, when Robert Dear attacked the Planned Parenthood clinic in Colorado Springs, Colorado. Over the course of five hours, Dear shot twelve people, injuring nine and killing three—Garrett Swasey, a police officer who was one of the first responders, and Ke'arre Stewart and Jennifer Markovsky, friends of clinic patients. As of the writing of this updated introduction, Dear's trial has not yet happened, but information has surfaced indicating that Dear harbored intense anti-abortion sentiments and was motivated to attack the abortion clinic because of those beliefs.[15]

These murders have not been the only incidents of violence against individual abortion providers. Other providers have been kidnapped, shot, bombed, and attacked. Scott Roeder, Dr. Tiller's assassin, existed on the fringes of this violent anti-abortion movement in the years before he ultimately killed Dr. Tiller. After flirting with the militia movement in the early 1990s, Roeder began on his path of anti-abortion violence.[16] In the mid-1990s, he associated with several prominent violent anti-abortion activists and threatened a Kansas City abortion doctor at his clinic. In 1996, police found bomb-making materials in Roeder's car, which Roeder admitted he intended to use against an abortion clinic. He was convicted and sentenced to twenty-four months of probation for using explosives, but the Kansas Court of Appeals ultimately overturned the conviction.[17]

Roeder became more involved in the anti-abortion movement after this incident. He began associating with Operation Rescue and posting his thoughts about Dr. Tiller on various websites. In 2009, he was in the courtroom during the trial over Dr. Tiller's alleged relationship with a consulting physician and reacted angrily when Dr. Tiller was acquitted. Roeder picketed Dr. Tiller's clinic in Wichita and demonstrated outside of Dr. Tiller's church on Sundays. In the weeks preceding Dr. Tiller's murder, Roeder twice vandalized a clinic in Kansas City, something he had done multiple times before.[18]

After shooting and killing Dr. Tiller on May 31, 2009, Roeder was quickly apprehended and brought to trial. At his trial, he attempted to use a "necessity" defense, claiming that murdering Dr. Tiller was necessary to save the thousands of babies that he believed Dr. Tiller murdered with his abortion practice. The judge rejected this defense, and the jury ultimately convicted Roeder of first-degree murder. Roeder was sentenced to life in prison with the possibility of parole after fifty years. A federal grand jury investigated whether Roeder conspired with any individual or group to kill Dr. Tiller, but there is no public information about the results of that investigation.[19]

Until the 2015 Colorado Springs shootings, Dr. Tiller's murder had been the most high-profile act of anti-abortion violence to occur in the 2000s. With Robert Dear's attack and the number of abortion-related murders now at eleven, renewed attention has been focused on the most violent anti-abortion crimes. According to the most recent statistics available from the National Abortion Federation, from 2010 to 2015 there were 14 attempted or successful bombings and arsons; 145 acts of vandalism; 621 incidents of trespassing; 15 clinic invasions; 2 anthrax/bioterrorism threats; 21 incidents of assault and battery; 111 death threats or other threats of harm; 22 bomb threats; 36 acts of burglary; and 45 incidents of stalking.[20]

The spike in these numbers is partially attributable to a coordinated campaign against Planned Parenthood's abortion practices that emerged in the summer of 2015. The campaign was spearheaded by the Center for Medical Progress, a fake bio-tech company that infiltrated abortion clinics and abortion provider conferences. The Center surreptitiously video-recorded thousands of hours of conversations with abortion providers and their associates and then released several videos online purporting to show that Planned Parenthood violated various laws regarding fetal tissue donation.[21]

Despite being repeatedly discredited as deceptively manipulated and false, the videos continue to have a profound effect on abortion clinics and providers. The individual abortion providers who appeared in the videos have been threatened and harassed. Clinics, both Planned Parenthood and independent, have been victims of arson and vandalism. States have launched investigations, all of which, as of the writing of this update, have found that Planned Parenthood has not violated the law. Congress has also jumped into the mix, with the House of Representatives forming the Select Investigative Panel on Infant Lives. The Panel's investigation is ongoing and has raised concerns about abortion providers' personal information being used against them in possibly nefarious ways.[22]

The National Abortion Federation has documented the effect these videos have had on anti-abortion violence and harassment. Since the videos were released, direct threats against providers have skyrocketed. Of particular note is the rise in online threats, which have gone from double-digit totals in previous years to more than 25,000 in the last few weeks of 2015. Perhaps most concerning though is that Robert Dear's murder spree can be directly linked to the videos, as he reportedly screamed "no more baby parts" to police upon being arrested, a clear reference to the content of the attack videos.[23]

## Targeted Harassment of Abortion Providers

Extreme forms of violence and aggression against individuals involved in abortion care, like Dr. Tiller's assassination, make local, if not national, headlines when they occur. But these extreme examples hardly represent the full extent of the ways in which abortion opponents terrorize providers. Other forms of harassment occur much more frequently but go almost completely unnoticed in national headlines. While a media outlet will occasionally feature an in-depth story about a particular provider and her day-to-day struggles dealing with harassment from abortion opponents, this type of harassment usually flies under the radar of the national consciousness and discourse surrounding abortion. Based on interviews with abortion providers from around the country, this book rectifies this missing element in the national story about abortion by telling and analyzing providers' stories of the targeted harassment they face.

To the extent that people are aware of anti-abortion protest and harassment beyond the high-profile attacks and murders, they are most likely familiar with what this book calls *general clinic protest*. General clinic protest can take many forms, but the most common type occurs when abortion opponents protest in front of a clinic. They do so for many reasons, including to express their opposition to abortion to both clinic employees and passersby to try to change the minds of women entering the clinic so they do not obtain an abortion, to "bear witness" to what they believe is a mass slaughter, and to participate in the national movement to end abortion.[24]

General clinic protest has serious effects on women seeking abortion, people providing abortion, the clinics and offices where abortion occurs, and the national debate about the issue. These effects have been well documented.[25]

This book is about something different, what we call *targeted harassment of abortion providers*. This term refers to acts of anti-abortion protest that are or are perceived to be specifically focused on individual abortion providers. Two parts of this definition require explanation.

First, since targeted harassment of abortion providers is or is perceived to be directed toward individuals, this type of protest differs from general clinic protest, which is focused on the clinic, the clinic's patients, or the larger issue of abortion, not the specific individuals who work inside the clinic. Targeted harassment of abortion providers also differs from anti-abortion rallies or political events that are focused on the general issue of abortion. These categories are not hermetically sealed as general clinic protest and political rallies can also target individuals, but the distinction is important.

Data from the Feminist Majority Foundation confirms what is clear from the most recent report from the National Abortion

Federation—that individualized targeting has been on the rise. In 2014, the Feminist Majority Foundation surveyed abortion clinics in the United States and found that there are "significantly higher levels of threats and targeted intimidation of doctors and staff than in prior years." Moreover, "the overall percentage of clinics impacted by these types of threats and targeted intimidation tactics increased dramatically since 2010, from 26.6% of clinics to 51.9% of clinics."[26]

This increase is possibly explained by the fact that, as political scientist Alesha Doan has described, the people who work inside clinics are an effective target for anti-abortion protesters. Harassing them "is relatively cheap to implement, generates publicity, and introduces costs to clinic employees." It can also produce "more immediate" results than "long-term legislation aimed at incrementally restricting services." Moreover, abortion providers are nongovernmental actors who often do not have the resources or political pull to effectively curb harassment and are vulnerable because "they must contend with it on a regular basis."[27]

Second, the targeted harassment that is the focus of this book includes harassment against anyone who works in providing abortion care. Some people within the world of abortion use the term "abortion provider" to mean only doctors who perform the procedure. However, we use the term more broadly to encompass the many people who work to provide women a safe, caring, and medically-skilled environment in which to have an abortion. This includes not only the doctors who perform abortions but also referring physicians, nurses, physician assistants, administrative staff, counselors, clinic owners, security guards, and volunteer escorts and supporters. All of these people have been the subject of individualized targeted harassment by anti-abortion protesters. After all, in the brief account of abortion violence provided earlier, four of the eight murder victims who were abortion providers were not doctors. These four—a volunteer escort in Pensacola, two clinic receptionists in the Boston area, and a clinic security officer in Birmingham—were all murdered because of their role in providing safe and competent abortion care. Their deaths, along with the targeted harassment experiences of providers who are not physicians, are no less important in understanding the ways in which the lives of individuals involved with abortion provision are affected by anti-abortion protest.[28]

Based on interviews with abortion providers from around the country, this book seeks to show that targeted harassment of abortion providers has been and continues to be a serious issue. It exists in a wide variety of forms all over the country and can profoundly affect the daily lives of abortion providers everywhere. Contrary to some commonly held assumptions, this harassment is not a relic of some distant past, is not directed solely against high-profile doctors like Dr. George Tiller, and is not limited to only the most conservative parts of this country. Rather, it is a severe, ongoing, and nationwide problem that needs to be addressed.[29]

## Legal Response

In addition to highlighting abortion providers' experiences with targeted harassment, this book explores various legal responses to targeted harassment of abortion providers and ways to improve the law. Providers interact with the law in various ways. In a country like the United States in which federal, state, and local governments often tackle the same problems, the legal response to the targeted harassment of abortion providers invokes a patchwork of laws and people enforcing those laws. Even though law alone cannot stop the targeted harassment and violence that providers face, law can improve so that more abortion providers can perform this legal and common medical procedure free of fear and harassment.

Law can address targeted harassment in many ways. Basic criminal laws in every jurisdiction, such as laws that criminalize murder, arson, burglary, assault, and trespassing, can be an effective response to targeted harassment of abortion providers when that harassment constitutes a crime and when the person responsible for the crime can be identified. However, targeted harassment involving crime does not always end in a conviction. For a variety of reasons, many crimes against abortion providers remain unresolved—the suspect is unknown, the police refuse to take sides when the anti-abortion protester says one thing and the abortion provider says another, or the police have an attitude that pursuing such crimes is not worth their time or that abortion providers should expect to deal with anti-abortion crime specifically because they work in abortion care.

Beyond run-of-the-mill criminal law, there are other ways that law addresses targeted harassment of abortion providers. Perhaps the most important law relating to anti-abortion protest is the Freedom of Access to Clinic Entrances Act (FACE). Signed into law in 1994, FACE is a federal law that prohibits using force, threat of force, or physical obstruction to injure, intimidate, or interfere with anyone trying to provide or access reproductive health services. FACE violations can result in criminal penalties or a civil lawsuit.[30] In some circumstances, federal law also provides protection for abortion providers from the US Marshals Service.

State and local laws also address targeted harassment of abortion providers. Some laws regulate how close protesters can stand in relation to an abortion clinic, its patients, or its workers. Other laws address protesting in a residential neighborhood, with some prohibiting it altogether and others regulating it, such as requiring protesters to keep moving or to be there only during certain hours. Still other laws give providers the option to sue protesters for violating their privacy or harming them in other ways. Sometimes providers can also obtain injunctions from courts to prevent these harms from happening again.

This mix of legal response is subject to the usual vagaries of the legal system. Individuals within the legal system, from police officers to district attorneys to judges to politicians, are often constrained by time and resources. Moreover, they may have their own prejudices about abortion that influence how they respond to any situation. Lawyers usually cost significant amounts of money, which means it can be difficult for an abortion provider to access help in navigating the legal system. And all of this occurs against the backdrop of the First Amendment guarantee of freedom of speech, which protects abortion opponents in certain expressions of anti-abortion speech.

This description of the legal responses and issues related to targeted harassment of abortion providers just scratches the surface of the complexities that will be addressed throughout this book. Collectively, the abortion providers that we interviewed have experiences with almost every avenue of legal redress for the harassment they face. Their stories help inform the analysis in the second half of this book, which looks at how the legal system's different approaches work for abortion providers and then shows that these systems can improve.

## Current Significance

The two overarching messages of this book—that targeted harassment of abortion providers continues to be a serious problem and that the legal system's response can improve—are important for several reasons. First, targeted harassment of abortion providers left unaddressed by the legal system can drastically hinder abortion access. Many of the providers we interviewed told stories of colleagues they knew who would not work in abortion care because they feared the possibility of harassment.

A recent study by sociologist Lori Freedman bears this out. She looked at the reasons why doctors who were trained in abortion in their residency did or did not perform abortions in their practice. Freedman came across several doctors who voiced concerns about targeted harassment. One doctor who had previously provided abortions stopped doing so "because of the violence of the anti-abortion movement, which she felt could put her family at risk." Another doctor started a job in a new medical practice soon after Dr. Slepian was murdered and said, "[A]fter that experience … it wasn't worth it. [It's a] small town, and I didn't want to have to worry about all of that—you know, get a [bulletproof] vest and all that." Freedman concluded that, although fear of violence and harassment was not the most prominent reason doctors did not provide abortion, it was a serious concern for some doctors, particularly those in rural areas. Even though targeted harassment of abortion providers does not deter all providers, it does deter some, contributing to the decreasing accessibility of abortion.[31]

Second, people providing basic medical services should not be harassed for doing so, and law and society should understand the nature of this harassment and respond by protecting providers. At its most basic level, abortion is a medical procedure that more than 50 million women have obtained safely and legally since *Roe v. Wade*.[32] It is one of the most common procedures in the United States. Physicians and others who provide abortion should not suffer threats, harassment, intimidation, and violence for providing a basic and common medical service. The politicization and stigmatization surrounding abortion do not justify terrorizing the lives of the people providing this legal procedure. Moreover, harassment reaches beyond just the providers. Providers' neighbors and families, including young children and elderly parents, often feel the brunt of the targeted harassment as abortion opponents target them in an effort to coerce the provider. Very few notions of justice would countenance this type of harassment in the context of lawful medical care; yet despite the extent that anti-abortion harassment permeates providers' daily lives, few people and legal actors understand the true nature of life as an abortion provider.[33]

Third, in the midst of the current "war on women," it is important to understand yet another way that women's rights are threatened and how law plays a role. Women's issues have dominated the political landscape in the early 2010s, from issues of pay equity to insurance coverage for contraception to the definition of "rape" to whether immigrants and lesbian-gay-bisexual-transgender people should receive benefits under the Violence Against Women Act. Perhaps most prominent, though, have been issues of reproductive rights. Attacks on abortion have become commonplace in state legislatures. In fact, states enacted 288 abortion restrictions between 2010 and 2015, accounting for more than a quarter of all abortion restrictions since *Roe v. Wade*.[34]

The current political climate places this book's two messages in tension. On the one hand, understanding targeted harassment of abortion providers is undeniably important so that people are exposed to all aspects of this larger war on women. On the other hand, the argument that legal responses can improve to address targeted harassment is a difficult pill to swallow in an environment in which law is also being used to restrict women's rights, particularly around abortion and other reproductive health issues. If the political system is currently using law to restrict access to abortion, then how can we seriously hope that law can be used to help abortion providers and, by extension, help the women who need access to abortion care? There are two main responses to this conundrum.[35]

First, people providing medical care should never have to worry about individual safety and security because of their work, even in an environment seemingly opposed to abortion rights. Second, educating the general public about the ways that abortion providers are harassed, threatened, and terrorized could shift public opinion and encourage legal responses that better protect abortion providers, thus improving abortion access more generally. In other words, if people understood the truly unsettling extent of the methods of attack in this war on women, the entire war might not be so appealing.

## This Interview-Based Study

This book delivers its two messages by presenting and analyzing original research drawn from interviews with abortion providers across the country From the middle of 2011 through the beginning of 2014 (before the attack videos were released in 2015),[36] we interviewed eighty-seven abortion providers about their experiences with anti-abortion protest and harassment. All but five of those interviewed detailed experiences with targeted harassment. Of the eighty-two who spoke about their experiences as targets, seventy-five described experiences that occurred within ten years of the interview.

For a variety of reasons, including the privacy and safety concerns at the heart of this book, we were not able to interview a random representative sample of abortion providers from around the country; nonetheless, we culled a diverse cross section of abortion providers in the United States,[37] including physicians, other medical professionals, staff, executive directors, and volunteers. We interviewed people who were new to the field of abortion and those who had been working in abortion for more than half a century. We interviewed people who were young, old, and everywhere in between. We interviewed men and women of various races, religions, ethnicities, and sexual orientations.

The providers in this study have worked in the field of abortion in thirty-four states. Some have worked in the same state for their entire career, while others have worked in multiple states over the course of their time as an abortion provider, often working in more than one state at the same time. All of the providers worked in urban or suburban areas of various population sizes, which is consistent with the fact that abortion clinics are concentrated in only 11% of the counties in the United States.[38] Nonetheless, the providers live in every type of locale—from dense urban centers to suburban areas to rural farmland.

The providers also work or worked in a variety of abortion-care settings. For many reasons that have been documented extensively, abortion provision in the United States has moved away from the hospital setting and into separate clinics that specialize in abortion and reproductive healthcare.[39] Some doctors continue to provide abortions in hospitals or their own private practices, but most abortions occur in specialty clinics. These clinics can be divided into roughly two different types—those that are affiliated with Planned Parenthood and those that are independently owned and operated. The people we interviewed have provided abortions in all of these settings—hospitals, Planned Parenthood health centers, independent clinics, and private medical practices.

The interviews were structured, but open-ended. All but fifteen of the interviews were conducted in person and at the provider's preferred location, mostly in providers' places of business but also in their homes or convenient public spaces. We approached each interview with general topics to address but did not use a rigid format to be followed regardless of the responses. Rather, the interview subjects responded and told their stories as they saw fit, and we then asked follow-up questions as necessary to make sure we covered all of the topics. The basic topics we covered were providers' experiences with protest generally and targeted harassment in particular; their reactions to the harassment they have experienced; interactions with law, if any; and the providers' thoughts about their interactions with law. Given the nature of the topic, the subjects' varying approaches to being interviewed, and their different depths of experience with the topic, the interviews ranged from fifteen minutes to over two hours and revealed many unexpected aspects of life as an abortion provider.

Also, given the nature of targeted harassment, we offered the participating providers confidentiality and anonymity. Because we did not want this research to put any provider at risk, almost all of the names in this book are fictional and almost all of the descriptions of the providers are generalized and nonspecific.[40] To the extent that providers' stories have details that could possibly identify them, such information has been changed without any indication in the text that we have done so. We have not altered the nature of the stories told here, only identifying details.[41]

Participating in a study like this is risky for providers. A book detailing the ways that anti-abortion protesters harass abortion providers and then analyzing the effect of that harassment could inspire other protesters to pursue new avenues of harassment. This is not a risk that we take lightly, so we discussed it in detail with all of the people we interviewed. Not a single person declined to continue the interview after discussing this as everyone felt that the benefit of telling these stories and thinking about how law can better respond to this harassment was of utmost importance. The providers felt strongly that their stories needed to be shared with the public.

Before each of the interviews, we discussed another major risk with the providers. We warned the providers that talking about their experiences with targeted harassment could be emotionally difficult. For many people we talked with, it was just that. They opened up to us about some of the most difficult moments in their lives. They told us stories that they had told very few others. They cried about personal memories and became angry about the way they are treated. They trusted us with details of moments in their lives when they felt vulnerable. They welcomed us into their homes and offices, two places many providers vigilantly guard precisely because of the targeted harassment they face. Without any compensation in return, they were generous with their time and hospitality in ways we never could have imagined. And all this openness, trust, and generosity came to us even though we had not met most of the providers in person before the interview and had only corresponded with them for a short time by phone or e-mail. The providers participated in this manner because they trusted us to listen to their stories and use what we learned from the interviews to improve their lives. We hope this book does their trust justice.

## Key Findings

This book has several key findings. These findings are explained in detail throughout the book but summarized here to frame what will come in the following chapters.

First, targeted harassment of abortion providers takes an incredible variety of forms, from high-profile incidents like the murders described earlier in this introduction to more routine and private events like picketing at someone's home or church. The variety of harassment tactics detailed in the interviews is staggering. In almost every interview, a different type of targeted anti-abortion harassment emerged. Many tactics are repeated around the country, but many others are unique to particular individuals or locations.

Second, targeted harassment of abortion providers is ongoing and can happen to anyone associated with abortion provision. This finding calls into question many common misperceptions about abortion-related harassment. Many people believe that targeted harassment is a relic of a past when federal law was silent on the issue, Operation Rescue was more active, and doctors were more frequently being murdered.[42] These interviews show that this is not true; rather, targeted harassment continues today and can be a major aspect of abortion providers' daily lives. While some of the stories in this book are from decades past, the majority of the experiences told throughout these chapters are much more current.

Moreover, many people believe that targeted harassment is a problem only for doctors and occurs only in the most conservative states or locations in the country. In fact, many of the people we interviewed expressed these beliefs. However, the stories in this book reveal that this is not true. Doctors do experience a great deal of the targeted harassment that occurs, but so do nurses, counselors, administrative staff, executive directors, volunteers, and others associated with abortion provision. Targeted harassment is aimed at every type of provider all around the United States, from populous liberal urban areas to remote conservative rural areas.

The previously described murders illustrate these points. Of the eight murders of abortion providers that are directly attributable to anti-abortion violence, four have been of doctors and four have been of others who work at clinics. With respect to political leanings and geography, five occurred in Kansas, Alabama, and Florida, states generally considered more conservative, but three occurred in Massachusetts and New York, states generally considered more liberal. The stories in this book are likewise not tied to the general political leanings of a particular location.

Third, targeted harassment affects abortion providers' lives in serious ways and invokes a variety of reactions. Many providers report giving the harassment very little thought and just accepting its effects and the risks it poses as a normal part of life, like the everyday risk of being in a traffic accident. Others report a variety of negative emotions, such as being annoyed, angered, or frustrated by the harassment. Still others report much more serious emotions in response, such as living in fear or feeling terrorized.

Regardless of their specific emotional reactions to the targeted harassment, abortion providers report that it often substantially interferes with their lives. Because of targeted harassment, directed at both them and others in their profession, some abortion providers are hypervigilant, alter their routes to and from work and home, hide their identities, refrain from discussing their work publicly, and take other measures to increase their sense of personal safety. The harassment affects providers' personal relationships and home lives, affects their non-abortion-related businesses, and threatens their long-term emotional health. Fearing the worst, some providers wear bulletproof vests and carry concealed weapons.

Despite these negative effects, targeted harassment often strengthens providers' resolve as well as their commitment to providing abortion care. Many providers remain motivated to stay in the field despite the harassment because of their memories of a pre-*Roe v. Wade* era when women were injured or even died from illegal, unsafe abortions. Only a small number report thinking about leaving the work or actually leaving because of targeted harassment.

Fourth, law sometimes adequately addresses targeted harassment, but it can further improve. Many abortion providers told stories of law and law enforcement responding to targeted harassment in ways that significantly helped their lives. Positive responses and interactions occurred all over the country, not only in communities generally perceived as more supportive of abortion rights. The reverse was also true. Providers had negative interactions with law and law enforcement all over the country, not just in communities generally perceived as politically opposed to abortion.

Drawing from these stories, we ultimately propose several reforms. We recognize that these reforms alone are not likely to end targeted harassment, as legal reform cannot accomplish that by itself. But certain reforms can help, such as improving policing, adopting legislation that protects providers and punishes violations more severely, improving providers' access to and reception within the judicial system, and labeling targeted harassment of abortion providers as what it is—terrorism.

Ultimately, the last of these suggestions may be the most important. Though many abortion-rights advocates and some anti-abortion protesters have long used the term "terrorism" to describe the activities documented and analyzed in this book, it has not been universally adopted. In fact, in many contexts, it has been actively resisted. For instance, in March and April 2009, the Department of Homeland

Security released two documents that included "anti-abortion extrem-ism" within a larger discussion of domestic terrorism. As a result, the department faced intense backlash. Because of the public pressure, the department pulled both reports in May 2009[43]—just weeks before Dr. Tiller was murdered by anti-abortion terrorist Scott Roeder. Similarly, there was intense debate following the Colorado Springs kill-ings in 2015 over whether Robert Dear was a terrorist or "just" a crazed lone wolf.[44]

In light of the providers' lived experiences that are analyzed through-out this book, the answer to this debate should be clear—this kind of anti-abortion extremism is terrorism. Although there is no universally accepted understanding of terrorism, one leading definition that most relevantly captures the concept is "the deliberate creation and exploita-tion of fear through violence or the threat of violence in the pursuit of political change." Terrorist acts are so unsettling because they have "far-reaching psychological repercussions beyond the immediate victim or target."[45]

Scott Roeder's murder of Dr. Tiller is an excellent example of how terrorism works. Roeder shot and killed Dr. Tiller in the name of anti-abortion activism. Through this single and deliberate terrorist act, Roeder not only killed Dr. Tiller but also instilled fear through-out almost an entire field of medical professionals and volunteers. Anti-abortion protesters exploit providers' fear of extreme violence, a rational fear based on past violent acts, such as Dr. Tiller's murder, by following providers home from work, screaming at them with their private personal information, picketing their houses, or engaging in almost any of the activities documented in this book. Although a par-ticular action by an anti-abortion protester may not itself be violent, its effectiveness is derived from the threat that it could escalate into the violence to that other abortion providers have faced. As other scholars have demonstrated, there are many objectives and motivations behind the actions of anti-abortion protesters,[46] but one of the central goals is the political and social change of ending abortion. Deliberate creation of fear to enact change: simply put, this is a form of domestic terrorism.

If these interviews and this book could help to influence people in government, media, classrooms, and everywhere else to call targeted harassment of abortion providers "terrorism" rather than "protest," the societal approbation that comes with such a term could influence some people to stop engaging in this behavior. In the meantime, while we are under no illusion that the reforms discussed in this book will put a complete end to abortion-related terrorism, we do hope that these suggestions help diminish it while also helping to make abortion providers feel safer and more comfortable providing lawful medical care.

## Roadmap

The structure of this book follows its two main messages—that targeted harassment of abortion providers continues to be a serious problem and that the legal system can do a better job of addressing it.

The first half of this book describes and analyzes targeted harassment of abortion providers and the effect that it has on them, starting with Chapter 1, which has seven stories of abortion providers and their experiences with targeted harassment. Chapters 2, 3, and 4 then categorically break down the different types of targeted harassment abortion providers have experienced by examining where it happens, how it occurs, and against whom it is directed. These chapters present a comprehensive look at targeted harassment, answering the question, "What is the targeted harassment that abortion providers experience?" Chapters 5 and 6 finish this portion of the book by looking at providers' various responses to targeted harassment. Chapter 5 illustrates the range of their emotional responses, while Chapter 6 details the ways that abortion providers change their lives in response to targeted harassment. These two chapters answer the question, "How does targeted harassment affect abortion providers?"

The second half of the book focuses on abortion providers' experiences with the legal system. Chapter 7 starts by providing six stories of abortion providers and their experience with the law, and then Chapter 8 breaks down providers' different interactions with the legal system. These stories are supplemented by publicly available resources, such as cases and legislative responses to targeted harassment. Chapter 9 draws on the providers' reactions and thoughts with respect to the legal response to their targeted harassment and suggests reforms based on the providers' experiences.

The conclusion in Chapter 10 looks at reasons why abortion providers continue to provide abortions despite the terrorism they encounter. Though some providers knew of people who had stopped providing abortions because of targeted harassment and one of the providers we interviewed permanently left the field as a direct result of the harassment she endured,[47] everyone else explained why they stayed in this profession: their commitment to their patients, their commitment to women's rights, their refusal to return to the days when women were injured or died from illegal abortion, their refusal to let the terrorists win.

Easing this burden on these dedicated health care providers' lives is the reason we have written this book. No one should have to face this terrorism and exhibit such extraordinary resolve just to provide women with legal, safe, and basic medical care.

# I

---

# Seven Stories of Targeted Harassment

I often say that as an abortion provider, you lose your sense of perspective. You think everybody has the FBI on speed dial on their phone. Doesn't everybody have it on their phone? You forget that it really is a very unique set of circumstances that you work under.

—RACHEL FRIEDMAN

Eliminate the providers and you can have as many clinics as you want, but you won't have someone providing abortions.

—DUSTIN MENENDEZ

ABORTION PROVIDERS FACE RISKS in their lives that most people in most jobs do not. Each of the stories below highlights different parts of the life of an abortion provider who is targeted by anti-abortion protest.

Taken together, the seven people featured here have dealt with arson, murder, assault, stalking, home picketing, business loss, death threats, community protest, religious and racial attacks, hate mail, and targeted Internet postings. They have altered their lives because they are targeted by anti-abortion protesters. Their families and neighbors have also been affected by the targeted harassment in serious and life-changing ways. They have all learned how to live with the risk that comes with their profession, a risk foreign to most other people, especially most other medical professionals. Yet, notwithstanding the widespread effects of the targeted harassment, they all continue to work as abortion providers because they feel it is the right thing to do.

In other words, targeted harassment takes its toll on providers, but it does not stop abortion. In fact, for some providers, targeted harassment increases their resolve and motivates them to continue. These seven abortion providers tell this story.

### Kristina Romero

Kristina Romero has worked in the field of reproductive healthcare for over three decades. She started as a receptionist in a clinic that did not perform abortions and is now a regional director for multiple clinics, a small subset of which offers abortion services. Her clinics serve people from urban, suburban, and rural parts of her politically conservative West South Central state. Though Kristina is responsible for many clinics, her home base is a clinic in the same suburban college town where she has spent her entire career.

Kristina did not experience much protest until the clinic began performing abortions in the late 1990s. Before then, the clinic where she worked provided basic family-planning services and was rarely targeted. "No protesting. Nothing. We were just providing family planning, and the protesters maybe didn't like that, but it didn't motivate them."

When the clinic decided to start offering abortion care, Kristina's nearly twenty years of peace and quiet working in family-planning clinics came to an end. Kristina's "under the radar" clinic was transformed into a focal point for local anti-abortion sentiment. The anti-abortion protest was instantaneous: "When we did our first abortion, which the protesters figured out before we were done with construction of the clinic, they were outside waiting." The new level of protest bothered Kristina's employees, and the first group of them, who had been working with Kristina for years, could "only take so much" and eventually left.

Over time, the protesters began using tactics both to shame patients and to target the clinic's employees. The protesters stand at the entrance to the clinic's parking lot and badger the patients when they come in. "They get screamed at. The protesters write down their license plates. They send them cards. They make phone calls to their homes." Protesters also swarm the clinic and harass the people who work there. "These window blinds," Kristina explained while pointing to the huge windows that surround the conference room table in one of her clinics, "you can pull them down, you can look through them, and you could find the protesters at the windows, looking in."

Kristina herself has been and continues to be subject to targeted harassment. When entering or exiting the clinic, the protesters use Kristina's personal information against her. "They call you by name. They know your kids' names. They know your mom and dad's names. They know where you go to church." Kristina has also received cards in the mail that describe what type of car she drives and where she drives it. To Kristina, this information is proof that someone is following her.

One protester who frequently targets Kristina is a doctor who works at a local hospital. Some of the nurses who work at the same hospital as the doctor also work at Kristina's clinic. When the protester-doctor sees those nurses at the hospital, the protester warns the nurses that he is keeping close tabs on Kristina. He has told the nurses that he knows Kristina's kids' names and where they go to school and that he wants the nurses to let Kristina know that he knows this information about her.

Protesters also individually target others who work with Kristina. She and her coworkers regularly receive e-mail from protesters at their work and personal e-mail accounts. "You'd be sitting there doing your normal work and an e-mail from a protester pops up. That's a little freaky." The protesters have even targeted a volunteer who works at Kristina's clinic. "She was in her eighties, it was her birthday, and the protesters cut the heads off of a bunch of roses and put them on the fence around her home with a card that said, 'Hopefully you'll have another birthday and here's your dead roses.'"

Kristina tries to be civil and ignore the protesters calling her name and addressing her directly, but one day she found it hard to ignore them:

> I came into work one day and there was this guy standing at the end there. They like to hang on the fence. I told him to get off the fence, and he yelled, "Suck my dick." Of course, I went, "What did you say?" Like an idiot. And he screams it again. I'm like, okay, he didn't really say that? But this guy would see me other places outside the clinic and he'd walk by me and say, "I'm still waiting."

Perhaps the riskiest part of Kristina's job is when she drives the doctor to and from the clinic. Because of past violence against abortion providers, the doctor does not drive directly to the clinic. Instead, the doctor drives to another public location to meet Kristina, and then

Kristina drives the doctor to the clinic in her own car. For extra security, Kristina and the doctor vary the locations where they meet. Kristina hopes that with this system in place the protesters do not see the doctor's car, so they cannot use the car to discover the doctor's identity or follow the doctor. This system is not foolproof, and Kristina understands the risks. "That's always that moment when your heart starts beating a little harder."

One of the more vocal protesters at Kristina's clinic has followed Kristina to a pickup location. On more than one occasion, the protester was there with a camera. Kristina joked, "He'd always shoot, but he was luckily shooting with a camera, not a gun." One time, the protester discovered that Kristina's pickup location was going to be a grocery store parking lot. The protester went into the grocery store and tried to convince the store manager to take action because abortion providers were in the parking lot. Luckily for Kristina, the manager did not heed the protester's request and instead called to Kristina to warn her about what was happening.

Because of this protester's attempts to follow her, Kristina has tried even more deceptive measures, including using someone as a decoy. "One time when we went to one of the pickup locations, there was a decoy. I didn't have the doctor. And the protester who had followed me was running through the parking lot down low with his camera." The decoy doctor yelled, "Some guy's running between the cars," so Kristina drove to where the protester was running and pulled up alongside him. Thankfully, the incident did not escalate. When Kristina reached the protester he stopped and "just stood there with his camera."

Kristina has also been followed home. Sometimes when Kristina drives to pick up the doctor, she leaves from her home instead of the clinic:

One day I left to pick up the doctor and I got to the corner of my house and there's a big picture of the doctor with a bullseye on him, and every corner that I turned was another picture, so obviously they'd followed me. And that was probably one of the creepiest days. The pictures were all up the main street I travel on, all the way back to my house.

The signs on Kristina's route were similar to the signs that had appeared before the murders of several of the doctors around the country—large "Wanted" signs with the doctor's name and picture.

Even though the signs showed the doctor's picture and name, it was clear to Kristina that they were targeted at her as well. The posters were stuck in the ground all the way from Kristina's house to the clinic. The doctor would never see the signs; rather, the signs lined the route that Kristina traveled. "It was for me to be scared. It was for me," Kristina said in recalling the signs. "There's nothing in my experience with the protesters that stands out more than that morning when I got up to go get the doctor and saw the doctor's picture all over town."

This targeted harassment has taken a toll on Kristina and has affected how she lives. She installed a security system in her house. When she drives home from work, she consciously tries to take different routes so that protesters cannot follow her and learn her routine. "It's stressful. You get sick more. It gets into your head, it gets into your heart. It gets to be really hard to take." This perspective on life is one that most healthcare providers would likely consider completely foreign to them, but for Kristina, targeted harassment has become a normal part of life.

Kristina is concerned not only for her own safety but for her children's safety as well. As a result of the targeted harassment she faced, Kristina moved her son from public school to a private school where the administrators were aware of her profession. "They knew not to let him go with just anybody and that if somebody came to pick him up that wasn't me, they would call." The school was supportive, and thankfully nothing ever happened there, but Kristina's children were affected. "They would get scared. They would get upset at times when they'd hear or see things."

Kristina is "totally aware" of anti-abortion violence elsewhere. Her clinic started providing abortions not long after Dr. Barnett Slepian was murdered by a sniper while standing in his kitchen in his home in Buffalo, New York. Though Dr. Slepian's murder happened far away from Kristina, she thinks about it every day. "I cannot sit down at my kitchen table without thinking of Dr. Slepian's murder, because we have a big backyard and I don't have any coverings on my windows. It goes through my head on a regular basis that there could be somebody out there with a rifle." When Dr. George Tiller was murdered in 2009,

Kristina had a hard time dealing with it as well. "We had a memorial for George in one of the cities nearby. I went to the funeral in Wichita, and I think it's hard to think that could happen to you. That was tough."

As a result of anti-abortion violence around the country, Kristina obtained a bulletproof vest. Kristina had been cautious in the past, but "there was just a different reality when doctors started getting shot." Kristina wonders, though, whether it will make any difference. "I think you can wear a vest, but most of us now think that they're going to shoot you in the head. Unless they're shooting from a distance or something with a pistol, they're going to walk right up and shoot you in the head." Kristina has not bought a gun, even though she has been told to do so by others:

> They wanted me to get a gun, but I would probably shoot one of the protesters, and I'd be in jail. So I don't want to have a gun. The most I have is a baseball bat, and I don't know what I'm going to do with that. And I've had pepper spray, but I have asthma so I'm afraid I'm going to shoot myself and then I'm going to be rolling around on the ground. I'll just take my chances.

Despite the harassment, despite being followed, despite the bullseye signs throughout her neighborhood, despite purchasing a vest and considering carrying a gun, despite playing cat-and-mouse games to transport medical care providers, and despite the toll all of this takes on her children, Kristina continues to work in this field. "I finally just had to get to the point where I asked myself, 'Are you going to do this, or are you not going to do this?' If you're going to do it, you can't let them run your life. You can't let them dictate everything that you're going to do." She copes by compartmentalizing her life and having other outlets for enjoying life, such as her dog and her grandkids. Kristina does not think it would be healthy for her to be consumed with the harassment "24/7," so she intentionally works to avoid feeling that way.

Ultimately, Kristina reflects very positively on her work as an abortion provider:

> I never thought I would be doing this type of work, but it's been the most rewarding thing I've ever dreamed of doing. It hasn't always

been easy, but you always get something back from clients and from women and their stories. You know what the truth is. You know how difficult this is for them. They know what's happening. They're not idiots. They know that there is a pregnancy there, it will end, and there will no longer be a baby. They cry and they're sad and as long as it's legal, maybe even if it wasn't, I'd feel a need or a want to try to continue to do this work.

Kristina insisted that she will not back down because she is confident she is doing the right thing. "If I quit, maybe there's not somebody else wanting to do it. I'm also stubborn. I'm a little pigheaded. I don't want them to win. I think what I'm doing is right. I think what we're doing is right. I think a choice is right."

## Rodney Smith

Rodney Smith has worked in abortion care for decades. He went to medical school for general surgery while in the Air Force and then served in the Air Force until the mid-1980s. When he retired from active duty, he opened his own private general surgery practice. In the late 1980s, Rodney started performing abortions part time for a West Midwest clinic that was separate from his own practice; he has provided abortion care in many different regions of the country ever since. Given the length of time that Rodney has worked as an abortion provider, his stories with targeted protest range from very recent to over two decades old.

Rodney's first experience with targeted protest came as a result of the regular large-scale protests outside of the clinic where he first worked as an abortion provider. Two of the regular protesters were the parents of Rodney's son's fiancée. When they learned that their daughter's soon-to-be father-in-law was a doctor at the clinic, they forced her to move out of their house and cut off their support. When the two were finalizing their wedding plans, protesters made it clear that they planned to target the wedding. The priest for the wedding threatened to call the police if the protesters interrupted the services and told them, "If a priest has you arrested, it's not going to do your cause any good." The priest did not allow any protest but allowed the protesters to stand in an ante-room where they could see the services but could not be heard.

By the early 1990s, the protesters started targeting Rodney in a much
more direct and violent manner. One day, Rodney was working at the
clinic when he received a call from a police officer who told him that
his house and barn were on fire. The fire was so large that an Air Force
plane flying over the scene saw the fire and reported it. Rodney said
that despite the call from the pilot, it took three calls before firefighters
appeared. By the time the firefighters arrived at the scene, the fire had
been burning for nearly two hours. Rodney and his family lost everything they owned other than what they were wearing at the time. They
lost their house, their barn, and three separate outbuildings. Their dog,
cats, and seventeen horses were killed. Thankfully, the human members of Rodney's family were not injured because none were home at
the time.

Rodney was in disbelief when everything he owned was destroyed.
Before the fire, he did not think that anything like this could be possible. Looking back, Rodney remembers that the arson occurred on the
same day that anti-abortion legislation went into effect in his home
state. Rodney had testified against this law and thinks that the arson
occurred in response to his public opposition.

The authorities never caught the arsonist. Someone mailed a letter
postmarked the morning of the fire, justifying killing the animals on
Rodney's farm because Rodney "murdered little children"; however,
the letter was untraceable. The investigation into the fire revealed that
it originated from thirteen different sites on Rodney's property, but
beyond that, Rodney explained that the investigation was thwarted by
city incompetence or maliciousness. For example, rather than preserve
the crime scene for a full investigation, the city demolished the property the day after the fire. When the state fire marshal arrived, at first
he wanted Rodney arrested for destroying the crime scene. When he
learned city workers had done this at the behest of the chief of police,
the fire marshal left and the investigation ended. Rodney attributes this
mix-up to confusion between the city and county over responsibility
for fires as well as to his identity as an abortion provider:

I don't think the abortion issue helped a heck of a lot either. And I'm
sure that's why they pushed everything in a pile, so that there was no
way that anybody could be prosecuted. I mean, there's just no doubt

in my mind about that. And the fact that the fire was called in by the air force at 12:28, and they didn't respond until five minutes after two, when they finally got a third call from a passerby.

Rather than deterring Rodney, the fire that destroyed his home and left him with nothing strengthened his resolve. "That was the last day that I did abortions part-time. I quit doing the general surgery practice. I went to the hospital and told them I was going to resign my privileges on the staff there and I was going to travel and do abortions." From that point until now, Rodney has been a full-time abortion doctor who has provided abortions in many different regions of the country for his own clinic as well as other clinics that need his assistance.

The targeted harassment did not end with the arson. Immediately after the fire destroyed their home, Rodney and his family rented an apartment. The first weekend they were there, protesters broke into their apartment and wrote all over the walls. Rodney's new neighbors identified the people who broke in, but the police never prosecuted them. It was then that Rodney realized just how vulnerable he was as an abortion provider. He likened his vulnerability to his time in the Air Force during the Vietnam War when he knew that any day he could be killed. Nonetheless, he found himself more committed to the cause because of the high stakes.

In the 1990s when anti-abortion extremists started murdering doctors and clinic workers, it was obvious to Rodney that the anti-abortion movement's goal was to frighten everyone in the field into not working. "No matter who you were, a nurse or a staff member or an anything, you were vulnerable. If you can agitate or put fear into all the workers, you do a lot more damage than if you just make the people at the top of the organization worried." He understood this plan but insisted on continuing "to help carry on the movement." Though he recognized that the people who opposed him "were crazy," he was willing to live with the risk:

I've always said, if you work at the post office or the 7-11, you probably had a higher chance of getting murdered or shot in a robbery than you do doing abortions. That's probably still true today. Not every career field has its risks, but many of them do, and if you believe in what you're doing, I think that it's worth taking those risks.

Over the years, Rodney has become more and more visible as an abortion provider: he has been involved in high-profile court cases, worked with other high-profile doctors, and become known as a doctor with expertise in late abortion care. He has had several death threats, mostly during the time of the fire and then again in the late 1990s. Much more recently, a protest organizer told him, "You're not going to be here to do this much longer." This comment may have referred to Rodney's age or to some sort of violent crime that the protester planned to commit against Rodney. Either way, Rodney explained that he was not going to take any chances, so he notified the FBI, federal marshals, and local police, who investigated the comment.

Rodney's involvement in high-profile court cases has also placed him at the center of anti-abortion protesters' attention. Rodney and his lawyers have hired personal security to guard him during court appearances and events related to the cases. The security could not help him, though, in the US Supreme Court courtroom, where a few years before we interviewed him, Rodney was physically attacked by a protester:

He was wearing one of these very anti-choice T-shirts. He pulled a chair up. There wasn't even a seat there, but they let him bring a chair up and sit in the aisle behind me on the right-hand side. And my wife and I were sitting there. I thought that just seemed really strange because nobody else was doing it. But the case was going on, and he stood up and yelled some kind of a profanity at the Court; and he grabbed me, pulled me off my chair, and knocked me to the ground.

While Rodney was on the ground, the protester pummeled him with a chair. Luckily, the courtroom deputies were able to stop the attacker before he severely injured Rodney. "The deputies immediately swarmed all over the protester and arrested and took him out, and I had to go fill out all this paperwork. We pressed charges and he was convicted." Rodney attributes the attack to the fact that the Supreme Court did not allow Rodney's private security inside. Rodney had been assured that "nothing ever happens in the Supreme Court."

In the 2000s, Rodney worked with another high-profile doctor performing abortions in a very conservative West Midwest state. The protesters there were relentless. Rodney stayed in the same chain hotel each time he traveled to the clinic, and the protesters staged anti-abortion demonstrations outside of the hotel. The protesters also wrote to the hotel's corporate headquarters saying they were going to protest all of that chain's hotels around the country. Eventually, the tactics worked, as the hotel prohibited Rodney from staying there in the future.

The protesters have also targeted Rodney's family. The day after Dr. Tiller was murdered, someone called Rodney's daughter in the middle of the night and said, "Your mother and father were both just killed." For some reason, Rodney's and his wife's phones were not working that night, so their daughter could not contact them immediately. She finally tracked them down through one of the women who worked at their clinic, but for a period of time she panicked because she thought both of her parents had been murdered.

Rodney started working for a clinic in a South Atlantic state about a year before we interviewed him. Once Rodney started working there, the protesters targeted the clinic in ways they had never previously done. In the past, the clinic rarely saw protesters; now, the clinic is under siege. Protesters appear in numbers approaching fifty or sixty, and they show up all the time. They bought an office in the building across from the clinic so that they can continuously monitor Rodney. They come right up to the door and incessantly scream at Rodney when he comes and goes from the clinic.

From his long career, Rodney is used to this type of verbal abuse and sometimes reacts in kind. When a priest called him a murderer, Rodney responded by calling the priest a child molester. When protesters told Rodney they were praying for him, he responded, "You mean you're preying upon us. There's a difference."

Rodney also described his extensive experience with law enforcement. For example, within an hour of Dr. Tiller's murder, US Marshals were at Rodney's clinic to protect him. Rodney explained that they had a list of a small number of doctors around the country who they believed were "significant risks." Rodney had a full detail of marshals protecting him for the next three months:

> We didn't get to drive anywhere. It was nice. I suppose you could ask
> them to do anything and they would have, but it just was easier to

stay home and call somebody and have them pick stuff up at the store than to go out and go shopping or go out to dinner or anything. So it was quite restrictive that way, but, again, it was quite reassuring to have somebody that seemed like they cared. That was cool.

For reasons they never disclosed to Rodney, the marshals stopped their detail after three months but restarted for another six weeks later in 2009. They ended their detail by the end of the year, but they still check in with him almost every week to make sure that there are no problems. He feels that the Department of Justice under President Obama is "really very aggressive" with their counterterrorism efforts in this regard. "They've told us about problems before we even knew there were any plans." Rodney appreciates all the work they are doing to make him and others safe.

Rodney's experiences as a target of this anti-abortion protest have made him significantly alter his life. He does not eat at the same restaurants on a regular basis, and when he does go to a restaurant, "I try to be in and out within 30 minutes so that if somebody sees me and calls, before somebody else can be there, then we're not there." He does not use his real name to make reservations. He has an arrangement with airlines so that he can fly on a different flight from the one he reserved without telling them ahead of time. The most important thing, according to Rodney, is to vary your routine so that there is no plan that others can discover.

When he first considered incorporating abortion care into his medical practice, Rodney discussed the risks with his family, but none of them anticipated the extent of the crime and violence that would occur. "When it got to the murders, I think I was surprised by that." Nonetheless, Rodney takes a very calculated view of the risk he faces. He does what such as can to improve his security, but he also accepts that life has risks and that targeted harassment is one of them:

Relatively, I mean, you can't drive without being aware that something can happen. You know? And I think that my whole family knows that something could happen because of the abortion issue, but something can happen for a number of other reasons too. I think I'm probably almost at as great a risk of a car accident or something while working here as I am from the protesters here. It's just a risk that I have to take. Maybe ignoring it is my way of coping with it.

Looking back on his career, the only thing Rodney would do differently is that he would have started working in abortion immediately after his residency rather than waiting fifteen years. He articulated a very simple, yet powerful, reason for this and for continuing to work in this field despite everything he and his colleagues have been through: "The patients. It's clearly the patients."

## Howard Stephens

Howard Stephens is an obstetrician-gynecologist whose original medical practice did not regularly include abortion, although he occasionally performed one if needed. After leaving his practice, he began counseling part-time at a local abortion clinic and enjoyed the work. "It's something that is really necessary. People like me, somebody who could sit and talk with somebody and be personable with them and not judge them. They were going to get as personal care as they could possibly get."

A few years before we interviewed him, Howard became a full-time abortion provider and has been doing it ever since. "I've been extremely happy doing what I'm doing. Part of it is being able to provide a service that I know is really needed." When he switched to providing full-time abortion care, Howard thought he would miss the gratitude that his obstetrical patients would show after he delivered a child, but he gets similar, if not more frequent, expressions of gratitude from his abortion patients. Howard now works at and runs two clinics in two different East Midwest states and performs abortions through about twenty-two weeks of pregnancy.

After performing abortions for three years, Howard became the target of the local anti-abortion protesters. They started targeting him by demonstrating outside of his house. At the first home protest, between thirty-five and fifty protesters walked down Howard's street holding signs Howard described as "graphic." Howard was "taken aback" by this first protest and "to some extent freaked out." His wife was "spooked" as well. Howard was surprised that protesters started targeting him in his neighborhood and at his house because he thought he had been keeping a low profile. For instance, the clinic never put Howard's name on its website, instead using "Dr. S." Nonetheless, the protesters discovered Howard's identity as the clinic's physician and began to target him.

On the day that Howard's son graduated from high school, the protesters again staged a demonstration outside of Howard's home. Because Howard lives close to the high school, he was scared that the protesters would follow him and his family to the school for the graduation ceremony. Howard called the school and explained, "This is what's going on, there may be people going over there to protest because of me." Luckily, the protesters did not follow the Stephens family to the high school.

About a month after the protesters started picketing Howard's house, Howard took his red Toyota to his mechanic to be serviced. The mechanic needed the car for several hours to do the repairs, so he gave Howard a loaner car, a dark green Toyota. Howard drove the loaner home and parked it in his driveway. Later that day, Howard discovered a leaflet in his mailbox that he was sure was in other mailboxes in his neighborhood as well. The leaflet said, "There's a murderer that lives in your neighborhood who kills babies out to 24 weeks. The house he's living in is paid with blood money from abortion and his dark green Toyota is paid with blood money too." Howard was shocked to read this description of the loaner car. "I'm thinking, that car's only been in the driveway for two hours, three hours tops. So it made me think, God, who is watching?"

Howard and his son have received anti-abortion mail from fake return addresses. The mail to his son was particularly concerning, because the names written on the return addresses were the names of Howard's son's friends. That protesters had somehow found out the names of his son's friends and used those names in their protest was "really kind of spooky."

The home protests and mail affected Howard and his home life. Recalling the way that Dr. Slepian was shot in his home in Buffalo, Howard explained the effect on him:

> Before I go to bed I always fill my water bottle up and I keep it by my bedside and I typically go to bed 11:30, 12:00. I'm a late-night

person. When I'm in the kitchen, and it's dark outside, and I'm standing in front of my kitchen window, more than just a couple of times I'm thinking is there going to be a rifle shot coming through this window? And I never used to think that. That was furthest from my mind until these protests started.

To deal with these new concerns, Howard obtained an unlisted phone number and started leaving the lights on around his house. In addition to making these changes, he considered protecting himself with a gun and a bulletproof vest but ultimately rejected those options because he did not want to "fall prey to the paranoia that goes on." Eventually, "little by little," this increased awareness became a normal part of life for Howard and his family, and they adapted to the changes in their lifestyle.

The home protests also made Howard nervous about his relationship with his neighbors. When the protesters first came to his house and neighborhood, he thought his neighborhood was too conservative to support him. Instead, he found support in unexpected places:

> I had people calling me saying, "What can we do? Is there something we can do to help you? We are so on your side." And I thought, "In my neighborhood?" There are people in my neighborhood I know that supported the anti side but I was just really surprised at the number of people in the neighborhood who came through and said, "If you need something, you let us know."

The protesters have targeted Howard outside of his neighborhood as well. After the first two home protests, the protesters twice demonstrated outside of Howard's church. The first time they appeared at his church, Howard was out of state; he later heard about their demonstration from members of the congregation. The second time, Howard found out about the protest before it was going to happen and decided not to go to church that day. He alerted his minister, who warned the entire congregation. On the day of the demonstration, the protesters showed up in force, lining the street for about an hour and a half with sixty or seventy people holding anti-abortion signs. The demonstration did not disrupt church services, however, as attendance was higher than usual that morning thanks to the congregation showing up to support Howard.

Although the protests at the church affected Howard, he was grateful for the support his fellow churchgoers had shown him. The minister later told Howard that he appreciated the way everyone supported not only Howard but also the church. According to Howard, the minister joked, "Maybe they should protest here more often. Our collections plate was really good that week."

Not long before we interviewed Howard, the protesters began to target Howard on the Internet. One of Howard's patients had a medical complication from her abortion as a result of a weakened uterus from a past pregnancy. Following proper medical protocol, Howard called a doctor at a local hospital who agreed to take the patient. An ambulance arrived at the clinic to transport the patient to the other doctor. As the ambulance arrived, the protesters were demonstrating outside of the clinic, "watching everything." The ambulance transported the patient to the other doctor, who successfully performed minor surgery on the patient the with no further problems.

About three or four weeks after this incident, protesters posted images of the ambulance outside of Howard's clinic to the anti-abortion website that they maintain, with a caption claiming that Howard's clinic is "killing women." Protesters continue to repost these images and caption, which Howard, as one of the owners of the clinic and the woman's doctor, perceives as a personal attack.

Howard has also been targeted on anti-abortion websites that specifically reference him. The sites mention Howard's name, as well as that of the owner of the building. They also call Howard an "instrument of the Devil" and say that Satan will enjoy having Howard visit him.

Out of fear that protesters will try to escalate their harassment tactics, Howard feels that he has to protect his identity as much as possible. For instance, he feels constrained in how he can talk about his work as an abortion provider because abortion care is "unfortunately a field of medicine that you can't broadcast what you do because you never know who is listening." When asked his profession, he responds, "I do women's health. I do reproductive care. I do family planning." Howard explained, "I would love to be really open with what I do." He wants to be able to proudly say, "'I do abortion care.' However,

I can't because I'm worried about folks like Scott Roeder. I'm worried about Eric Rudolph[1] coming to my house." Because he has to be so circumspect around others, he said that he "lives for" abortion provider conferences. "When I'm there, I am surrounded by people who are like-minded, who know what we do and appreciate what we do for women in general in the country. I can say, 'I do abortion care.' But not to somebody I don't know."

Beyond not talking freely about his work, Howard also tries to protect his identity while coming and going from the clinics. Dr. Tiller was Howard's friend, and following Dr. Tiller's murder, Howard has started taking extra precautions:

> Dr. Tiller's murder was unnerving, and we changed policies at the clinic. I used to park in the driveway in the parking lot at one clinic. But the owner of the building gave me and the other doctor a garage door opener. As soon as we get into the driveway and push the button, the garage door opens. I drive in and before I turn the car off, I push the button and the garage door closes. So they don't have the opportunity to really see me that much anymore. And I always drive into the parking lot with a baseball cap on, pulled down to my eyebrows, and whether it's sunny out or not I have sunglasses on. And I always drive with one hand on the wheel and one hand over my face so they don't have a really good chance to see me. They do try to take pictures. But I mean, how much of me do you know when I have my hand over my face?

That clinic is located in an area that Howard described as much more conservative than his other clinic's location. At the more conservative location, when Howard approaches the clinic,

> that's when I get my cap on, that's when I get my sunglasses on. In wintertime I'll put my hood up or a scarf and I'll bring my scarf up over my mouth and nose as well as I come in. It's almost a visceral feeling. And even though I feel reasonably safe, you just never know. George Tiller was supposed to be safe in his church. You just never know. Some of the folks out there are just really insane and the world is so black and white to them. Baby: Good, Abortion: Bad.

If abortion is bad, then God is telling you that you have to use everything you can to stop them.

In the short time that Howard has been an abortion provider, he has been targeted in multiple ways, which has affected his life and family. He is not going to stop though. Because there are few people in the United States who perform abortions, Howard reasons, "If I stop doing it, who is going to take my place? Who is going to take care of these people?"

## Lucy Brown

Lucy Brown has worked at an abortion clinic in an East Midwest state for a decade. She started working at the clinic because her sister Alana had previously worked there. Lucy is a certified nursing assistant who has been a "Jill of all trades" at the clinic. At the time we interviewed her, she worked primarily in the lab, but Lucy has also worked in the recovery room, with patient transport, in the instrument room, in the procedure room as an assistant, and as a secretary.

Protesters target Lucy on a daily basis when she comes and goes from the clinic. Protesters yell at her and call her by name. Lucy believes they learned her name from a protester who was in one of Lucy's college classes. Although the protester never said anything to Lucy in class, she demonstrated at the clinic and yelled at Lucy there.

Protesters use other personal information to target Lucy. When Lucy was pregnant several years ago, the medical scrubs that she wore when she entered and exited the clinic hid the fact for most of the pregnancy. When the protesters eventually figured out that Lucy was pregnant, they started using that information when they screamed at her and the patients entering the clinic along with Lucy. Lucy remembers the protesters saying things like "Lucy's saving her baby, you save yours" or "Look at Lucy, she's keeping her baby."

About a year before we interviewed Lucy, one of the clinic employees and Lucy's close friend, Jim, died at a young age and for reasons unrelated to his profession. The protesters had targeted Jim for a long time, including at Jim's home and other workplace, which was completely unrelated to the clinic. When Jim died, the protesters celebrated his death on the anti-abortion website that they maintain. The protesters also started yelling at Lucy about her child and connecting Lucy to Jim by yelling, "What's your son going to do when you end up like Jim?" This line of attack "shocked" Lucy:

> Jim passed away recently, and do you take this comment as a threat? How do you take it? Are they threatening me? That was the first time they brought up my son. And I thought, "Wow. Where'd they get this? How all of a sudden do they know I have a son?" He's five now. It's been five years.

Lucy went back and forth over whether the incident bothered her: "I don't know how to take it. Sometimes you get to the point where you get upset and then you just get over it and you just think, 'Eh, they're crazy.' You don't know what they mean." She was clear though that if protesters went further with bringing her son into their harassment tactics, things would change. "I think if they would ever bring up a picture of him on their website or anything, I would probably freak out. That would probably be it for me."

Lucy's personal information has appeared elsewhere. The protesters' website displays Lucy's name and picture. The website says that she has "butchered babies" and had to take people to the hospital because of substandard care. Several of Lucy's friends also told her about a sign with her and her sister's names on it that protesters displayed at a local parade and at various locations around town. The sign said, "Lucy Brown and Alana Brown kill babies at The Women's Center."

Lucy expressed the same mixed reaction about the sign that she expressed about the protesters using information about her son. She said her initial reaction was "wow," but she was eventually not as bothered by the signs because her name was already on the website. Lucy and her sister considered bringing a slander lawsuit against the protesters based on the signs but decided against it. Instead, Lucy feels resigned to this being the way her life is: "We figured they're always going to be doing this kind of stuff. And they have a free lawyer. It's pointless to go in and fight when it seems like they get away with a lot."

Lucy explained one incident that made her feel particularly threatened. Lucy and a coworker drove into the clinic's private employee parking lot after a trip to the store. "I was in her passenger seat, and as I went to open my door, a guy grabbed my arm. And of course I went off. I freaked and went off on him. 'You shouldn't be in this parking lot. You're trespassing.'" While holding on to her arm for what seemed like a long time, the protester said something to Lucy about abortion. The protester eventually let go, and Lucy was able to squirm away. This was the first and only time Lucy ever saw this particular protester at the clinic, which caused her to worry about him even more. "You worry about the people who aren't from around here. The few strange ones." Lucy recalled, "You could tell he wasn't right."

Though there were witnesses, Lucy decided not to press charges. She feared that if she did, the protesters would obtain her address and then come knocking on her door, scaring her and her elderly grandmother who lived with her. The whole incident disturbed Lucy and made her think, "Hmm, do I want to continue doing this?"

Lucy has continued, with a mix of nonchalance and bravado but also with caution and vigilance. She talks openly about where she works and even purchased a vanity license plate with her name on it, in a sense toying with the protesters, saying, "Oh well, you know my name. Big deal, here it is." She says that at this point she has worked at the clinic long enough to "pretty much ignore them and not pay attention to anything they say."

On the other hand, Lucy takes precautions in her daily life. In order to make sure that protesters do not follow her, she watches to see if anyone is behind her when she drives and is on alert for strange people. When she parks in the clinic parking lot, she looks around before she gets out of her car and makes sure that there are no papers visible in the car that have her or her family's names on them.

Despite these precautions, a strange car once parked outside Lucy's home. Inside the car was a woman Lucy did not know, "just sitting there":

It scared me so much I took my cell phone out and actually took a picture of the woman in her car and her license plates. Because I thought, "What do I do?" I left my house and got into my car, and she was just sitting there the entire time. By the time I got home, though, she was gone. But you always think, "Who was that?"

After the incident with the woman in her car, protesters started shouting to Lucy about her son, so Lucy speculates that this woman somehow learned her address and was staking out her home to find out personal information about her.

Like other abortion providers around the country, Lucy was rattled when Dr. Tiller was murdered. Her clinic referred many patients to Dr. Tiller, so she knew his work well:

> That may be what makes me start taking it a little more seriously. "Oh, this does happen." It makes you think back to that guy that grabbed me in the car. This was some random guy who walked into Dr. Tiller's church. And that's when you start thinking about, "Oh my God, I've got these plates. Am I asking for that? Am I asking for that one random person who just takes it too far?"

Despite these thoughts, targeted harassment has become a normalized part of Lucy's everyday life. Yet she is concerned that she perceives the harassment as something so normal:

> If we don't do something and let them continue, it makes you worry about the fact that when something does happen everyone's just going to respond, "Oh, well it happens daily, we go through it daily, getting harassed." I don't know how many patients come in here and say, "You have to deal with that every day?" We respond, "We're used to it. We get it every day." I think sometimes mentally that kind of wears you out, but it stresses you out every single day you walk in the door; and then by the time you get into the door, you don't even pay attention. You're here. You do your job and it's fine.

Lucy explained that the targeted harassment she has faced does not scare her enough to leave her job. She has a very rational explanation for that attitude: "I know that sounds really bad because it probably should scare me enough to quit, but I think anything could happen anywhere, anytime, from anything." Plus, Lucy does not want to give the protesters the satisfaction of being successful. "I feel like why let them win? I never want to be that person that'd say, 'Oh, you guys won.'"

## Dustin Menendez

Dustin Menendez is an obstetrician-gynecologist who has been an abortion provider for almost two decades. He completed his medical training in a Middle Atlantic state but has provided abortions at a clinic in a South Atlantic state for the entire time he has been an abortion provider. He also has a solo obstetrics and gynecology practice. Unlike some of the providers who talked at length about their experiences, Dustin was very concise and matter-of-fact about the many ways he has been targeted by anti-abortion protesters.

Like others, Dustin has been targeted while coming and going from the clinic where he provides abortions. Protesters yell at him, "Dustin, you're out there murdering again." The protesters have slashed his tires, which he notes is frightening "because what do you have to do if you have a flat? You have to change it, which makes you vulnerable." One time, a protester hid behind a garbage bin outside the clinic and took pictures of Dustin. Dustin walked over to the protester and, while the protester was running away, said to him, "Next time you point something at me I'm going to point something back, and it's not going to be a camera, because I have no idea what you're doing."

Over a decade ago, protesters followed Dustin as he drove away from the clinic:

> They were following me and I drove into the mall, pulled into the parking lot, and slammed on the brakes. I walked out of my car and pointed my gun at the driver. They took pictures and I told them, "You better move, you better get the hell away, because the police are already on their way and they know I have a gun out." And they move a little quicker when they hear that, they do. After the police arrived, I stayed there, they took off.

Dustin's private medical practice is in a separate location from the clinic where he provides abortions. Despite the fact that he does not perform abortions at his private practice, the protesters who target Dustin regularly demonstrate nearby. He chose the specific location of his private practice based on the protesters: "The office is set up so that it's actually on a large parking lot, so they cannot actually picket in front of the office itself, because the parking lot is private grounds. And it's intentionally on a second floor, because people do weird things." Sometimes the protesters come on to the private property around his office, so he requested that the building provide extra security.

The protest has affected Dustin's relationship with his landlord. At one point, the landlord asked him to leave. "A lot of the other tenants got together and basically insisted that they kick me out." Even though other doctors in the building that housed Dustin's private practice were themselves quietly performing abortions, Dustin was targeted because he also works at an abortion clinic. After discussions with the landlord, Dustin was able to keep his private practice at that location but had to sign a commitment in his next lease that he would not perform abortions there.

The picketing also affects the business side of Dustin's private practice. Some patients become angry; others have left the practice or never come to Dustin in the first place because they want to avoid the protesters. "I mean, the husbands, who wants to go through that? They have ugly signs, ugly statements. If you don't have to, why would you want to?" As a result, his private practice has been hurt economically.

Outside of the work environment, protesters have targeted Dustin where he lives and on the Internet. When Dustin started performing abortions, the protesters found out where he lived:

> My father ran a hotel in another town, and so when I first came here I lived with them for a while. They had about fifty to a hundred protesters along the highway in front of the hotel, and no one could figure it out, because there was no hospital close by, no medical offices, nothing. And my father even said, "What are these people doing around?" It was not until I said, "Because I am using this as my address" that he figured it out.

With this experience in mind, when Dustin was looking to move, he intentionally sought and purchased a home in a gated community. For many years, he tried to hide from the protesters by using his office address as his mailing address. Eventually, though, the protesters found him once again. He now regrets that he did not have the foresight to place his house under someone else's name.

When protesters descended upon his private residence, they appeared in front of the gated community in a group of about twenty or more. They carried large signs stating that Dustin was a "murderer" and displaying abortion-related pictures. Protesters would "congregate and make a nuisance of themselves," and in the process they slowed traffic on a main street in front of Dustin's community. For a while, the demonstrations occurred weekly, usually on Saturday mornings. They continued until one of Dustin's neighbors threatened legal action against the protesters.

Dustin described how the protests made him feel "lousy" because "you'd like to think that your home is your private protected space." Based on the extreme harassment and violence against abortion providers around the country, Dustin feels that home protesting "can be life-threatening because protesters are not logical, and they don't really have boundaries."

The protests were also alarming to other people in Dustin's community, though his neighbors never took issue with Dustin because of the protests. In fact, the protests may have even helped people who needed abortion care connect with Dustin. Neighbors have left notes on Dustin's car seeking help for themselves or a friend. "Please call so and so, a friend of mine. I know you provide abortion services and she could use your help."

Protesters have also mailed letters to Dustin's home, which Dustin considers threatening. The letters typically call Dustin a "murderer," say that he is going to hell, and try to persuade him to stop performing abortions by quoting religious passages. He has also received a few letters with not-so-veiled threats, such as "you better be careful when you're walking around."

Dustin has not received quite as many letters over the past couple of years, which he attributes to retaliatory action that he took against one of the most aggressive protesters. Dustin traced the license plate of this aggressive protester and parked his car in front of her home so that she could see him. Dustin felt that if she could park in front of his house, he could do the same to her. According to Dustin, she was not happy about it and eventually stopped coming to his house. The letters to his home also slowed down afterward.

The protesters have also targeted Dustin on the Internet. They have designed a website that calls him a murderer, has pictures of him and his car, and lists his home and office addresses and phone numbers. He worries about the people who "spend too much time on the Internet" finding his information because "people are wacky." The same information has appeared in pamphlets that protesters distributed around his private practice and mailed to all of his neighbors.

The personal targeting has taken a serious toll on Dustin's relationships. His young niece found the protesters' information on the Internet, which has negatively affected his relationship with his niece and nephew. His fiancée called off their engagement. Dustin explained that one of the reasons for the breakup was that she felt unsafe. According to Dustin, "she realized the harassment was an ongoing thing, it was not just for a day, it was not just for a weekend, it was going to be all the time." This problem continues into his current relationships: "Anyone now that I date or see, I say that right up front, because it's going to be an issue." Because Dustin knows the protesters will say "all sorts of nasty things," he asked one woman he dated who wanted to have children, "You need to tell me what you're going to tell the child when they come home and say, 'Why is Daddy a murderer?'"

To feel safer, Dustin has a concealed weapons permit and a bullet-proof vest. He carries the gun and wears the vest regularly, even during our interview with him. He obtained both because of his line of work. Dustin usually parks his car in the back of the building where there are cameras watching at all times. Dustin knows other abortion providers who use decoy cars to travel to or from work or have someone else pick them up for work, but Dustin cannot take this added precaution because he often needs to travel from the clinic to his private practice to see patients.

Toward the end of the interview, we asked Dustin whether he felt threatened. He replied incredulously, "Yes. I mean, do you walk around with a bulletproof vest? Or carry a gun? Yeah, I feel threatened." He knows what the protesters are trying to do: "Eliminate the providers and you can have as many clinics as you want, but you won't have someone providing abortions." Nonetheless, he has questioned whether he should continue because "it's affected my practice and it's affected my personal life." He calls the harassment "personal and a half" and understands that this is a unique form of medical work: "Any other line of work, you go home and it doesn't follow you."

At the same time, Dustin explained that he has figured out how to live with targeted harassment. "Once someone told me it's not what's right and it's not what's wrong, it's the way it is. And you simply learn to live with it." He continues working in abortion care because he is "doing a good service" and his patients are "always thankful." Emblematic of that, he described one patient who wrote him a card that said, "I just want to thank you. Eight years ago you helped me out. Currently I'm finishing my ophthalmology residency."

## Danielle Figueroa

Danielle Figueroa was a homemaker for much of her life. About ten years ago, a friend told her about a receptionist position at an abortion clinic in a Middle Atlantic state. She had no medical office experience but applied for the job after her friend suggested it would be a good fit for her. Danielle has worked at the clinic ever since. In that time, she has worked her way up to become one of the main administrators for the clinic. She also helps with patient counseling.

Danielle explained that when she started at the clinic, she had no idea what she was getting herself into. For the first several months she worked at the clinic, she went home every day and cried:

> I don't know if it was the idea of abortion. I don't know if it was getting out of my car and being called some horrible things. So I really had to give it some thought. Then the thought that I gave it was, "Man, these women need me. This is exactly where I belong." I found it. I knew where I belonged, and it wasn't home baking cookies. [Laughter] So, that's how I ended up here.

She has found her "calling" in helping the women who come to the clinic. She is able to talk to patients not as "Danielle Administrator" but rather as "Danielle Person," saying to them, "Why don't we just have a talk like friends? Tell me what's going on."

Despite the comfort and fulfillment that Danielle feels from her interactions with patients, her experiences with the protesters targeting her have been an ordeal. At first, her interactions with protesters were limited to them yelling general anti-abortion statements at her when she entered the clinic. She sometimes ignored them. ("Sometimes I can't waste my breath. I don't want to be bothered today.") But other times she yelled back at them. ("Sometimes I feel feisty and I need to fight, I need to argue, I need to say they're stepping over boundaries.")

One of the protesters, whom Danielle believes is violent, once said "vile things" as she entered the clinic. She responded by "giving him the bird." Protesters standing nearby videotaped Danielle's gesture, focusing only on Danielle, not what the protester said to prompt her. Protesters then put the video on YouTube, where it attracted widespread attention from anti-abortion activists. Nonetheless, despite having regular interactions with Danielle, until recently the protesters did not call Danielle out by name when they were yelling at her.

This changed about a year before we talked with Danielle. The police arrested one of the clinic's regular protesters for violating a local ordinance while demonstrating outside of the clinic. Danielle witnessed the violation, so she testified at the hearing. Like any other witness, Danielle had to identify herself in court before testifying. Danielle testified, and the court ultimately found that the violation occurred and fined the protester.

After Danielle testified in court, protesters started targeting her in a much more personal manner. According to Danielle, the protester who was fined is "trying to get back at me" for testifying. Since Danielle testified in court, the protest signs have identified her by name and accused her of being an accessory to murder and working for a serial killer. One protester even showed up to protest the clinic wearing a T-shirt with Danielle's name and picture on it.

Protesters' signs have also included personal information about Danielle's family. The signs have included her son's name and picture as well as information about an unrelated legal dispute involving her son and her grandchildren. The day we interviewed Danielle, one of the protesters had all of the legal papers related to Danielle's son's legal dispute and waved the papers at Danielle as she entered the clinic, yelling, "Don't you think people should know that your son's just as bad as you are?" Danielle knows that these new tactics are the result of her participation in the court proceeding: "The signs with my name on them appeared after we went to court, never before then, only after." She feels that this level of personalization is not right. "What do my innocent grandchildren have to do with the protester or my job? You are pushing me. That is so wrong. Leave my children out of it, and leave my grandchildren out of it. If you want to fight with me, fight with me. Don't go there."

Protesters have also threatened to direct their attacks at Danielle's husband. Protesters learned that Danielle and her husband own a restaurant and bar in a town about half an hour from the clinic and have told Danielle that they are going to protest in front of the restaurant and bar. They use Danielle's husband's name and shout at Danielle, "I wonder if Scott knows that his wife murders children for a living?"

Danielle became extremely emotional when describing something that had occurred less than twenty-four hours before we interviewed her. Danielle had been a member of the same church for over forty years. She is not a regular churchgoer, but she enjoys attending on occasion. The day before we interviewed her, she received a call from the priest, who told her that she was no longer welcome at the church:

> I got a phone call from my priest that the protesters went to see him and told my priest what I do for a living, and he threw me out of the church. It's not that I'm a holy roller but I do believe that there are times that I need to go to my church. And they've now seen to it that I don't go there. I am very angry. I am immensely angry. But the priest told me, "I'm sorry, if something should happen to you, you cannot come to our church and I cannot do a mass for you. In good faith, I cannot do a mass. And if I ever see you come here for communion I cannot give it to you until I know that you have left your job." And I'm mad. I'm really mad.

Danielle tried to reason with the priest, asserting that she was helping women who needed her, including many of his congregants. The priest did not care: "Well, I know your name. I don't know their names."

Danielle traces all of this targeted harassment to her testimony in court. She told us that she has asked the local authorities to pursue charges for intimidating or retaliating against a witness, but they have declined out of fear of a retaliatory lawsuit from the protesters. In hindsight, she now questions whether she should have testified:

> If I knew what was going to come, I would really have to think about it. Because of my family, not for me. But then I just might be mad

enough to say, "You know what, I'm not backing down from you."
That's what they want me to do right now. They want me to back
down. And then I have a priest calling me. You're really, really hitting
me in the knees. And that's sad.

Looking at the entire scope of what has happened to her, Danielle
feels threatened by the protesters. She fears for her physical safety. "If
you know where I live, and you know where my businesses are, and
you know where I work, and you have my license plate, and you know
my grandchildren, you know my son, you know too much about me."
In her mind, the protesters have "stepped up their game," which makes
her frightened about what will happen next. "Let them know that I am
frightened. I feel physically threatened, I do."

Because of the targeted harassment, a security adviser warned
Danielle to be aware of her surroundings and always look around at
who might be near her. Nonetheless, she does not necessarily fear the
protesters coming to her home: "You know what, don't come to my
house because I live in a farming area. I know all the farmers. If you
come to my house, your ass is going to be so full of buckshot it ain't
even funny. You'll be sorry you ever walked on my street. Don't go
there."

Despite the harassment, Danielle continues in her job because of the
patients. Because of them, she feels that she has "found where I need
to be." Danielle relayed emotional and heartbreaking stories: patients
who wanted their pregnancies but had fetal anomalies, so they had to
have an abortion; teenagers who were in awful situations and could not
have a baby; and patients who came to her thinking their only choice
was to have an abortion, but Danielle counseled them about all of their
options and they chose to have the baby or put it up for adoption.

She even recounted a story from her family's past that "not a lot of
people know" but she saw as important in relating why she continues
to provide abortion care despite the personal attacks from anti-abortion
protesters:

I'm pretty old, so it took me a long time to find this out. My father's
mother had five children at the time she was twenty-nine years old,
the youngest being five months old. And she finds herself pregnant

again. Her husband—my grandfather—as I understand, was a tyrant. He was a strict old Italian man. Mean. So she found the backdoor alley butcher for an abortion. She took the horse and buggy, went to the city. Found the doctor. She went with my other grandmother, they were neighbors. They took the horse and buggy down, and then the doctor said, "You know, you have to stay overnight, I want to watch you." She said, "There's no way I can stay overnight, I gotta be in that house by the time my husband comes home from work." So they left, took the horse and buggy back. She got into bed and when my grandfather came home from work, she was lying in a pool of blood. He didn't know what happened. They get the horse and buggy, they take her to the hospital, the doctor said, "What happened?" He said, "I have no idea. I don't know. I came home from work, this is what I got." Three hours later the doctor came out and said, "I'm sorry, your wife is dead." I never knew that story until I took my job here and then one of my brothers told me. He said, "That's why you're working where you are. God led you there to help women."

Danielle summed up her conviction: "Women need me. They really do need me. Because there's not a lot of empathetic people out there. And I know I'm one of them." Danielle stands up to the protesters because of her patients. "I can't in my good conscience just walk away."

### Inez Navarro

After medical school, Inez Navarro completed a fellowship in obstetrics in a West Midwest state. As part of her training, Inez learned abortion care and worked at one of the local abortion clinics. Following her fellowship, Inez moved to a New England state, where she has been for over a decade and is now the medical director of a series of clinics.

Before Inez started her fellowship, she did not know much about targeted harassment of abortion providers or general clinic protest, even though her fellowship was located in a place that had a history of anti-abortion harassment:

I grew up maybe in a sheltered fish bowl of my culture. I didn't know it was a big deal until I started working for my fellowship director and I thought, "Oh my God. These people are protesting what I do." Because in the country where my family is from you can drive down the street and there'll be a sign, "Abortion, go here, with an address listed." It's all over the place, nobody cares. And when I did some work with some people from where my family is from, people would be in the elevator saying, "So I had eight abortions, and I was just wondering . . . ." They talk about it, it wasn't like a big deal, and nobody fears the judgment from other people that happens in America. So when I got here I was flabbergasted, "Oh, wow, people actually care too much about the stuff going on in other people's lives." To the point that your life could be in danger. I guess I finally realized I was getting into a controversial field.

As part of her fellowship, Inez became well trained in the world of anti-abortion protest. Her fellowship program director regularly lectured about the issue and made it a central part of the program. The director even took the doctors in the fellowship to meet some local protesters. When Inez tried to talk with them, she found doing so to be useless. "No matter what I said or tried to say they still, literally, said the same thing back to me, repetitively. To the point where I realized, 'Okay, so I can't really have a logical discussion or debate with you because it's not about logic.'"

These past interactions help Inez handle the protest that she now experiences. "So that really gave me a different lens when I came here. This is not an approachable issue, this is not a logical argument that's going on. These are some people really entrenched in whatever is driving them ideologically to be out there, and there's nothing that I can do to change that." Given the ideological conviction the protesters appear to have, Inez considers it "ironic, hypocritical, immoral, and mean" that, as she later learned, many of the protesters had themselves previously had abortions.[2]

The clinic where Inez has worked for the past decade has been in several different locations within the same state, resulting in very different experiences with the protesters. The first building's parking lot was small, and the layout of the parking lot, the public street, and the building allowed the protesters to have direct confrontations with people parking in the lot. "The protesters at that point could be right in front of your car. You would park, and they could be right there trying to take a picture of you. It was a little scary." The clinic gave Inez a bulletproof vest, though she never wore it. "My goal was just to get inside as soon as possible." Inez felt at the time that the protesters were not targeting her personally but instead were going after anyone who was an abortion provider at the clinic.

The clinic has since moved. The newest location has made the situation worse for Inez. The parking lot is now very large, and the protesters have to be far away on the public street. Inez initially thought this layout would improve the situation, but it has not. "I didn't think about things like they have zoom lens cameras that they use to get pictures. Now I might as well pose because I walk into the building carrying so many things in my hands, I can't really cover my face. Moreover, I shouldn't have to." The protesters also stand at the entrance of the parking lot and come close to providers' and patients' cars as they drive into the lot. As a result, whenever Inez drives in, the protesters stand almost against her car and yell directly at her.

To avoid the protesters, some of the providers at the clinic speed down the street to get to the parking lot. The protesters contacted the police about the speeding, and the police told the providers they would be ticketed for going over the speed limit. Inez responded, "Well have you ever thought that we're speeding because we're frickin' scared for our life and trying to get through the gauntlet?"

Earlier in the year that we interviewed Inez, the protesters' tactics became much more personal. At the start of the year, they "ratcheted up" their attacks and, for the first time, started yelling Inez's name and directing their comments at her as an individual, not just as someone entering the clinic. She has two theories on why things changed. First, she believes that the political climate contributed to her being targeted. "The only thing I can think is a national sentiment building around abortion. It's not like I was that under the radar before. But something changed in January." Second, she believes the protesters took advantage of her being less than completely vigilant about her online presence. After being prompted by some longtime friends, Inez put a photo of herself on a social networking site. Soon thereafter, that photo appeared on a website that the anti-abortion protesters maintain. She thinks that this slip contributed to the protesters attacking her more directly.

Part of the personal targeting against Inez has included racial attacks. Protesters have called her racial epithets from time to time, but their efforts in this regard have not been very successful at bothering her. She laughed after telling this story: "They used to call me 'amigo' for a while. I think once or twice someone called me 'sand nigger,' which isn't even right. If you're going to use a racial slur, get it right."

One day about a month after the protesters started using Inez's name, as Inez was coming into the clinic, one of the more vocal and prominent protesters yelled at her, "No one is going to protect you." To Inez, this was the "big day where everything really changed." She decided that she needed to call the police about this incident. "If anything did happen, I wanted them to know there was a history; it wasn't just a one-time, random incident." The police did not take her complaint seriously and instead laughed at her. The combination of the threat and the police reaction left Inez "irritated and pissed and emotional all at the same time."

She did not back down though. "I thought, 'I am a brown person who grew up in America, and if you think that's the end of it, that's not going to be the end of it because I have fought for everything.'" Inez decided to fight back until someone makes her stop. She ultimately contacted police internal affairs about the threat and lack of police response and in the meantime has lost faith in the local police. "Maybe I had a naive faith that the police were there to protect me. I can tell you right now, I no longer trust that this police force is here to help. That was kind of my eye-opening experience with them." As a result, she has been working with federal authorities on matters that she could not detail for us in the interview. The protesters have not issued any threats to her since, but they continue to yell that she is going to hell and needs to stop killing babies.

Protesters have targeted Inez in other ways. She has received hate mail at home that implored her to "stop killing." Although she took the letter to her clinic's security guard out of caution, she said that receiving the letter at home did not scare her. Inez did wonder how the protesters knew where she lived but attributed that to not being diligent in protecting her personal information on the Internet.

One day, when Inez was driving home from work, a man chased her car into the gated complex where she lived. The man followed her to her home, waited for Inez to go inside, and then knocked on her door. She yelled at him through the door that she would not open it. He claimed he was selling magazines and then left. Inez felt unsettled by the incident and thought it had something to do with her job. "You get that feeling. The hair on the back of my neck was standing up. It was just that gut-sinking feeling of 'this is just weird.'" Immediately before this incident, the clinic's security guard learned that people had been searching the state's online databases for information about the doctors who work at the clinic. In light of that discovery, Inez suspected that the magazine salesperson was really an anti-abortion protester who had followed her. The authorities investigated the incident but were unable to pursue anything.

Inez and her husband have had very different emotional reactions to the targeted harassment. Inez does not feel that she lives in fear but, rather, that she has "fear moments." For instance, Inez enjoys most of her commute to work; however, the last two minutes are completely different:

> The minute I get off the highway and I am getting close to the clinic I start thinking, "Where are the protesters? Where are the police?" That's where it kind of sets in that I just need to get through this little gauntlet, and then I'll be okay. For a while after the threat, it was fear, and it was also anger like, "Really?" I don't think this is what I should have to go through if I come to work every day. And I was angry—why do we tolerate this?

Her husband has had a much stronger reaction. He is often fearful and has nightmares about the harassment. He worries about Inez and wants her to contact him when she arrives safely at work, like a new teen driver would have to text her mom when she gets to school.

Inez and her husband have altered their lives to protect themselves. When buying a house, they spent years looking for a sufficiently protected space and ultimately bought a property in a gated community. The local police department, which is a different police force from that for the clinic, has been receptive to Inez's and her husband's concerns. Inez's husband told the police chief about Inez's job, what she has faced, and how the harassment has gotten worse. He also told the chief, "We're sort of fearful and just want to be really proactive about everything." The police chief gave them his cell phone number, offered to help anytime, and told Inez and her husband that the department would identify their house for special emergency assistance. A detective helped with a home security assessment that identified problem areas. As a result, they installed a security system with indoor and outdoor cameras in their house. The police also suggested that Inez and her husband obtain concealed weapons permits and assisted them with the process. As an added level of protection, the police also helped Inez and her husband mark their license plates in the state database so they are notified if someone tries to search for their information.

Inez and her husband also take precautions with their online identities. They have Facebook pages that are not easily associated with Inez's professional identity and have increased privacy settings. They also use Reputation.com, an online service that scrubs their information from the Internet. Inez tries to educate her colleagues about taking similar precautions and being proactive in these ways.

Other members of Inez's family have had strong reactions to her situation. Some of her relatives, particularly those who live outside the United States and do not understand the American controversy over abortion, are shocked that this type of harassment takes place at all. After Dr. Tiller was murdered and an anti-abortion extremist in another part of the country tried unsuccessfully to shoot providers at an abortion facility, Inez's mother called her and told her, "You should make sure you wear your vest." Despite her mother's concerns, Inez does not wear her bulletproof vest:

I just think if they're really going to try and shoot me, I'm going to see a little red light up here on my forehead. They're going to assume that I have a vest on. There's also that religious side of me that thinks if I'm really supposed to die, then I'm really supposed to die. I can't live my whole life around trying to protect myself, so I don't.

In other words, as Inez sums up her feelings, "everything happens for a reason, and I just have to accept it and try to do the best that I can."

Armed with this attitude, Inez continues her work despite the ever-increasing harassment that she faces. To Inez, "what the protesters do is wrong and irrelevant." She strongly believes that she should not have to work under these conditions, but at the same time, these conditions drive her to work harder. "I'm not doing anything wrong. I work very hard, I pay my taxes, I want the best for my family and children, and I am making a positive, productive contribution to society. Can the protesters really say the same, especially with their hypocrisy?" The escalated attacks on Inez have backfired. "They fired me up more to continue the fight against them."

## Conclusion

The stories of these seven individual providers help paint a picture of life in the face of targeted anti-abortion harassment. These stories show the variety of terror tactics employed against providers as well as their cumulative effect on particular individuals. Without these full stories, some readers might think that the different types of harassment detailed in this book seem individually insignificant. As seen here, the aggregate effect of the various types of targeting takes an extreme toll on providers.

Although these full stories paint a complete picture of the lives of the seven individuals profiled and give rich context to the problem of targeted harassment, the individual stories do not cover the entire landscape of anti-abortion terrorism faced by the abortion providers we interviewed, nor do they provide an easy way to think about the different types of targeted harassment. The next three chapters aim to accomplish these two things, ultimately answering the question, "What is the targeted harassment that abortion providers experience?"

# 2

## Where Targeted Harassment Occurs

We go to the homes of abortionists and to places they work other than the clinics precisely because they don't like it.

—JOSEPH SCHEIDLER[1]

THE BEST WAY TO understand targeted harassment is by thinking about three things: (1) where it occurs, (2) how protesters do it, and (3) who is being targeted. The first category, broken down in detail in this chapter, refers not only to different physical locations where targeted harassment takes place but also to virtual locations, such as online or in other media. The second category, the focus of Chapter 3, covers the various tactics protesters use to target abortion providers. The third category, discussed in Chapter 4, may seem obvious as the abortion providers are the protesters' ultimate target. However, protesters sometimes target abortion providers by harassing their children, their family, their friends, their neighbors, their clients, and others.

This chapter focuses on where providers are targeted. The abortion providers we interviewed described experiencing targeted harassment both where they work and away from work. Harassment that occurs where the providers work, which we call *on-site harassment*, is sometimes targeted directly at the provider. Other times, on-site harassment is, on the surface, general clinic protest against the clinic or the topic of abortion; however, when a particular provider has a special connection to the clinic, the general clinic protest can be perceived as targeted harassment.

Targeted harassment also occurs in places other than where the provider works. This type of harassment, which we call *off-site harassment*, can occur anywhere. The most common location the providers discussed was their homes, but providers also shared stories of harassment at schools, in convenience stores, at churches, at other jobs, and anywhere else they may be.

Finally, harassment also occurs in various media, such as on television, in the newspaper, and online. We call this last type of harassment *media harassment*.[2]

## On-Site Harassment

Shortly after Dr. George Tiller was assassinated, Thomas Andrews, a physician at a clinic in a Middle Atlantic state, tried to enter his workplace:

> I was going to park in the regular parking lot. The protesters saw me coming, so I drove to another place. They raced around the building, and then I called someone to come and pick me up. There was a lot of going back and forth trying to catch me. So I went in through a third entrance, and right when I was closing the door I saw one of them standing there, and I can't remember exactly what she said to me but it was some kind of "you can run but you can't hide" type of comment.

*On-site harassment* is targeted harassment that occurs where the abortion provider works, much like the pursuit and threat that Thomas experienced. Depending on where the target provides abortion care, this can occur at a clinic, a more general medical office, or a hospital.

### Coming to Work

The most common form of on-site harassment that providers face is the harassment Thomas experienced—harassment targeted at individual providers when they come to the medical facility to start work for the day. In fact, the first three abortion providers who were murdered—Dr. David Gunn, Dr. John Britton, and volunteer escort James Barrett—were all murdered on their way into work.

For some providers, this type of harassment begins with the simple task of trying to pull their car into the parking lot at the clinic. When

Marshall Cook, a physician who has worked at clinics in four different states in the Middle Atlantic and East Midwest regions of the country, tried to enter his clinic's parking lot, a protester lay on the ground with his body outstretched in front of Marshall's car. Similarly, when Olivia Armas, a clinic administrator who has worked at clinics in both a New England state and a South Atlantic state, drove into work one morning in the early 2000s, one of the main protesters at the clinic blocked her car with his body:

> He didn't allow me to go into the parking lot. And I was just like, "Hello, I work here. Let me in." Sessions started at 7:00 in the morning. So this was at 6:30 in the morning, so I thought, "Really? On a snowy day, this is what you're doing?" Eventually he moved out of the way, but that got my blood boiling the whole day.

Even when the provider's travel is unimpeded, targeted harassment can occur as the provider approaches the facility and sees protesters holding signs prominently featuring his name, photo, and other personal information. Paul Fortin, a physician at a clinic in an East Midwest state, comes to work frequently to see a barrage of signs displaying his name. The signs contain all sorts of epithets and derogatory statements about Paul, and one sign even displayed his picture in crosshairs.

Providers then get out of their cars and face the most common form of on-site targeted harassment—protesters relentlessly yelling at providers as they enter the building. Eva Sager, a clinic director at two different clinics, one in a New England state and the other in a West South Central state, described how the protesters always "lined up on either side of the barricades, everywhere. Just screaming and yelling and carrying on with megaphones." Eva explained that she experienced this "every single day. It never stopped."

This overall experience of trying to get into work can be very difficult for many providers. Roberta Keller, a physician who performs abortions and does not want even the region of the country where she works to be identified, described her experience with on-site harassment when she comes to work each day and concluded, "I always say that the hardest part of my job is getting in the front door." Ruth Hicks, a new physician at a clinic in an East Midwest state, summed up many others' feelings about the simple act of going to work by turning the tables on us during the interview: "You guys don't go to work to have someone yelling at you as you walk in the building."

## While Working

Just getting into the seemingly safe office environment does not spare providers from being targeted. Three of the eight murders of abortion providers have occurred while the provider was working—Shannon Lowney and Leanne Nichols were murdered in 1994 while working as receptionists and Robert Sanderson was murdered in 1998 while working as a security guard.

Anti-abortion extremists have found various ways to seriously harass and threaten providers at work. Lowell Taylor, a longtime abortion physician who has worked in clinics in the South Atlantic, West South Central, and West Midwest regions of the country, described a chilling incident. A protester, who would later murder another abortion provider, appeared at Lowell's clinic and asked for Lowell. At the time, the clinic receptionists did not know this protester, so they paged Lowell. He responded and went into the clinic waiting area, where the protester stated menacingly, "I know what you look like now," and then left. That same protester subsequently threatened Lowell, saying, "We're justified in killing you to prevent another murder."

Others described receiving similarly chilling communications from protesters while at work. Warren Hern is a physician in Boulder, Colorado, who has been performing abortions since before the Supreme Court decided *Roe v. Wade*. Three weeks after Dr. Tiller was murdered, one of Hern's administrative assistants received a call at work. The caller said, "I'm just calling to let you know that there are two men currently leaving Utah to come to hurt Dr. Hern's family." The caller then immediately hung up. Similarly, Cynthia Kendrick, a longtime clinic director in a Middle Atlantic state, described receiving a menacing flower delivery at work. The flowers were all black, and the attached message read "for your grave."

Another way that protesters can target providers while they are working is through their cars, which are often exposed to the public during the workday. John Steele is a physician at a clinic in a Pacific West state who has received several "pretty nasty notes" on his car while working. He recalls notes saying things like "How do you feel about the fact that you butcher babies daily?" and "I hope Satan can appreciate you in hell." Several other providers explained that protesters have placed tacks or nails near their cars, giving them flat tires when they left work.

### Leaving Work

Protesters tend to leave the facilities as the day progresses, so providers generally feel that they are at less of a risk when exiting the building at the end of the workday. Nonetheless, some protesters still target providers at the end of their workday, oftentimes using the same tactics that they employed earlier in the day.

Targeting at the end of a provider's workday poses a unique and serious problem that harassment earlier in the day does not—the risk that the protester will follow a provider home or chase the provider upon leaving work. Sarah Haupt is a longtime clinic director in both the South Atlantic and the East South Central parts of the country. She described a protester she considers to be "possibly violent" who began following her on a regular basis when she left work at the end of the day. Sarah lives in a neighborhood that is separated by a bridge from her city's downtown area. The protester used to follow Sarah through the downtown part of the city and toward the bridge to her neighborhood. Sarah said, "Luckily, I knew how to lose whoever was following me. I knew their cars. I mean, it was kind of obvious."

When Lewis Turk, a longtime abortion physician who has provided abortions in states in the Middle Atlantic, West Midwest, Mountain West, and Pacific West regions, left work one day, protesters began to follow in their car. Lewis explained that he was able to evade them because of his "high-powered sports car," a car he justified purchasing as necessary for his protection. Lewis insists it has helped him avoid protesters on multiple occasions.

### General Clinic Protest as Targeted Harassment

Separate from on-site harassment specifically targeted at a particular individual, general clinic protest can also sometimes constitute targeted harassment. As we are using the term in this book, general clinic protest is protest outside a clinic that is directed at the clinic as a whole, the issue of abortion as a general matter, or the women who go to the clinic for abortion or other services. Protests in front of clinics can be relatively nonthreatening, such as when a nonaggressive protester stands near the clinic praying quietly. Or protests can be very aggressive, such as when large numbers of protesters shout directly at women entering the clinic, hold signs of bloody fetuses, admonish women that they are going to hell, and videotape or photograph patients. Alan Stewart, a longtime clinic volunteer in a West South Central state, captured this difference:

> Some of them like to talk about peaceful prayerful protest, and there are some that stand out there and don't do much of anything. And there's others that are more vocal and active, and I mean, compared to other medical clinics in town or other businesses, you don't have people regularly standing in front of it trying to convince you to shop somewhere else or go to another doctor.

Almost every provider who talked about general clinic protest expressed serious concern about how this type of protest affects their patients. For instance, Kristina Romero explained what women entering her clinic have to put up with. "These women get hounded when they come in. They get screamed at. Protesters write down their license plates. Protesters send them cards. Protesters make phone calls to their homes. Women will do whatever it takes to get an abortion. They're the ones that are really brave, to fight through that." Lauren Henry, a clinic administrator from a Middle Atlantic state, echoed this sentiment forcefully:

> Once the patients walk in here, even though they're sometimes fully in tears and really upset because of the protesters, we sit them down privately and we just talk with them. And they're fine. They know what's going on in their lives. Nobody else does. They know why they've decided to go through with this procedure. Nobody else does. They are the ones in control of their circumstances.

Protesters also target clinics through criminal activity and tactics more extreme than general yelling and large gatherings. These tactics include bombings, arsons, anthrax scares, and mass blockades. Extremists have also thrown butyric acid into clinics, glued clinic locks shut, locked themselves to clinic property using items such as bicycle locks or chains, drilled holes into clinic roofs so that the clinic floods, invaded clinics, vandalized clinics, made threatening phone calls, tried to persuade patients to go to fake clinics, put spikes in driveways, talked outside clinics about bomb-making chemicals, laid down on sidewalks, jumped on cars, camped out in front of clinics for multiple-day stretches, and sent decoy patients into clinics to disrupt business.[3] Jennifer Young has worked for decades with abortion clinics in the South and the Midwest in various capacities, including as a counselor and director. Jennifer reflected upon the overwhelming nature of these tactics: "We were used to it every single day. When I look back on it I think, 'Oh my God, I can't believe this.'"

But most of the providers we talked with had grown accustomed to general clinic protest and maybe even dismissive of it. Rebecca Lane, a former Planned Parenthood executive director in a Middle Atlantic state, said that, though "it is awful for the patients and the families," for her the protesters became "like wallpaper." She understands and accepts that people are opposed to abortion but thinks that the people who take that opposition to the extreme of protesting in her parking lot are "a bunch of wackos."

Sometimes, however, providers view general clinic protest as individually targeted harassment. These abortion providers, particularly clinic owners, clinic directors, and certain doctors, are so deeply associated with a particular clinic that they perceive attacks on the clinic to be personal attacks. Cynthia Kendrick described having this perception when her clinic was firebombed in the late 1980s after moving to a new location:

When I think about the emotional effect on me, the firebombing didn't affect me nearly as much as all of those protesters, because there wasn't anybody that could help me with the protesters. I felt like I was the person in charge. I was responsible to the patients, to my staff, to the physicians, to everybody. It was a job that I had accepted and wanted to be doing, and I wasn't able to do it. So I had lots of sleepless nights. I don't even know, when I think back, whether I was depressed or anxious or both. Somehow, I don't know how, all the staff stayed, nobody quit.

Warren Hern described his experiences similarly. After a national anti-abortion figure announced that he was going to lead a huge demonstration against Hern in front of his private medical practice, one of the national figure's supporters threw a stone through Hern's clinic window. To Hern, because he is the public name and face of the clinic, this violence was targeted not at the clinic generally, not at the larger issue of abortion, and not at his patients but rather directly at him as a physician specializing in abortion services. In that sense, this act of violent vandalism targeted Hern, not the clinic, and is an example of how general clinic protest is sometimes perceived as targeted harassment.

## Off-Site Harassment

Harassment does not always occur at the abortion clinic, something that Tami Madison knows all too well. Tami is a clinic director in a Middle Atlantic state who has worked in the field for over a decade. Protesters regularly picket Tami at home. They also distribute flyers to her neighbors, drive through her neighborhood with anti-abortion signs and props, and confront her when they see her in the community. Tami described the protesters' determination to target her and her colleagues anywhere they happen to be:

> A number of escorts have also reported that they've run into the protesters in various places, like when we're going down the street to the corner store or the diner to get lunch, they might be in there. I feel like anywhere around here I have to look over my shoulder. When staff have walked down the street to go to the fast-food restaurant to pick up lunch, the protesters have followed them into the restaurant and shouted in the restaurant that "so-and-so kills babies" while they're picking up lunch. When they follow you outside of the workplace and do something like that, it really goes beyond what's normal.

The type of targeted harassment that Tami described, harassment that occurs away from the provider's work environment, is referred to as *off-site harassment*.

*At Home*

Based on the interviews conducted for this book, the most common location of off-site harassment is the provider's home. To many providers, this is also the most invasive and threatening form of targeted harassment because they perceive their homes to be a private and safe space away from work. Home targeting pierces this sense of privacy and security. The Supreme Court has referred to this sentiment as "residential privacy." Residential privacy, according to the Court, is "the well-being, tranquility, and privacy of the home," where people "retreat . . . to escape from the tribulations of their daily pursuits."[4]

The most extreme form of targeting at a provider's home occurred in 1998 when Dr. Barnett Slepian was murdered at his home in Buffalo, New York. On that fateful evening, Dr. Slepian was preparing dinner when a sniper shot him through his kitchen window. That sniper was James Kopp, who, in the years before murdering Dr. Slepian, had shot other abortion providers in their homes along the US/Canadian border, though the other providers survived.[5] The previous murders of abortion providers had occurred at the providers' workplaces;[6] with Dr. Slepian's death, murders of abortion providers had taken a serious new step—from the workplace to the home.

Many providers have dealt with less violent targeted harassment at home as abortion opponents commonly stage anti-abortion demonstrations outside of providers' homes. In fact, thirty-six of the eighty-seven people interviewed for this book experienced such home protest. Providers shared their experiences with home protest that involved anywhere from one person picketing outside with signs drawing attention to the provider's house to groups almost one hundred strong marching in front of the provider's residence, chanting, singing, and demonstrating against the "murderer" who lives inside. Some providers told us that protesters target their homes sporadically and unpredictably, while others told us that some protesters have developed a regular home protest schedule.

Samantha Newsom, who lives in the East Midwest state where she has worked as a medical professional at abortion clinics for decades, described her experiences with home picketing. One Saturday morning, Samantha woke up and saw fifteen people walking in front of her house. "They had signs that said I was in a bloody business. Very visible signs. They were walking back and forth and shouting." Given where Samantha lives, the protesters had to park on a side road and then walk "the length of a cornfield" to get to her home. Her home fronts on a state highway, which created an intimidating visual effect: "You could see the lineup of vehicles slowing down on the highway to look at the demonstration. So this was intimidation by the amount of people that would go by on a state highway. Their attempt was to bring attention to what I did, thinking it would affect me."

Ellen James, a director of multiple clinics in an East Midwest state, experienced home picketing most holidays, including Super Bowl Sunday, over the course of the two years before we interviewed her. Each time protesters stage a demonstration, they line both sides of the street in front of Ellen's house and arrange themselves so that Ellen can see and hear them from everywhere in her house. They sometimes park their cars on her neighbor's front lawn without her neighbor's permission. They have even set up a grill in Ellen's neighbor's yard, taunting Ellen to "come out and have a hotdog with them."

Sometimes protesters bring additional props to intensify their demonstrations, which makes these home protests even more threatening. Tamara Cocci, a physician who owns abortion clinics in a New England state and performs abortions at them, has experienced many anti-abortion demonstrations at her home. Protesters use a bullhorn to amplify their message as they yell ethnic slurs about her and call her "murderer." Sadie Hay, who worked as a medical professional at a West Midwest clinic for decades, explained how protesters targeted her by driving around her neighborhood in three large trucks with pictures of bloody fetuses on either side and ultimately parking near her house.

Living in an apartment building with many other people does not immunize providers from being picketed where they live. Charles Slattery, a longtime abortion physician who has worked and lived in states in the Pacific West and Midwest, has experienced protest at his homes in both locations. Most recently, protesters came to his mid-rise apartment complex. "They actually came and marched outside our condo a few times." According to Charles, however, "the whole thing backfired because it got on the news and everybody thought that they were just being stupid and they were shooting themselves in the foot."

Protesters target providers at home even when they live in remote or private residential communities. Kevin Bohannon, a physician who has performed abortions in a South Atlantic state for decades, lives on a private road with a long driveway. Protesters sometimes come to his house and stand on the main road leading to his private road. Other times, they parade around the small traffic circle that leads to his private road. "It is sort of silly since nobody comes down here, so it's not like they're showing the world what they're doing. But there have been as many as forty or fifty protesters on some occasions." Even though these protesters do not stand directly in front of Kevin's house, they still talk to people who drive by, pray with rosary beads, and carry signs that say, "Do you realize your neighbor is a killer?"

Protesters target providers at home in ways that extend beyond in-person demonstrations. They also send hate mail to providers' homes, make threatening phone calls to providers' home numbers, stalk providers to their residences, vandalize providers' property, and trespass on providers' grounds. As will be described in more detail in the following chapters, these different methods reach into the provider's home space, sending the message that protesters are not afraid to breach the provider's sense of residential privacy and safety.

*Other Places of Business*

Protesters do not just target providers at their homes or where they perform abortions; they also target providers where they work when they are not providing abortions. For instance, William Byers is a physician in a South Atlantic state who had not been personally targeted when we first interviewed him. However, when we checked in with him just before finishing writing this book, protesters had begun picketing his private medical office, which is in a different location from the clinic where he provides abortions. Protesters come to the office "once every couple of weeks for an hour." During their demonstrations, about ten protesters picket on the sidewalk along the office parking lot. Some of the protesters drive cars with out-of-state license plates, which worries William because, though he believes that the local protesters are not violent, he is wary of the protesters who have no ties to the local community. When the protesters are at his office, they hold up signs with his name that call him a murderer. Looking on the bright side, William says that these demonstrations advertise his abortion practice as he now has patients at his private clinic, where he does not perform abortions, asking him for an abortion.

Other providers shared stories that involved harassment at jobs completely unrelated to direct medical services. About a decade ago, Rebecca Lane left her job with an abortion clinic and started work with a charitable health foundation. People mailed letters to the board of the foundation, saying they would not support the foundation because of Rebecca's previous work as an abortion provider. Similarly, Diane Dell, a counselor and volunteer for two clinics in West Midwest and East Midwest states, told stories of former colleagues who were targeted at their outside jobs a couple of years before we interviewed her. One of Diane's colleagues ran a company that threw parties for children. Protesters showed up to the party space and demonstrated with gruesome signs while four- and five-year-old children walked into the facility for a birthday party. Similarly, protesters staged demonstrations outside of an ice cream shop that employed Diane's other colleague. The manager of the ice cream shop eventually fired Diane's colleague because the protesters were disturbing the customers.

*Elsewhere*

Off-site harassment also includes harassment at physical locations besides the provider's home or other place of business. As noted earlier, the first six murders of abortion providers occurred on-site, and then Dr. Slepian was murdered off-site at his home. The most recent murder took place off-site as well, as Dr. George Tiller was murdered at his church. This progression sends a message that abortion providers are not safe anywhere—at work, at home, or in their communities.

As the stories in the previous chapter make clear, George Tiller was not the only provider targeted at his church. Constance Phillips, an administrator for multiple clinics in a West South Central state, described something similar. Protesters at Constance's clinic recently started targeting one of her colleagues at her church prayer group. At first, the other members of this colleague's group did not know anything about her work. Once they found out, they began harassing her to the point she began to question her church community and ultimately decided to join a new parish.

Several providers told stories of being targeted at shops and businesses in their towns. A protester targeted Penny Santiago, a clinic administrator in a West South Central state, when she was at a local hardware store:

> I was minding my own business and one of the picketers recognized me and stopped in the middle of this store and started calling out to the other customers saying, "this young lady is a baby killer" and "she's evil" and that kind of thing to the customers. People just stood around and looked at us in shock, trying to figure out what was going on. I think the cashier knew this particular picketer and was kind of aligned with him, kind of waiting to see what other people were going to do. It didn't last very long, but I felt very nervous and I just left my things and left the store.

Protesters similarly targeted Nellie Wayne, an administrator in a South Atlantic state clinic, while she was at a local restaurant. "Two weeks ago I was at the restaurant and they came up to me and talked to me about Jesus."

Providers who speak out publicly as part of the political process are sometimes targeted where they speak out. For example, protesters followed Miriam Dixon, who owns and operates several clinics in South Atlantic, West Midwest, and South West Central states and lives in a particularly conservative South West Central state, around her state capitol. In the early-2000s, the state where Miriam lives tried to pass anti-abortion legislation. When Miriam testified against the legislation, she was repeatedly followed by anti-abortion protesters, including in the capitol building's elevator, bathroom, and parking lot. She relayed one potentially dangerous story: "A member of my staff jumped out in front of an oncoming car in the parking lot, because she felt like the car was coming at me. She was a roller derby girl, and I think she was right even though I didn't move. But it didn't occur to me until that moment that we might not be safe in that parking lot."

Protesters have targeted providers at the protester's own house. During the week before we interviewed her, Lauren Henry received two separate phone calls from family members to tell her about something they separately saw while driving through town. One of the most vocal protesters from the clinic where Lauren works lives on a main thoroughfare in town. This protester erected a large sign on his front lawn that had Lauren's name on it and identified her as someone who works for a "serial killer."

Even funerals are not off limits. Protesters picketed Eva Sager's husband's funeral because of Eva's job as an abortion provider. Eva recalled how the anti-abortion protesters "basically tried to obstruct the street."

In the past, when airport security was more lax, airports also used to be a place for off-site harassment. Lewis Turk told a story of flying to work in a West Midwest state:

> I got to the airport, and when I got off the plane and headed to the car rental place, there was a lot of noise. I saw placards and yelling and screaming. Then I realized that all of those signs had my name on it. Apparently somebody at the car rental business was in a pro-life group and had recognized my name. That's when the harassment started in that city. After that, whenever I flew, airport security took me down the runway, the way the pilots go on the staircase when they inspect the underbelly of the plane, and they would have a car waiting for me there.

## Media Harassment

Targeted harassment also can occur in various media outlets that are distinct from on- or off-site harassment. Providers experience targeted harassment in traditional media, such as radio, newspaper, television, and books, and, more recently, in online media.

### Traditional Media

Abortion providers have been personally targeted and harassed in traditional media, such as radio, newspaper, television, and books. For instance, a protester who regularly targets the clinic where Diane Dell works recently appeared on "the local shock jock radio drive time program" and called out Diane by name as someone who worked at the clinic. The radio show host urged listeners to call the clinic because Diane worked there, which they did en masse that day. More directly, almost two decades ago, a prominent anti-abortion extremist appeared on a Christian radio station and talked specifically about Warren Hern. Hern explained, "He invited his listeners to assassinate me. By name. Mentioned my name, quoted scripture, said that I should die."

Sarah Haupt described how a regular protester at one of her clinics gained prominence in the 1990s and appeared on a nationally televised show with a famous host. During his interview, the protester showed an Old West "Wanted"-style poster featuring Sarah. The poster said "Wanted: Dead" above a digitized photo of Sarah's face. Though her face was not recognizable because of the digitization, the protester talked about Sarah by name. Sarah recalled the television appearance:

> The protester told the host that he owned guns, and I think it was the host who asked him, "Would you shoot her?" And he said, "Not today." The protester then said that if the poster incited someone else to do it, then he would have accomplished his goal, but that he himself wasn't going to kill me that day.

Though this incident occurred in the early 1990s, the protester continued to target Sarah for years and still maintains an inflammatory anti-abortion website.

Local media outlets can also be a vehicle for targeted harassment. Several providers recounted seeing their names in local newspaper stories that identified them as abortion providers and connected them with allegedly improper medical practices. Peggy Gifford, a physician who provides abortions in three states in the Mountain West and West Midwest regions, was subjected to an investigation from local political forces about whether her medical license had expired. Peggy's name and picture appeared regularly in local media, both newspapers and television, with headlines that she felt reflected a clear bias against abortion providers. After her photo and name appeared in the local media, they made their way onto anti-abortion websites as well. As a result of the investigation, Peggy faced felony charges, even though she quickly remedied the license issue and no patient ever complained. The attorney general for the state ultimately dismissed the charges.

Constance Phillips described a unique form of media harassment. After trespassing on Constance's property and facing criminal charges as a result, one extremely vocal anti-abortion activist self-published a book that specifically discussed Constance in detail. Constance had testified against the protester at the trespassing trial and then experienced more targeted harassment from this protester and others afterward. In his book, the protester describes Constance and how he targets her, as well as the clinic where she works.

*Online Harassment*

With the huge proliferation of online resources, protesters have taken to the Internet to target providers. Probably the most high-profile form of targeted harassment in this realm occurred in the late 1990s in the form of the Nuremberg Files. The Nuremberg Files was a website that listed approximately two hundred "abortionists" by name in one of three fonts, as explained by the site's legend: "Black font (working); Greyed-out Name (wounded); Strikethrough (fatality)." The site used the strikethrough font for the names of providers who had been murdered, implying that these providers' names had been crossed off a list with more to come. In effect, the site was both keeping score and encouraging others to harm the rest of the providers on the list so that more names could be crossed out.[7] Many of the people interviewed for this book were listed on the website.

Although the Nuremberg Files website lives on only in Internet remnants hosted by anti-abortion extremists, protesters continue to post information, pictures, and videos of abortion providers on their own websites. Protesters take photos of providers and post those pictures online. They also post providers' identifying information, such as their names, addresses, and phone numbers, which they find by tracking providers' license plates or through other databases that make biographical information available to the public. For instance, Marietta Spring is a physician who has worked at clinics in the West Midwest, Mountain West, and Pacific West. One particular anti-abortion website contained all sorts of personal information about Marietta, including her medical school, the names and occupations of certain family members, and to whom she donated money.

Dustin Menendez shared a conversation that illustrates just how detailed this information can be:

The young lady I'm dating currently asked me, "I thought you had a blue Acura?" I said, "How did you know?" At this point I know why, because there's a picture of me on the protesters' website getting out of an Acura. They put my office address down, my home address, my phone numbers, everything. They say "murderer" this and that, and people are wacky, especially those that spend too much time on the Internet. She said, "I googled you, and that's what came up."

A friend of Dustin's tried to use his computer expertise to "knock down" the website. He had some success, but the site reappeared after protesters moved it to a different service provider.

Some protesters have created entire websites devoted to individual providers. Protesters created a website targeting Rachel Friedman, a longtime clinic owner and director in a South Atlantic state. The URL was her name followed by ".com." The website had her photo, her home address, and other information about her. It also linked to a separate "horrible bloody holocaust 'abortion is murder' site." Other protesters similarly created an entire website devoted to Anthony Ward, an obstetrician-gynecologist who has performed abortions at clinics in the South Atlantic and Middle Atlantic for almost four decades. The website displays Anthony's name, address, detailed biography, and photos of him and his house. The site urges Anthony to retire and encourages others who oppose abortion to take action against him, including by protesting his neighbors.

Protesters have also recorded abortion providers and put those videos on YouTube. Paul Fortin explained how the protesters at his clinic use YouTube:

If you go to YouTube and put in the clinic's name, there are quite a few things. I don't know if you've ever gone and looked. There are clips of this clinic. For a while there, the protesters said there was no film in their cameras, but there is. They get you coming in, they're standing in the aprons. There is a guy who just stands there, so unless you hit him, you have to stop your car. And the guy is right in your face with a camera. I've seen my car on YouTube, and the guy with the camera saying, "I'm going to get you." They think my name is "Forman" so they chant in the video, "We're going to come to your house, Forman."

Because the virtual world is so varied, there are many other forms of online harassment. Targeted harassment can appear in e-mail, such as the e-mail Penny Santiago received. "It said that they knew who we were and who our families were and that our families were going to pay the consequences for our actions." Calvin Litwin, a physician who has performed abortions in a Pacific West state but now works at a clinic in a Mountain West state, explained how the websites that allow patients to comment about particular doctors can be the site of targeted harassment: "At one point on one of those review sites, there were a whole bunch of nasty things written from the protesters about me." Chrisse France, a clinic director in an East Midwest state, told us that one of her staff members wound up in an exchange with somebody on Facebook who was "pretty threatening," saying things like "you should all die—you people that murder babies."

## Conclusion

By targeting, harassing, and terrorizing abortion providers at work, at home, in the community, and in the media, anti-abortion protesters send a very clear message to providers: "You are not safe anywhere." Even in places where providers may least expect to face harassment—such as in their house of worship or at the homes of family members—they are vulnerable. Not all providers face harassment at each of these different sites, but almost all of them understand that they can be targets anywhere.

# 3

## Tactics of Targeted Harassment

If you do abortions, the way I look at it, you can't be scared because they know who you are. They know where you live. They know where you walk. They know what cars you drive. They're not stupid. So you can't hide.

—ANTHONY WARD

It could have been mass murder, it could have. We just all would have been guinea pigs. His statement had said that he didn't really care who he shot. I think some of the attention went towards the doctor because he mentioned wanting to shoot a doctor, but he also said, "I'll line them all up."

—SAMANTHA NEWSOM

PROVIDERS ARE HARASSED on-site, off-site, and in the media. But what exactly do protesters do when they target abortion providers? This chapter dives deeper into how providers are targeted by categorizing the general tactics that protesters use.

The first distinction that this chapter draws is between criminal and noncriminal methods of targeting abortion providers. Many types of targeting constitute criminal behavior. The most extreme form of criminal targeting is one of the most serious acts of violence—murder. Other criminal behavior that targets abortion providers includes kidnapping, physical assaults, vandalism, trespassing, and stalking. These criminal acts not only harm the victims but also send a message to other providers that they should live in fear because it could happen to them too.

Other harassment tactics fall short of overt criminal behavior (though they can become criminal in some circumstances), such as certain communications from protesters. The best way to think about communicative harassment is to distinguish between the form and the content. Verbal attacks are the most common form, but protesters can also harass providers through writing, such as mail, signs, posters, or print and electronic media. The content of these targeted communications can include threats, exposure of personal information, derisive comments, anti-abortion messages, and identity-based harassment.

After exploring communicative harassment, this chapter then highlights two other types of noncriminal targeted harassment—professional harassment and harassment through the legal system. Professional harassment occurs when members of an abortion provider's professional community harass her because of her association with abortion or when protesters attack the provider's professional status. Harassment through the legal system occurs when protesters or government officials use law to target abortion providers.

## Criminal Behavior

Crimes against abortion providers are probably the most offensive and high-profile forms of targeting. This section describes different types of crimes that have been committed against abortion providers.

### Murder

David Gunn. John Britton. James Barrett. Shannon Lowney. Leanne Nichols. Robert Sanderson. Barnett Slepian. George Tiller. As recapped in the introduction of this book, these eight abortion providers were murdered because of their profession.[1] Among the people interviewed for this book were several who had direct knowledge of and experience with each of these murders. Those providers opened up about these shocking acts of violence.

Sarah Haupt unfortunately had personal memories of several of the murders. Sarah worked with Dr. Gunn and Dr. Britton before they were murdered in March 1993 and July 1994.[2] The murders happened over such a short period of time, which for Sarah was "pretty hard to take." Sarah reflected on Dr. Britton's murder:

He lived in Jacksonville and after protesters found that out, they were saying things to him about where he lived, his other life, his real life. But he was killed right there at the clinic. Paul Hill shot him there, with a shotgun, which is horrible. And I think that's part of the terrorist tactics, is any personal information they can find out they then throw that out there and it is unsettling.

Sarah did not have as close a relationship with Robert Sanderson or the clinic where he was murdered in 1998, but she has a distinct memory of it because she had clinics in the same region of the country:

We got the call, we actually were in clinic one morning, and my front office person came back and told me, "The Birmingham clinic has just been bombed." Or that's what they suspect, they didn't know who did it, no doctors were there. The building's got some damage, but nobody was hurt. And then the second report we got was that the police officer had been killed and the security guard was hurt so bad. We didn't know how bad. So that just took over a period of a few days to learn what it really all meant.

Eva Sager was a clinic director in a New England state when receptionists Shannon Lowney and Leanne Nichols were murdered in 1994. She described that day in detail:

We actually were in flight from down South. I was on the plane with my family. I was paged over the intercom on the plane to come forward immediately. One of the head stewards said, "We have contact from the FBI and were alerted that when you get off the plane your family must leave immediately, you need to be escorted by police to your office. A very grave emergency has occurred, and you will need to have police protection." I had no idea what happened. I got to the luggage area, I had somebody come pick up my family, and I was whisked away with the state police.

My family went home, and I went to one of the clinics and realized at that point that mayhem had occurred absolutely everywhere and the administrative assistant, who I was very fond of, was dead. And three of my associates were in the ICU and the OR. A huge number of other clinic employees were in understandable disarray, and their families were withholding their ability to go to work.

I had patients who were booked to come for surgery but had no idea what to do. It was December 30, 1994. It was a busy period of time. Christmastime could be busy with people who had work time off or a little bit of a break and so forth. At that same time, a call came in on a switchboard saying that that director of yours who has the blue eyes, I'm going to make sure she'll be dead. So Donna Shalala, who was the Director of Health and Human Services, came and met with me, and US Marshals were assigned to me, as were state police.

Robert Burton is a physician who has performed abortions for almost two decades at clinics and hospitals in two Middle Atlantic states and one South Atlantic state. He described Dr. Slepian's murder in the Buffalo area in 1998:

There were some shootings that had occurred on the Canadian border for the last three or four years—starting in the mid-nineties. And they all had the same kind of m.o. And I had known, even though it was not public knowledge, that one of the physicians in an upstate New York town, kind of on the Canadian border, had a bullet put through his window. He had a lovely home, wooded backyard, and he had a pool in his house and a lot of windows. And he was there and a bullet went through. He was also an abortion provider, and I knew this. I also know he was going through a divorce. So I tried to rationalize it. I thought, it must have been related to his divorce. Bizarre in my thinking, right? Anyhow, I knew that happened, and a year had passed and then one Friday night I started getting calls at home that Dr. Slepian was killed. So the first thing I did was I called my friend, and I said, "I think that shot a year ago was part of this." Over the phone he says, "You dumbass, of course it was. The FBI's been working on it." I didn't know. Right? So Slepian was actually the fifth person shot in the same way, and he was killed. My friend was one of them, and I didn't know this. Some denial.

Well, at that point, I'm on the phone, and I'm probably starting to shake a little bit. Because we all have windows in our home. And if you don't have enough shades in your windows . . . . Well, anyhow, at that point I got on my belly and crawled around my house. Just to give you an idea what that was like. Someone was out there, and we didn't know who it was.

Finally, Amanda Williams, a clinic administrator in the West Midwest who worked very closely with Dr. Tiller, explained her experience the day he was assassinated:

I can remember the morning when one of my colleagues called me. It was about ten thirty, and I said, "But they've caught them, haven't they?" We always talked about "they." You know, it was "they."

I was home by myself, my husband was over at the lake, and I can honestly remember thinking when she said "No, they don't know who it is, they got away," I can remember looking out the kitchen window and thinking, "I don't think I'll go outside." Besides being in a total state of shock, that was my first conscious reaction, so I guess probably I had more fears than that maybe, but you just put that all in perspective because you have to. I have good training for that. You just have a way of dealing with fears differently than I think other people do.

It was about two o'clock in the afternoon when they arrested him. By then enough people were here, everybody had a different television station on, and just listening to it because there was pretty constant local news about it. And of course the name, Scott Roeder, you're trying to place who it is and everything.

This was Sunday, so we had patients from out of town scheduled to start treatment Monday. We scheduled two weeks out for our afternoon clinic, so we always had a full calendar. So my colleague called and said that Dr. Tiller's wife was adamant that she wanted the clinic canceled, and so I called a couple other coworkers and had them meet me at the clinic Sunday night. I was in touch with the security guard on and off all day. In fact, I'm the one that had to call him and tell him what had happened. So he was at the clinic and so we went there, I think it was about six o'clock that night, and started making phone calls and got everybody canceled. Some people were already in town; they'd flown in. God, it was awful.

*Attempted Murder and Other Physical Attacks*

Providers also told stories of anti-abortion protesters physically attacking or attempting to kill or otherwise physically harm them. Physical attacks of every variety have occurred, from attempted murder and infliction of serious injury to simple forms of unwanted touching.

Several attempted murders accompanied four of the murders detailed above. When Paul Hill murdered Dr. John Britton and James Barrett in 1994, he also shot James's wife, June Barrett. Luckily, June survived the shooting. John Salvi's attack at two Boston clinics not only killed Shannon Lowney and Leanne Nichols but also injured five others who worked at the clinics. The 1998 bombing in Birmingham that killed security guard Robert Sanderson also seriously injured nurse Emily Lyons. James Kopp, the anti-abortion extremist who killed Dr. Barnett Slepian in 1998, is also suspected of shooting four other providers, all between 1994 and 1997. These four providers were all seriously injured but survived: Dr. Garson Romalis in Vancouver, British Columbia, in 1994; Dr. Hugh Short in Ancaster, Ontario, in 1995; Dr. David Gandell in Rochester, New York, in 1997; and Dr. Jack Fainman in Winnipeg, Manitoba, in 1997. All four were shot in similar circumstances as Dr. Slepian—a sniper used an assault rifle to shoot each of them through a window in his house.[3]

Several other attacks have already been detailed in this book, such as the anti-abortion protester who shot Dr. George Tiller in both arms a decade and a half before he was murdered, the man who attacked Rodney Smith in the Supreme Court building, and the protester who grabbed Lucy Brown while she was trying to exit her car.

Other abortion providers have been physically attacked as well. A protester once hit Bruce Steir, a physician who performed abortions for decades in multiple Pacific West states, over the head with a sign as he was entering the clinic. "The protester had a big sign with a handle and dead fetuses or something on it, and was waving it back and forth, and then as I approached the doorway, he hit me on the head." Bruce was fine as the poster was only cardboard. "It didn't hurt, but it was just very annoying to be smacked over the head by somebody you don't like."

Volunteer escorts who assist patients entering clinics are at particular risk of being physically attacked on site, since their job is to put their bodies between the patients and anti-abortion protesters. For instance, a protester attacked Debra Fulkerson, a volunteer escort who has helped coordinate security for multiple clinics in an East Midwest state for decades. Debra was assisting a patient getting out of her car, when the protester started to kick her. "He wears steel-toed boots, and I had four layers on because it was winter, but the leg was pretty bad. I still have scar tissue on my shin."

Anti-abortion protesters have attacked other abortion providers at off-site locations. Ryan Christopher, a medical professional who worked at clinics in East and West Midwest states, was attacked in the back of his apartment building. Although the authorities never officially identified the person who attacked Ryan, he, his colleagues, and his friends firmly believe the attacker was an anti-abortion protester.

Sharon Rhoades, a director of several clinics in the Midwest, provided an example of how protesters' attempted attacks sometimes fail. Only a few months before we interviewed Sharon, the local police thwarted a serious attack on her clinic. A man who was a frequent protester at one of Sharon's clinics was captured when he misfired his gun at a motel. The police called Sharon in the middle of the night and told her that the man had detailed plans to travel to Sharon's clinic the next morning and shoot everyone there.

Warren Hern now owns the parking lot next to his clinic, but he did not several years ago when a hostile anti-abortion demonstrator parked his car in the parking lot. Hern went outside to write down the protester's license plate number so that he could notify the police that the demonstrators were using the lot to harass and threaten patients. The protester, who was in the car, started the car and tried to run Hern down. "He tried to kill me."

Protesters have also attempted to seriously injure abortion providers at their homes. Bruce Steir explained that anti-abortion protesters set a trap at his house that could have seriously injured him:

> I went home one day from work and in order to get to my home
> from my garage I had to walk down 20 cement steps, a railing on
> both sides of the staircase, and I went skipping down those stairs and
> somebody had put a wire from one railing to the other railing at the

level of my feet. I saw the wire at the last second as I was coming down because fortunately the western sun was shining on the wire.

*Kidnapping*

Anti-abortion extremists have also kidnapped abortion providers. While there have only been a small number of reported abortion provider kidnappings, none of which occurred in recent years, the past kidnappings are still burned into the memory of many providers, especially those who knew the people involved.

The most high-profile kidnapping occurred in the early 1980s, when the owner of a clinic in Granite City, Illinois, was kidnapped at gunpoint along with his wife. Anti-abortion extremists held them for eight days. During this time, the kidnappers planned to kill the doctor and his wife. As the kidnappers later wrote, "We all agreed that the will of God would be carried out if they were executed, and we were planning for the procedure." The kidnappers did not follow through with this plan, and they ultimately released their captives.[4] Lewis Turk remembers the kidnapping:

> That was a little bit unusual because the radical anti-abortion group Army of God was the group that was implicated in kidnapping Dr. Hector Zavalos. They captured him and his wife and held them captive for about a week, but apparently he was able to escape with his wife, although I guess the trauma cost him his marriage. It was a very sad situation.

Diane Dell talked about the kidnapping as well. She said that she had originally thought the Zavaloses had escaped, "but actually the kidnappers told him, 'If you promise not to do abortions any more we'll let you go.'" He agreed, so "they drove him someplace and they did let them go, and the next day he wanted to be back at the clinic." According to Diane, Dr. Zavalos and his wife "were sure they would be killed. It was that bad."

Protesters have also kidnapped at least one provider's child. Many years ago, in the South Atlantic region of the country, protesters lured a provider's son who accompanied his mother to work one day. Jennifer

Young, who worked at the clinic where the kidnapping occurred, described what happened:

> My friend was actually working at the same clinic as me, and she brought her son to the clinic. She didn't have childcare that day, and he was about twelve, and so she brought him to the clinic with the warning not to go outside. Of course he went right outside when she was in with patients, and the antis said to her son, "Gee, you look hungry, do you want to have something to eat?" He didn't think or know or whatever and got into a van with these people, and they took off down the road.
>
> My friend came looking for him, couldn't find him, and the police started looking for him, and it was a pretty frantic few hours before they found him, and when they found him the van was just pulling up to a fast-food restaurant. Nobody knows where they had him before. My friend's son says they were driving him around, and they were saying things like, "Your mother does this because she doesn't know a better way, and if she really believed in abortion, you wouldn't be here. She would have aborted you. I know you don't want your mom to kill babies." They did that to him for several hours.

Jennifer concluded, "When he came back, he was pretty shook up, and she was ridiculously shook up."

*Vandalism and Other Property Crimes*

Much of the vandalism and other property crimes abortion providers described to us tend to fall into the category of general clinic protest. Providers detailed stories of protesters vandalizing clinics using extreme means such as arson, putting glue in the door locks, spraying butyric acid into the clinic building, shooting bullets or other projectiles through the front window, and inducing a flood in the clinic. Many of the anti-abortion vandalism stories are from the 1980s and the 1990s, but some are more recent, such as the fire bomb that gutted the clinic in Pensacola, Florida, on New Year's Day 2012 or the vandalism that destroyed a clinic in Kalispell, Montana, in March 2014.[5]

For instance, Amanda Williams explained how the clinic where she worked suffered three extreme incidents of vandalism in the years before we interviewed her. The first involved protesters setting fire to the clinic's fence in the middle of the night. The second incident occurred when protesters plugged the downspouts on the clinic roof after a big snowfall. When the snow melted, the water poured through a hole that protesters had cut in the roof membrane and damaged the inside of the clinic. The third incident was the most substantial. Protesters drilled holes in the ceiling of the clinic and ran a garden hose through the hole. The clinic flooded, and the repair work caused the clinic to close for two weeks.

Beyond clinic vandalism, providers also told stories of vandalism that involved protesters slashing or puncturing providers' car tires while the provider was at work. Donald Yates, a longtime clinic owner and physician in a South Atlantic state, routinely ended his workday to find his car tires punctured. Protesters placed drywall screws in the middle of his tire's center groove, which indicated to Donald that "there's no question that they just didn't happen to be there." Donald explained that these "suspicious flat tires" are a regular occurrence for him and others at the clinics where he works. Tonya Villa, a medical professional at a South Atlantic clinic, experienced her first flat tire from a protester's nail a year before we interviewed her. She now checks her tires whenever she leaves work.

Off-site vandalism and property crimes occur as well. Julie Burkhart, a clinic administrator who has held various positions at clinics in the Pacific West and West Midwest and is now the director of a clinic in the West Midwest, came home one day and discovered a large crucifix draped with cloth erected in her backyard. "Somebody was back there digging a pretty deep hole to stick this, literally, life size crucifix in the ground. It was, frankly, chilling." A protester came onto Rachel Friedman's property and spray-painted "Murderer" on her driveway. On multiple occasions, protesters also left dead animals in her mailbox with notes calling her a murderer. Milton Correll, a physician who has provided abortions for decades in three different East Midwest states, described how protesters came to his house and planted signs in his front yard. These signs were such a normal occurrence that when Milton put a political sign in his front lawn, his grade-school child asked, "Is that a good sign or a bad sign?" Protesters also put glue in Milton's car locks and hid nails underneath the leaves on his driveway in the fall.

Protesters have also trespassed, both on private clinic property and elsewhere. Albert Tall, a physician who performs abortions in a Middle Atlantic state, described how protesters invaded and blocked the hallways of the hospital where he sometimes practiced. Mildred Randolph, a clinic director in a Mountain West state, explained how protesters incorporated a large number of small children into one of their demonstrations at her home during Christmas:

> They were all on my steps, which is clearly on my property. But they were little kids and I'm thinking, "Really? On Christmas you're out there with your kids sitting on somebody's sidewalk with those ugly signs?" I talked to our security person about it a little bit, and he said, "Well, you know they're on your property, we could pursue that." But—they're kids. That'll look good in the papers, won't it? I'm alleging trespass by a bunch of four-year-olds. So I just moved on.

*Stalking and Following*

A surprisingly large number of the abortion providers told stories of being followed by anti-abortion protesters. This often starts on-site when the provider leaves work. Daniel Martin, an obstetrician-gynecologist who has provided abortions in the Pacific West, East South Central, Middle Atlantic, and East Midwest regions of the country, was recently followed while leaving a clinic to get lunch:

> I walked across the street to a sandwich shop, and one of the protesters, who had been conducting a vigil and probably heard that I was new, saw me walk out the door and walk over to the sandwich shop. She followed me with her camera and proceeded to come into the shop and take pictures of me while I was in line. And when I realized what she was doing, at that point I didn't react other than just to raise my hand to block her so that she couldn't take a picture. The clerk said, "What is she doing?" I said, "I work at the clinic across the street." She said, "You should have said something because we don't allow them to do that in here." Then the shop workers asked her to leave.

Well, she waited for me outside and then she proceeded to walk step-in-step with me all the way back into the clinic, and to say berating things to me like, "You should be ashamed of what you do. Why are you so afraid for me to take your picture." I said, "I'm not afraid for you to take my picture. I'm just not accustomed to people I don't know taking my picture for unclear reasons." And she said, "How much are they paying you to kill your race? You know, you should be ashamed. Doctors should give life, not take it." That constant barrage of verbal harassment, walking literally next to me until I re-entered the clinic. At the time it didn't occur to me, but I mean, had she had the intention to injure me, she would have had complete access to me.

One week in the early 2000s, Olivia Armas's coworkers noticed that a car left the clinic at the same time as Olivia every day that week. Olivia did not notice at first but became much more vigilant when the car continued to follow her. At some point during that week, "I just started taking different ways home, the extra long way home, making stops, going to the grocery store." After several more days, "it just fizzled out on its own." Olivia suspects the protester probably grew tired of following her and then stopped. Looking back, Olivia thinks that she should have been more concerned about the incident than she was at the time.

Sometimes protesters follow an abortion provider when they recognize the provider at an off-site location. Constance Phillips had trouble at a local gas station:

A protester followed me from a gas station around a grocery store, and then back in my car towards my house. It did not seem that he specifically planned to target me. It was more of an opportunity for him. He ran into me at the gas station and thought, "Oh, I know who this person is. I can mess with her." So he followed me around for a while, until I drove up to a local police station. After I had a frustratingly unhelpful conversation with the police, the protester was no longer around. He had seen that I'd gone to the police, so I was able to go ahead and drive home.

Protesters also exploit providers' fears of being followed by mimicking that behavior. Tracey Carter, an administrator and medical professional who has worked at a South Atlantic clinic for almost two decades, described her experience with protesters when she exits her car and walks to the clinic: "I park in the front. They also park there, and they literally sit in their car and stare you down. And then when you get out, they get out. And when you start walking, they start walking. And they'll walk with you along the whole building just to intimidate you."

## Communication

Most of the abortion providers that we spoke with face some form of harassing communication from protesters every day they go to work, and many face it on other days of their lives as well. This type of harassment takes almost every form that verbal or written communication can take. The messages delivered range from the mundane, such as generic anti-abortion statements or religious messages, to the shocking, such as racist comments and even death threats.

### Form

The most common form of harassing communication is verbal harassment. This can range from protesters making somewhat civil comments in a normal speaking voice to protesters repeatedly screaming and yelling aggressive and threatening messages. Sometimes verbal harassment is even amplified through the use of bullhorns or other devices. Protesters often deliver their verbal messages face to face and in person, but other times they try to reach providers on the phone or leave voicemail messages.

Providers distinguish between these different types of verbal harassment. Albert Tall explained how he shares his disdain for the more aggressive and vocal protesters with another protester who is more civil:

> There are almost two factions of protesters here. It's not like an organized group. But there are two factions. We have Barney, who is out here sometimes with his wife, sometimes he brings his kids and he's a pretty passive guy. He says hello. He asks me when I'm going to stop. He says I'll pray for you, and I tell him I'll pray for you too, Barney. But he's not threatening at all, and I'm not afraid of him. I feel like if he passed out in the summer heat I would resuscitate him.

And then we have another group who are angry and yelling and loud and megaphone-y and they're yelling and screaming. There's a couple guys who are younger, in their thirties and forties. I guess they don't have jobs, but they're here and they're yelling. They're sort of threatening and I just ignore them. I walk in and I come in quickly, and the clinic has a guard that walks in with me so I don't feel too threatened, but they're a little scary. When they're really loud and yelling and screaming, I walk in and I'll look over at Barney, and Barney will even roll his eyes like, "it's okay to make your point, but I don't agree with the way that these other people are doing it."

For some providers, the verbal harassment can be quite difficult to take. Victoria Gates, a medical professional who has worked at a South Atlantic. A clinic for over a decade, explained that "even just the verbal conversations or the words, it's just as powerful as someone throwing things at you or falling in front of your car." Verbal harassment can be even more difficult when it comes with intimidating physical behavior. When Tami Madison arrived at work after talking about abortion on a local radio show, protesters "pounced" on her as soon as she opened her car door. "From all sides. There were people at the gate where cars drive in. And people at the door and they just were on me until I walked in."

Protesters also use written forms of communication to target abortion providers. Written harassment can appear on signs at protests or flyers distributed on- or off-site. It also appears in hate mail sent to clinics, hospitals, offices, or the provider's homes. Protesters can also use the Internet or e-mail as a platform for their written harassment. Some providers bear the brunt of many of these forms of written harassment.

After being targeted verbally at her clinic for years, protesters started harassing Tami Madison through various written communications. First, the protesters distributed flyers throughout Tami's neighborhood, including one at Tami's door. The flyer listed Tami's address, identified the make and model of Tami's car, and listed a telephone number purporting to be Tami's number. Then, the protesters appeared at her home with signs displaying her name that said she "kills babies" and "hires the baby killers." While they were outside Tami's house, they handed out flyers about her to anyone walking by. One particular protester published information about Tami in his newsletter, which he both printed and published online. Tami described other "weird" and "creepy, creepy" anti-abortion websites that have also published information about her and her family, such as their names and license plate numbers.

Among the providers interviewed, signs, flyers, mail, websites, and e-mail were common forms of written harassment, but Tamara Cocci experienced an especially unusual form of written harassment. Protesters plastered stickers with Tamara's name and address on state highway tollbooths as well as on shopping carts at her local grocery store. She remembers that the stickers called her a "child murderer." Tamara perceived the stickers to be an invitation to harm her.

Picketing is a unique form of targeted harassment that combines both verbal and written harassment with harassing conduct as well. For instance, protesters picket a provider by standing outside the provider's house or marching up and down the street while yelling and carrying signs with identifying information about the provider. Charles Slattery described such a scene when protesters picketed his house: "Just parading up and down the block in kind of a long, oval type pattern, they would reach the end of the block and turn around and come back. Maybe there were fifty people carrying the usual signs. I don't think there were any with my picture on them, but my name was certainly on the signs."

## Content

The content of harassing speech can generally be grouped into six categories: generic anti-abortion statements, the use of personal information, connections to current events, attempts to interact, identity-based comments, and direct threats.

### Generic Anti-abortion Content

Protesters commonly direct generic anti-abortion statements at abortion providers. Anti-abortion statements are "generic" when they are not specifically about at an individual provider but instead condemn abortion generally. These statements can also be directed at an abortion care facility or providers generally and are usually offensive or insulting.

Almost every abortion provider is familiar with these generic anti-abortion comments from this sampling culled from our interviews: "We can get you another job." "You don't have to do this."

"We're here praying for you." "We care about you." "How many babies did you have to kill today?" "Ca-ching, ca-ching, ca-ching. You have to murder babies for money. Can't you do something else?" "You're hurting women under the guise of pretending to help them." "You're lying to women." "Dear heart, you need to leave this place of death." "You must really hate children." "You will burn in hell for your actions." "God's going to judge us." "You will meet your maker on Judgment Day, and you will atone for all these babies you've put to death." "You don't need to do this." "We can help you find a job." "You're a murderer." "You're a killer." "Everyone deserves to have a birthday." "Why are you doing this?"

Images of bloody fetuses, which have long been a standard feature of the anti-abortion literature,[6] sometimes accompany these remarks. Maggie Sims, a doctor who has performed abortions in Middle Atlantic, West Midwest, and East South Central states, explained, "Over time I got two postcards at home about baby killing. I guess they're common postcards that are sent to abortion providers and their neighbors. One has a picture of a ten-week-old fetus, very bloody. The other has a picture of a much older fetus's head being held with forceps. I guess they are very standard."

We refer to these common messages as "generic" because, though conveyed to individual providers, they usually do not reference anything particular about the provider. Mildred Randolph reflected on the tedium of the generic literature and verbal comments. "Every once in a while they say something a little different, and it kind of makes you think, 'Well, that's a new one.' But with the usual ones, you're almost thinking, 'Could you get a different sign? Could you come up with something creative? Don't you get tired of shouting that every day?'"

### Current Events

Protesters occasionally include references to tragic current events when generally protesting the clinic as well as specifically targeting abortion providers. These references play on the immediacy of the event and increase the provider's sense of fear. For instance, soon after Representative Gabrielle Giffords was shot outside Tucson, Arizona, in early 2011, protesters referred to the shooting while addressing Mildred Randolph. "I think most people's nerves were on end by the end of that weekend, so I came in and they were shouting at me, alluding to the Tucson shooting. It just gave me goosebumps."

Kristina Romero told a story of a protester linking what she and her doctor do in performing abortions to Osama bin Laden and the attacks of September 11, 2001. "There were people outside yelling at us that day, and that really upset me. The next morning they've got a picture of our doctor and Osama bin Laden, and it says, 'What's the difference? These are murderers.'"

At Tami Madison's clinic, protesters seem to use any current event they can connect to their harassment. After Dr. Tiller was assassinated, protesters mentioned his murder to several people who worked there. Protesters also alluded to the shooting of a security guard at the Holocaust Museum in Washington, DC, when speaking to the clinic security guard.

### Use of Personal Information

The content of harassing speech goes beyond generic when it includes personal information about an abortion provider. Protesters seek out information about providers—their name and other identifying information, their picture, information about family members, and details about providers' past—and then try to incorporate that information into what they say or write about the provider. Kristina Romero explained the protesters' comprehensive knowledge of her: "They call you by name. They know your kids' names. They know your mom and dad's names. They know where you go to church if you go to church." This lack of privacy, according to Anthony Ward, comes with the territory. "If you do abortions, the way I look at it, you can't be scared because they know who you are. They know where you live. They know where you walk. They know what cars you drive. They're not stupid. So you can't hide."

Providers often suspect that the protesters use providers' license plates to search for personal information about their lives. Staci Hagler, a clinic administrator in an East Midwest state, believes that this is precisely how protesters discovered details about her. Staci lives a few towns away from the clinic where she works. One day, a protester called out to Staci by name and told her to "go back" to the town where she lives. Staci's name and hometown also appear on the protesters' website. "I think they have connections, and they can get our license plate numbers and find out our personal information."

Protesters may also learn about the providers' personal information through more involved ways. After protesters at the clinic where Thomas Andrews works settled a lawsuit with the city over protest restrictions, they used the settlement money to dig up information about the people who worked at the clinic. "They hired a private investigator to figure out who the physician was, who I was, and shortly after that a hundred and fifty of my neighbors received a letter from one of the protesters with some pretty horrific things in it."

Providers also shared their experiences with protesters digging even deeper into their personal lives and using this information in their harassment. Before he died, protesters put information about Ryan Christopher's childhood on their website, including details about Ryan's religion as well as his role in the church he attended. Sharon Rhoades described protesters publishing her salary and her clinic's net assets in the newspaper.

As a complement to their harassing words, protesters use pictures of the providers or the providers' property. Ruth Hicks described how protesters use their phones to take pictures of her, her car, and other people coming and going from the clinic. "You can see it. You know someone's messing with their phone taking a picture." Melinda Birkland, a medical professional who works at a clinic in an East Midwest state, explained the use of photographs to harass the doctors who work at her clinic. "They've got a million pictures of one doctor. They've got several pictures of another, and they've been really targeting her lately. Probably not a week goes by on the website without some mention of her or a picture of her in the car."

Finally, protesters also seek information about providers' family members. Sadie Hay's husband has come under attack from protesters. Along with putting Sadie's name, address, and phone number on their website and in the bloody-fetus postcards they sent to her neighbors, protesters also included information about Sadie's husband and where he worked.

Even providers' children are not off limits. Penny Santiago explained what happened at one of the clinics where she works:

They've made very specific references to our clinic manager's child, saying that they are going to go talk to the child's teachers and sports coach. They say that they will go to the games and "make sure that everybody knows that you're a killer." It can get that personal, to the point the protesters learn about your family and they use and threaten your family to inflict fear and try to stop us from doing what we do.

Gail Weaver, an administrator with an East Midwest clinic, relayed a similar story about protesters using information about her daughter in a way that deeply troubled her:

My daughter is a basketball player, and I had a little sticker on the back of my car that has a little basketball girl and her name underneath it. One morning I was walking in to work and one protester asked me how Samantha was doing. I looked at her and I said, "I'm sorry?" She goes, "How was Samantha's basketball game this weekend?" That turned me right on my heels. My reaction was probably wrong. I said, "Don't you ever talk about my daughter. You can bash me all you want, but you leave my daughter out of it."

We bought our car at a car dealership in a different town than where we live, so she assumes that my daughter goes to school in that town, and she said that she thought it would be a really fine idea for her and her group to go to that town's high school and start protesting, making sure that everybody in that high school knew that Samantha's mom was a murderer. There were a couple months that she would be very snide about it. Like "How's Samantha?" Just to let me know that she's very aware, but she's also very unaware, of where I live and where Samantha goes to school.

Gail's story about the protester having the wrong information about her daughter's school is similar to several stories we heard about protesters with incorrect personal information about providers, which provided a rare moment of levity in the interviews we conducted. In fact, the picture of Gail that appears on the protesters' website is labeled with the name "Gail Lewis" rather than "Gail Weaver." The name "Lewis" appears on her license plate because it is her husband's "joke nickname." The protesters have mistakenly assumed that name is Gail's last name. "They think my name is Gail Lewis, which is even better because they don't know my real last name. And they think I live in this other town too."

Protesters also exploit providers' sense of privacy by hinting that they know or are trying to obtain personal information about a provider, even without explicitly referencing a provider's personal information. For instance, sometime within the year before we interviewed Maggie Sims, who lives in a different part of the country from where she provides abortion care, a protester yelled at her, "We know where you live." As described to us by several of the providers we interviewed, protesters commonly shout these exact words to other providers across the country. Regardless of whether the words are true, the clear message is one of intimidation.

Protesters also intimidate providers by engaging in tactics that make it appear as though they are collecting various pieces of information about the providers. Alan Stewart explained how protesters stand outside the clinic with little notepads and appear to write down information, such as license plate numbers, about him and the other people who work at the clinic. Ruth Hicks similarly discussed how protesters appear to photograph everything: "People take pictures. Of the car. Of me coming in. Other people coming in. Just in general." Regardless of the protesters' ultimate use of the photographs or notes, collecting this information is menacing and is a way to intimidate providers.

The reasons that protesters go to such lengths to learn and then publicize providers' personal information are not hard to fathom. In publicizing providers' personal information, the protesters are, as Paul Fortin explained, trying to bully the providers. "They think that if people are identified, if videos are put on YouTube, if they have our license plate and home address, it's just a way of bullying and harassing people." Daniel Martin called the use of personal information an "intimidation move." As he explained, "The protesters make the assumption that abortion providers are intimidated when personal information is in the hands of antis. It is never with the intent of 'I know you're an abortion provider' but more specifically, 'I know who *you* are and *you* should be concerned that I know who you are.'"

Some providers see an even more sinister motive behind protesters' use of personal information—as a harassment tactic that extends beyond intimidation. To Miriam Dixon, the use of personal information is "terrifying" because "what they're doing is trying to provoke nutty people to take action," like they have before. Teresa Spellman, a physician who has worked at clinics and hospitals in states in the Middle Atlantic, South Atlantic, and Pacific West regions, agrees. She believes that protesters who use her personal information are "facilitating the crazies."

### Attempts to Interact

Harassing speech can also include attempts by protesters to interact with abortion providers and bait the providers to respond to them. Most of the providers interviewed explained that they resist as much as they can because they believe that nothing positive can come from interacting with protesters. Nonetheless, protesters frequently try to speak to providers to goad the providers into interacting with them. Gail Weaver explained what commonly happens:

> One protester would ask me why I work here. If you turn around and respond and say something like, "I have bills to pay." He would be like, "Blood money." You know, all that stuff. "Why are you going in there?" Most of the time you just don't respond. You don't lower yourself to their level. A few times you'll say, "Because women have the right to choose. Women are strong, they're going to do it one way or another. If women have decided this isn't right, they'll figure out a way because women are strong; and if you don't have someplace where they can get proper medical care, bad things happen." But you can't say that to them because they don't allow you to say words. Once you say something they start bantering back at you, so there's not intelligent conversation back and forth with them.

Protesters can be persistent when trying to interact with providers. Constance Phillips discussed one protester who tries repeatedly to talk with her. "He keeps saying, 'But I just want to talk to you, but I just want to talk to you. Please just listen to me, I just want to talk to you.' I'm like, 'I have nothing to say to you. I have nothing to hear from you. I have no relationship with you. You are to leave immediately.'"

Tami Madison described one protester who uses a bait-and-switch tactic to try to harass people at her clinic. The protester tries to talk with the clinic workers about topics completely unrelated to abortion, such as the weather. "Then, when he gets your attention, all of a sudden he unleashes his vitriolic and hateful rhetoric and screams things at you like, 'Mommy, Mommy, don't tear my arms and legs off.'"

### Identity-Based Comments

Anti-abortion protesters also target abortion providers with comments about the provider's race, religion, or sexuality. Religion and race are common elements of general clinic protest. Many people have a religious opposition to abortion, and an increasingly common anti-abortion refrain is that abortion is a form of eugenics against the black community.[7] What distinguishes targeted harassment based on race, religion, or sexuality is that the identity-based comments are targeted at the identity of a particular abortion provider.[8]

Protesters target abortion providers using race, religion, and sexuality both directly and indirectly. The clearest form of direct targeting occurs when protesters direct epithets at the provider. Daniel Martin explained how one protester regularly calls him "a filthy negro abortionist." At one point, the protester challenged Daniel to a fight, and when Daniel ignored the challenge, the protester said, "What do I have to say to you? What do I have to do, call you the n-word?" Rachel Friedman described epithets hurled at one of the doctors working for her: "We came to work on a Saturday, and we had skinheads in the parking lot with big signs that said, 'Abort the Jew doctor.'" Tamara Cocci explained how ethnic slurs were a regular part of protests at her house. "We would have sometimes ugly, big protests outside our house with signs saying that I was a murderer. Sometimes it was very ethnically negative. I'm Italian, and there were all kinds of really ethnic slurs about Italians. The protesters tend to be very ugly and nasty."

Epithets about sexuality can also be a part of targeted harassment. Diane Dell said, "They almost always call us lesbians. In that case, that's true for me, but some people are offended by that." Marietta Spring's sexuality became the focus of protesters' attention on their website. "They outed me too, as a lesbian. 'Marietta and her so-called wife.' We have a son, but he's not seen as my son, and 'so-called wife.' Just ugly. It's all outing."

More indirectly, protesters commonly comment on the provider's race and the protester's perception of a link between race and abortion. For example, Anthony Ward, who is black, explained how a frequent protester makes comments to him about his race: "She says, 'You're killing the black race.' She comes on Fridays. She says, 'Why are you killing all these black people?'"

Protesters also comment on their perceived disconnect between the abortion provider's religion and the protester's belief about the provider's religion. Camille Diaz, an administrator at a clinic in a West South Central state, attracted the attention of a protester who saw a rosary in Camille's car. Because of that sight, the protester latched onto Camille and began to target her. "He sent e-mails about the Virgin Mary, and then he started sending postcards to my house saying that he was sending them to all my neighbors." Other protesters call Camille by name, referencing her religion and sometimes even making comments about Camille's race.

Daniel Martin is a Christian and very open about his religion, frequently discussing publicly how his faith factors into the reasons he is an abortion provider. Some of the more hostile comments directed at Daniel came in the online comment section of a newspaper article that highlighted his faith as an abortion provider. "The commenters had direct issue with my claim of faith identity. They said that there's no way that I could be a Christian and do abortions. To them, those things are mutually exclusive, so they tried to let me know that if they controlled the thermostat of hell, my position there would be a little hotter."

### Threats

About a year before we interviewed Carolyn Barrick, a clinic administrator in a Pacific West state, someone called her house phone while she was out. Carolyn's young child answered the phone, and the caller asked to speak to an adult. When the child handed the phone to Carolyn's husband, the caller told him that the entire family was going to die by the end of the day.

Threats are perhaps the most serious message that protesters communicate to abortion providers, and the most serious threats are death threats like the one Carolyn received. Many abortion providers reported receiving death threats. Some of the death threats were direct and crystal clear, like Carolyn's; others were more opaque, but the abortion provider understood the protester's language as a death threat given the abortion provider's particular situation combined with her knowledge of the world of abortion-related violence. Unfortunately, stories of death threats were common.

For example, Stephen Tate, a physician who has been performing abortions in multiple New England states for decades, received a letter at work that explicitly said that he should be killed. Eva Sager received a death threat over the phone on the same day that an anti-abortion protester murdered multiple abortion providers in the Boston area. Then, in the months following the murders, Eva received letters threatening to "do the same thing next week, so get ready." She also received letters from the individual who was in jail for committing the murders, explicitly saying that he was going to kill her.

Providers also receive threats that are not as direct or explicit, but they understand the protesters' language to contain a death threat. For instance, a protester asked Thomas Andrews how he would like to die, with the protester offering "by knife or by . . ." and then trailing off. Just days after Dr. Tiller was murdered, the same protester approached a few of the clinic's volunteer escorts and asked, "How would you prefer to die? By knife or by bullet?" Sherry Bruner, a clinic administrator in a South Atlantic state, video-recorded an indirect death threat she received the year before the interview. The protester told Sherry, "The murder and the killing don't stop at this building, they follow you home." The protester then described details about Sherry's home to her.

One particularly frightening form of implied death threat is through protesters' use of a "Wanted" poster. "Wanted"-style posters have a frightening history in anti-abortion protest. Anti-abortion protesters created these posters featuring Dr. David Gunn, Dr. George Patterson, Dr. John Britton, and Dr. George Tiller, all of whom were later murdered. Protesters have distributed similar posters that display high-profile doctors' names, both individually and in a list. One such poster was called the "Deadly Dozen," which the American Coalition of Life Activists circulated in the mid- and late 1990s. The posters listed abortion providers, listed the providers' home addresses, and accused the providers of committing crimes against humanity.[9] Some of the providers we talked with were listed on this "Deadly Dozen" poster and described perceiving it as a death threat.

Although the "Wanted"-style posters still occasionally appear, they are now less common. Instead, protesters have used other tactics to convey threatening messages on their posters. For example, a few months before we interviewed her, Julie Burkhart, a longtime associate of Dr. Tiller, received multiple threats while protesters were demonstrating outside of her house. The first time the protesters appeared, they distributed a "Wanted"-style poster throughout Julie's neighborhood. "They can't say 'wanted' any longer, but it's the same thing." The poster asked the reader to "show Julie eternal life," which Julie understood as "code" for wanting her dead. Even more menacing, when the protesters appeared at Julie's house, they held a large sign with a bloody fetus on it that said "Where's your church?" on the bottom. Julie knew that this was a reference to her former employer, explaining, "Dr. Tiller was murdered in his church, and so I took that as a direct death threat."[10]

In addition to threatening to kill abortion providers, protesters regularly threaten to inflict other types of harm on abortion providers. Diane Dell described a threat a protester yelled at her only a few days before our interview with her. "This was Saturday, and he said, 'Your souls are all in danger tomorrow.' That was pretty scary, to be so specific. So I was thinking maybe he either knows something or he was talking generally about tomorrow, Sunday, as the day of worship."

Maggie Sims received a particularly concerning threat earlier in the year we interviewed her. She was working in a state across the country from where she lives and was in her hotel room for the night:

That Wednesday night, I was in bed, at nine or so at night I got a call on the landline of the hotel and they said, "Dr. Sims?" I said, "Yes, who is this?" The guy said, "How many babies did you kill today?" So I hang up and then my cell phone immediately rang and I thought, "Oh good, it's a friend of mine and I can tell her what a horrible call I just got." But no, it was the same guy. I said "Hello" and he went on and on and on. I didn't talk anymore, and he eventually stopped. Then he called again on my cell phone, and I didn't answer and he left a message.

Maggie saved the voicemail and played it for us:

> Yes, Dr. Sims, we'd just like for you to know that we're praying for you. We're praying that you get out of the business of killing children, not just for your salvation but also either to take care of your family and loved ones that you went to school for so long to have a medical license. It would be a shame for you to lose your medical license in this state doing abortions. You're going to make a mistake, and in this state we frown upon abortion. We love children. We also care about you. But in this state we have many attorneys waiting for a woman to be injured. The first woman to come forward we're going to go after your medical license. And not just in this state but throughout the country. We care about you, and we pray that you repent and do the right thing. Please don't injure somebody. God loves you, and you won't survive this. Please do the right thing. We have people at each emergency room throughout this city just waiting, waiting for one slip-up of yours. We will pursue it to the fullest extent of the law. We hope you get out and repent before that. God bless you, bye-bye.

Given the totality of the circumstances, Maggie viewed the calls and the message as a threat:

> He was not in any way threatening me in a way that would threaten life and limb by what he said. But there was something creepy about the way that he said it, which makes one feel threatened, especially since he's calling a landline in a hotel where I'm staying and he shouldn't know I'm there. And then he's calling my cell phone, and he shouldn't know that number. So the combination of that invasion of privacy of finding me and the creepiness of the whole approach, and then they're lying in wait for me, yes, I did feel threatened.

### Professional Harassment

Abortion providers are also targeted by professional colleagues or protesters who attack their professional status. We call this "professional harassment" because it occurs within the context of the provider's

professional community based on the fact that the provider is associated with abortion.

Professional harassment is one of the reasons that freestanding abortion clinics exist. In one of her books exploring the world of abortion,
sociologist and reproductive health scholar Carole Joffe explains that
after *Roe v. Wade*, providers feared professional harassment in the hospital setting. In freestanding clinics, providers can be assured that everyone
working there supports abortion rights and will not make comments or
take adverse actions toward the provider because she is working in the
field of abortion.[11] Providers who work in nonclinic settings still experience problems like this. For instance, John Steele explained that nurses
he works with in nonclinic settings "won't support you because they
think of you differently because you're an abortion provider."

Nonetheless, despite the emergence of freestanding clinics, professional harassment continues to exist and can constrain doctors' career
choices. In her study of doctors who are willing but unable to perform
abortions, Lori Freedman discussed the effects of professional harassment on doctors working within general-practice settings.[12] Freedman
recounts one doctor explaining how difficult it was to choose between
a practice without abortion care or providing abortion care and risk
being labeled by his colleagues:

> Do I sacrifice myself for the greater good? But then I can't take care
> of my wife and kids? I don't like thinking about it too much. It sort
> of burns me when I have to think about it too much. . . . [T]o be
> labeled as the evil abortion doctor is a great way to make no friends
> amongst the OB/GYNs and to have no family practice docs refer
> patients to you.[13]

Particularly in small communities, professional harassment of abortion
providers has the potential to "result in professional failure."[14]

As Freedman discovered, professional harassment can come from
other physicians. Thomas Andrews explained that he previously worked
at a hospital; when his colleagues there found out that he worked at an
abortion clinic part-time, they tried to force him to quit working at
the clinic or leave the practice. Mathew Whitley, a longtime abortion
physician who has worked in the same city in a Middle Atlantic state

his entire life, has similarly worked at hospitals and recounted other hospital physicians who could not have civil conversations with him while at work because they were opposed to his abortion practice.

Sometimes, professional harassment comes from the top. For example, against the recommendation of his hospital's medical staff, the board of the hospital where Milton Correll worked revoked his hospital privileges because the board did not approve of his abortion work.[15] After Roberta Keller was offered a new job as the chair of an obstetrics/gynecology department at a university hospital but before signing her contract, she made a passing comment that she was looking forward to "teaching all these family practice doctors to do pregnancy terminations." The president of the hospital did not approve, so the hospital rescinded the job offer. "Basically I was God's gift to their program," she explained. "They liked me as a person. They liked my credentials. They liked how I got along with people. They liked my ability to teach. They liked everything about me until I brought up the word abortion or pregnancy termination. And slam, the door shut."

Thomas Andrews described a more modern type of professional harassment resulting from protesters targeting his professional identity:

> Once I came in to work and one protester said, "Is it true that you ripped out someone's bowels and then sent them home to die like it says on the Internet?" I didn't know what she was referring to, and I went to the Internet, and they've got all sorts of medical, "Rate your doctor" websites and I found a post like that, which was dated December of last year, when I hadn't done surgeries in five years. So in my mind the protesters are filling those "Rate your doctors" with fictitious things.

Warren Hern faced a unique form of professional harassment because of his national and, apparently, international reputation. "I went to Florence to attend an international meeting, and the Vatican denounced me. They made an announcement that people shouldn't go to those meetings because I was there. Hello? Wait a minute. What does the Vatican have to do with this meeting? It's an anthropology meeting. But I was on their list."

## Harassment Through the Legal System

Anti-abortion extremists sometimes use law and the legal process to target and harass individual abortion providers. These uses of law to target providers are distinct from the headline-grabbing legislation that restricts abortion access, because such legislation is not specifically targeted at individual providers.[16] Nonetheless, some providers are convinced that targeted harassment is connected to these legislative restrictions on abortion. Kevin Bohannon noted that, despite all of the legislative restrictions proposed and adopted in this country, anti-abortion advocates "haven't quite succeeded at what they want to accomplish, so they are trying new methods and getting more radical about it."

Researchers have also made this connection. A recent study found that states with the most restrictive laws concerning abortion have the highest reported incidences of harassment and vandalism directed toward abortion providers, though there was no such correlation with acts of violence against abortion providers. They described the harassment and vandalism connection as a "great concern" because "[e]ven minor harassment implies the threat of murder, given the history of violence in the United States."[17] As this study shows, legislation restricting abortion is burdensome not only in the way it affects abortion access for patients but also in the way that it is connected to targeting abortion providers.

This section focuses on a more specific use of law—when law and legal institutions are used in a deliberate way to target abortion providers.

### By Anti-abortion Protesters Themselves

Protesters sometimes target abortion providers by invoking the judicial process, such as by suing them. Often, the lawsuits arise from the tense interactions between protesters and abortion providers that occur right outside the clinic. For instance, the year before we interviewed Edwin Abrams, a volunteer for a clinic in an East Midwest state, a protester pushed Edwin while he was trying to give directions to a patron of another business. "I was trying to give her directions. The protester also wanted to give her directions, and he started to growl at me, telling me to get away from the car and she doesn't want directions from me. I told him I was on clinic property, and then he just pretty much put his arm out and pushed me." The police arrested the protester for assaulting Edwin. The protester then sued Edwin for emotional distress, claiming that he experienced distress as a result of spending a night in jail after being arrested. The case was eventually dismissed, but Edwin, who was a student without much money, found the protester's lawsuit against him to be "nerve-racking" and "stressful."

Others have similar stories. A protester sued Marshall Cook, claiming that Marshall ran him over when he pulled his car into the clinic parking lot. "The protester laid down in front of my car, then called the ambulance and went to the hospital. He then sued me in a civil action and lost. It's all part of the harassment." More recently, the same protester sued Marshall again for "creating an atmosphere" in which a clinic volunteer allegedly ran over the protester when coming into the clinic. Marshall had to spend thousands of dollars to defend against the lawsuit.

Protesters and others opposed to abortion have exploited the legal relationship between landlords and tenants as a way to harass providers, particularly when providers own their clinics but not the building where the clinic is located. Milton Correll tried to move his clinic to a "more upscale" office. However, he was blocked from moving to the location he wanted because "when the landlord found out what we wanted to use it for they wouldn't rent to us." Rachel Friedman had a similar experience. When she was on the verge of renting new space for her clinic in a large medical complex, the doctors in the rest of the building "found out and they really had a mutiny, and they threatened the owner of the building that they would not renew their lease, so the owner asked if I would please let them out of the contract," which Rachel did.

Protesters have also used the criminal process to harass abortion providers. The morning we interviewed Miriam Dixon, a protester at one of Miriam's clinics called the police about one of the staff members there. The protester claimed that the staff member ran into the protester on the way into the clinic and was going to press charges. Miriam stated, "She didn't run into him, but the harassment is just constant." Sarah Haupt also faced false criminal charges. The local police issued a warrant for her arrest because two protesters claimed that Sarah had brandished pistols at them when she drove away from her clinic. The local judge dismissed the charges once it was clear from one of the protester's own testimony that the protesters were fabricating the claim.

Even if a protester's claim against a provider is genuinely untrue and ultimately thrown out of court, by merely initiating the lawsuit, the protester often succeeds in targeting a provider. For example, many providers explained how protesters have used the litigation process to discover providers' identities and other personal information. Soon after Diane Dell began working at an abortion clinic in the early 2000s, she testified in court about anti-abortion protesters harassing one of the clinic's patients. As part of her testimony, Diane had to state her name in open court. From that point on, protesters knew Diane's name and used it against her when harassing her at the clinic and online. The same thing happened to Nellie Wayne after she was deposed in conjunction with a lawsuit that the Department of Justice filed against a protester. Nellie told us that when she entered the clinic before her deposition, the protesters initially thought she was a patient. However, because of the deposition, "they finally figured out who I was."

Kris Neuhaus, a physician in a West Midwest state who has worked at various clinics in that state, explained how protesters persuaded local authorities to initiate criminal charges against the security guard at one of her clinics. In negotiating with the security guard over these charges, the protesters convinced the guard to reveal all sorts of information about the clinic, including Kris's name and biographical information. This information was leaked "strictly because of the protesters, because they already had charges against him for something, so they basically were shaking him down, that's what they did. And it worked. Of course, he got fired after we found out, but it took weeks to figure out."

## By Government Officials

Some of the gravest consequences for providers occur when government officials use the law to harass individual abortion providers, oftentimes at the prompting of anti-abortion activists. With the power of the state behind them, government officials can take away providers' licenses, levy fines, impose criminal penalties, and more. Providers shared how anti-abortion protesters often take the necessary steps to initiate investigations into abortion providers and force government officials' hands. Several providers shared their experiences with government officials who reluctantly go along with the protesters because they are required to do so by law.

Others told stories of government officials who themselves oppose abortion and then vigilantly target and harass the abortion provider with all the state power the official can muster. This latter type of harassment is similar to the prosecutions abortion providers faced after World War II but prior to *Roe v. Wade*. In that time period, when abortion was almost completely against the law but nonetheless only sporadically prosecuted, government officials who were particularly opposed to abortion rights selectively targeted and prosecuted abortion practitioners for providing medical care.[18]

Many providers have been harassed through these types of government investigations. Marietta Spring described an increasingly common tactic used against individual providers, which she has experienced in multiple locations. Protesters sometimes watch the clinic where she works and monitor its use of ambulances or 911 calls in emergency situations. As Marietta explained, providers call ambulances or 911 for emergencies as part of their medical care protocol. "That's what we're supposed to do. You know your limitations as an outpatient clinic, and you transfer people, and it's better to transfer them earlier than later."

Protesters use these incidents in various ways. They sometimes post pictures online to tarnish the provider's reputation. Other times, protesters file formal complaints to state medical boards against the individual abortion provider. The complainant in these cases is not the patient, the patient's family, or anyone connected to the patient. Rather, as Marietta describes them, "complete outsiders" file the complaints. Marietta has been subject to these complaints and the state investigation that follows. She is highly critical of these investigations because she feels that state officials allow anti-abortion protesters to drive the state's own investigatory process. "Isn't it convenient to have these little pests on the side who do your work so you don't have to come off as a crazy person? They do it, and you make sure that the work gets done because you have the power."

Miriam Dixon has struggled with multiple state investigations that have targeted her and her clinics. Although most of her clinics are located in the same state and are therefore subject to the exact same rules and regulations, the state has required different paperwork at different clinics depending on the inspector who visits. Miriam explained how some of the inspectors take their inspections beyond the state requirements. Particularly in the more conservative parts of her state, the inspectors usually hold personal beliefs against abortion and use their power to harass Miriam and her clinics.

The protesters also use the inspectors and other state entities to further harass Miriam and her doctors. The protesters, not Miriam's patients, have filed several anonymous citizen complaints about Miriam and her doctors. By law, the state must investigate any such complaint, and Miriam and her doctors must weather the attack and expend resources to defend against it:

> If you think about the resources that were spent on this, it's just incredible. I still can barely sum it up. We're still kind of in it, so I haven't been able to reflect enough about it to think about it strategically, the power of the state to harass and intimidate, how profound it is, and what a brilliant strategy it is on their part.

The harassing investigations ensnarled Miriam's staff as well. A report generated from one of the state's multiple investigations included Miriam's staff's names along with their office phone numbers. That report then surfaced on a national anti-abortion website. "I was furious. I am protective of my people. 'How dare you? I told you the risk that these people would be facing, and what part of this don't you understand?'"

Perhaps the most serious government targeting described during the interviews was aimed at Bruce Steir. One of Bruce's patients died as the result of an undiagnosed complication underlying an accidental perforation of the uterus that occurred during her abortion. The medical examiner originally determined the death was accidental; however, because of outside pressure stemming from anti-abortion protesters and a zealous anti-abortion state attorney general, the medical examiner took the unusual step of changing the original determination from accidental death to homicide.

The state's attorney general then led a criminal process against Bruce that dragged on for three years. Tired from the legal wrangling and concerned about a jury in a conservative part of the state, Bruce decided to plead guilty to involuntary manslaughter. As a result, he surrendered his medical license and spent six months in jail, where he was put in protective custody out of fear that other prisoners would harm him because he was an abortion provider. Even after being released from jail and performing the required community service, he has never again practiced medicine.

## Conclusion

Taken together, it is clear that the tactics used to target abortion providers take many forms. In fact, there seems to be no limit to the ways that protesters will terrorize individual abortion providers. This chapter is thus not meant to provide a comprehensive accounting of every form of targeted harassment that has occurred but rather an organized way to think about the different tactics anti-abortion protesters use to target, harass, and terrorize abortion providers.

# 4

## Secondary Targets

I knew the antis were right about one thing: the support or lack of support by a physician's family is often the salient factor hanging in the balance, the single thing that weighs most heavily on the decision whether to continue providing abortion services. Getting to the doctor through his or her children or spouse is a despicable tactic, but an effective one.

—SUSAN WICKLUND[1]

TARGETED HARASSMENT CAN OCCUR virtually everywhere and takes many forms, but who suffers as a result? At first blush, the answer may seem obvious: abortion providers.

While this is true for much of the targeted harassment that abortion providers endure, it is not true for all as protesters often direct their terror tactics at people close to a provider as a way to influence the provider. The apparent idea behind this tactic is that if protesters target those close to providers, such as family members or neighbors, then the providers might stop working in the field to spare their loved ones distress. In doing so, protesters also prey on providers' concerns about safety. While some providers might be too invested, committed, or stubborn to stop working out of concern for their own safety, protesters apparently hope that providers might stop working out of fear for the safety of their loved ones.

We call this type of targeted harassment *secondary targeting*. The term indicates that the abortion provider is the primary target of the harassment; however, in order to reach the provider, the protesters focus on a secondary target, someone close to the provider. This chapter looks at secondary harassment against four different groups of people: family members, neighbors, others, and mistaken targets.

## Against Family Members

Anti-abortion extremists do whatever they can to find out information about the families of the physicians who work at Tamara Cocci's clinic. "They run the registry plates. They run all of the different births, death, marriage, data registries to find out other names of people that are associated with this person or their children or their parents. Then they find them and harass them." Tamara gave one recent example. "One of the younger fellows that was working for us—protesters sent one of those fetal severed head postcards to the university office where his mother worked." Secondary targeting of family members like this often occurs against providers' children or parents, but other family members can also be targeted, such as providers' spouses and other loved ones.

### Children

As Susan Wicklund articulated in the quote that begins this chapter, targeting providers' children sounds like a despicable strategy, but many providers shared experiences with anti-abortion harassment aimed at their children. Protesters can target providers' children on-site when providers bring their children to work for a day, a common occurrence for working parents in many professions. For instance, on the day we interviewed her, Florence Davis, an administrator who works at a clinic in a South Atlantic state, brought her young daughter with her to the clinic. When she and her daughter entered the clinic, protesters began gesturing to Florence's daughter and telling her to come over to them. According to Florence, protesters were "waving to her with big smiles, and telling her, 'Come here, come here.'" Previously, whenever Florence brought her daughter to the clinic, she used an entrance that the public could not access, so protesters had never before targeted her daughter. However, the day Florence came into the clinic for the interview, she explained that she "didn't even think about it" and instead used the entrance in front of the protesters.

Florence was particularly disturbed by the protesters' beckoning to her daughter in this manner. As recounted in Chapter 3, many years earlier in Florence's region of the country, a provider's child was kidnapped under similar circumstances. Given this background, Florence's worry for her daughter's safety in the face of the protesters' luring behavior was understandable.

On-site secondary harassment of children can also involve the use of personal information. For instance, Sarah Haupt's daughter worked at the clinic with her and was also a provider, but Sarah believed that protesters targeted her daughter particularly as a way to target Sarah. Sarah's daughter is adopted, which the protesters discovered. The protesters routinely shouted at her, saying, as Sarah recalls, "You don't need to be doing this work. Your own mother didn't want you. You poor thing. Sarah adopted you. What a horrible life you've had."

Protesters have similarly tried to interact with providers' children at various off-site locations, such as the provider's home. When they were growing up, Cynthia Kendrick's children received multiple death threats over the home telephone. "My kids would be home from school, and some antis would call them up, and when they answered the phone they were told they were going to be murdered." Tamara Cocci explained that protesters learned her children's names and used that information when protesting in front of her home. "If any of the children came up the driveway or came back from school, the protesters would use their names and ask, 'Which one are you, are you this one or that one?'"

Off-site harassment that providers' children face can also be connected to the children's schools. Todd Stave, a property owner in Maryland who rents space to an abortion clinic, has two children who were targeted at their school. Just a couple of months before we interviewed Todd, the protesters who regularly protested at the clinic showed up at his children's school:

> The first day of school they went to my daughter's middle school and protested there. It was a mystery to everyone except me as to why they were protesting there. They protested as the children were arriving to school on the first day of school, but there was no mention of my name or my daughter's name or anything like that. Then they showed up at my daughter's school the next day with a poster with my picture and everything. The picture was four feet by two feet, I'd

say. So there was a picture of me on one side of it, and then it said, "Todd Stave, stop the child killing." And then on the other side of the street were a couple of people holding up the posters of aborted fetuses.

Todd's experience was not unique. One physician who wanted to be identified only as Dr. P. explained how his colleague was followed home by protesters. The protesters then discovered her children's identities and followed them to their school.

Schoolmates are sometimes the harassers. Lewis Turk related a conversation he had with his grown children about their experiences growing up with an abortion provider as a parent. "I said I hope it hasn't impacted you too much at school. And they said, 'Oh, Dad, you'll never know.' That kind of opened the floodgates of the harassment that they had at school. Their dad is a murderer, a baby killer and all that sort of thing." Eva Sager shared a similar story about her grown daughter. "Over time she sort of talked a little bit more about how it was for her to grow up with a provider as her mother." When she was in school, Eva's daughter's classmates taunted her, saying things such as "my parents told me that your mother kills babies" or "she's a baby killer."

The ways in which protesters have targeted providers' children are almost endless. Kristina Romero told us how one protester who has repeatedly harassed Kristina makes a point of menacingly saying hello to Kristina's son when the protester sees Kristina and her son around town. Camille Diaz's son was harassed when a protester discovered his school e-mail address and sent him an e-mail. The e-mail urged her son to force her to stop working at the clinic. Camille and her son knew that the e-mail was "just another tactic" to try to intimidate her into quitting.

*Parents*

Abortion providers' parents can also be secondary targets. Protesters have used the Internet and other media to publicly identify them as parents of abortion providers. For instance, Ryan Christopher's parents were identified not only by name on a website that targeted Ryan and others who worked at his clinic but also by name and hometown on signs that protesters displayed in various places throughout the community.

Protesters have gone even further and contacted providers' parents. Tami Madison's mother received letters from protesters, telling her that Tami was a "bad Catholic" and that Tami's mother should have done a better job raising Tami. Just days after Maggie Sims received multiple threatening phone calls in the East South Central state where she was working, the same person called her mother, who lives in a New England state. "She's an old lady, and she answered and talked to him briefly and then realized what his story was and hung up on him." Maggie explained further, "He called back, and he left a message on her voicemail, and I actually have that on my computer. It was very similar to the message he left me. Tell your daughter to get out of the business." Maggie found the calls particularly "creepy" because the caller knew very specific details about her mother's past and used that information to harass her. "He had done his research on her."

As with the use of providers' personal information, when protesters broadcast where a provider's parents live or contact a provider's parents at home, providers and their families fear that the protesters will act on that information by demonstrating outside of the parents' home, or worse. Two providers described experiences with this, and both incidents involved nursing homes. Samantha Newsom relayed such a story about a doctor who had previously worked at her clinic. The protesters used to "go to her mother's nursing home and would protest outside. She got phone calls there too. They would call and harass her mother."

Sarah Haupt explained an experience from a few years before we interviewed her, which turned out to be a very touching story. One day, Sarah was visiting her mother, who was in a nursing home after a hospitalization. An anti-abortion protester from Sarah's clinic saw Sarah's car parked in front of the nursing home. Recognizing the car, the protester stopped and entered the nursing home. "I was sitting in there with my mother, and I saw her go past the room, and I just thought she must have someone here too. In a few minutes she came back to the door and came into the room and addressed my mother by name and got kind of loud."

The protester began by saying she would pray for Sarah's mother despite her daughter's job, but then the protester's speech escalated to shouting at Sarah's mother that Sarah is a murderer. Sarah then confronted the woman:

> I got up and was walking towards her and saying, "You need to leave.
> You need to get out." My mother had already said, "I don't want
> to talk to you, I don't want you in here. Leave." And the lady was
> protesting and saying, "I have a right to be here, and I'm not going
> anywhere."
>
> Good old karma, here comes this big strapping nurse, and she
> stepped through the door and sort of pushed her back into the hall
> and walked out with her, and she was saying, "Oh, yeah, you're leav-
> ing. I'm taking you out right now." Then the nurse came back in and
> shut the door, and she said, "Security is coming to take her out of
> here, I'm so sorry."
>
> As soon as things began to calm down a little bit, the nurse said to
> my mother, "I want you to know that your daughter saved my life. And
> I am so glad that I was able to do something to help you." Then the
> nurse looked at me, and she said, "I know you probably don't recognize
> me, but I'll never forget you helped me." She said, "I came for an abor-
> tion, and I was really conflicted." She had lived with a man for several
> years, marriage was in the plan, and then she got pregnant. When she
> told him, he reacted badly. She was hurt and didn't know which way to
> turn, and she'd come into our clinic and I did the ultrasounds, so I was
> the first main staff person that she dealt with away from everybody
> else. She seemed a little conflicted to me, and we talked about it. I said,
> "You understand that you don't have to do this. Nobody is going to
> make you. We're here to help you whatever your decision is." She was
> pretty early in her pregnancy, and I said, "You've got plenty of time.
> You can think about this awhile. If you decide to come back, we'll be
> here for you. If you don't, that's okay too. Whatever you decide, make
> sure that's the best thing for you." And I hugged her.
>
> When she recited that back to my mother, she said, "When she
> advised me to do what was best for me and hugged me, I knew that
> this is where I wanted to be."

Sarah cannot recall whether the nurse ultimately chose to have an abortion but feels that is immaterial to her story. The nurse's help with

the protester invading Sarah's mother's room and kind words thereafter were "amazing" and "meant so much" to Sarah and her mother.

### Other Family Members

Spouses and significant others are sometimes targeted. For instance, Warren Hern told us that protesters have harassed his wife by following her to the hairdresser's salon. Sadie Hay's husband's name appeared on a protester's website. He was also specifically identified in a postcard that was distributed throughout Sadie's neighborhood. Julie Burkhart's husband has also been targeted. He has received frequent phone calls asking, "Do you know where your wife is? Do you know what your wife is doing?"

Protesters target other family members as well. After Elizabeth Moll, a physician in a Midwest state who has worked in family medicine since the mid-1980s, announced that she was going to expand her practice to provide abortions, protesters began picketing her god-brother's house. The protesters appeared at his house at least two times per week. "It was dark. It was a country road with not a whole lot of people on it, clearly just a group of people in the road to harass people that lived at that house." When protesters learned that Elizabeth's god-brother is gay, they added "God Hates Fags" signs into the mix with the anti-abortion signs.

## Against Neighbors

Neighbors can also be secondary targets. For instance, neighbors are often swept into protesters' targeting when protesters stage a demonstration outside of a provider's home or when they blanket a neighborhood with hate mail targeting a provider.

Rachel Friedman described a typical way that neighbors become secondary targets of anti-abortion protesters' harassment. "I lived in a gated community, so they would protest outside the gated community with signs that said, 'Rachel Friedman, your neighbor, is an abortionist.'" One protester who has been a particular problem for Rachel and her clinic has sent literature to Rachel's neighbors saying, "Do you know your neighbor is an abortionist?" The letters included Rachel's picture and address.

Chrisse France had a similar experience. One of Chrisse's neighbors was talking with her when protesters arrived to demonstrate in front of Chrisse's house. The protesters began their demonstration by yelling at Chrisse's neighbor because of Chrisse's job. Protesters have also leafleted Chrisse's neighborhood with information about what Chrisse does for a living, telling the neighbors that they should be horrified.

Hate mail directed at neighbors is a form of secondary targeting because the protesters' actions invade the neighbors' space and are apparently intended to scare them. Soon after Miriam Dixon bought a clinic in the West South Central state where she now lives, protesters sent hate mail to her neighbors:

> They circulated an eight-by-ten picture of me with my home address, calling me a serial killer of boys and girls. They circulated it to a hundred and eighty different neighbors, the school district, all the teachers. The photo they took of me in the parking lot of the clinic had my full name, my home address, but didn't have my phone number. A couple of people thought I was a serial killer who had been relocated to the neighborhood.

Thomas Andrews received mail from a protester warning him that the protester would show up at his house. The protesters then sent all of Thomas's neighbors the same letter saying that Thomas did "horrific things." The protester threatened that if the neighbors did not stop Thomas, the protester would come to the neighborhood on a regular basis. Thomas did not leave his job, and the protester has regularly protested in front of Thomas's house for years.

Stephanie McGoldrick is a physician who used to perform abortions in East Midwest and Middle Atlantic states. Her neighbors received the same type of mail the others described, but one neighbor wound up being targeted more personally. Because Stephanie travelled to and from work in a disguise, the protesters desperately wanted a picture of her without the disguise. They sent mail to her neighbors asking for pictures and, bothered by the letter, one of her neighbors responded. The neighbor wound up in a long back-and-forth exchange with the protester. As a result, the protester identified this neighbor by name in the online newsletter that the protester maintains and sends to people in jail who have committed acts of anti-abortion violence.

Protesters at Tamara Cocci's house have even harassed neighborhood children. The protesters picketed on Halloween as children were going to and from Tamara's house. The protesters stood in the driveway and stopped the children coming to the house. Protesters told the children that "a dangerous murderer lives there" and handed out "little religious cards" to the kids.

## Against Others

Other people and entities are also secondary targets. Protesters target some of these people and entities in an apparent effort to target clinics as a whole and not just an individual provider. For instance, Ellen James related a story about protesters targeting one of the donors to Ellen's clinic. About two years before we interviewed Ellen, protesters knocked on the donor's front door, and the donor's young adult daughter answered. Protesters screamed at her that her father supported killing babies. Afterward, the lead protester posted three photographs on his anti-abortion website: "The first photograph is this huge-bladed knife lying across a computer keyboard. The second photograph is a stack of boxes of thirty-eight bullets. The third photograph, the donor's daughter." Ellen's donor's daughter is not herself an abortion provider but was individually targeted because of her connection to the clinic.

Contractors and other service providers are also sometimes secondary targets. One provider, who does not even want his pseudonym used for this story, talked at length about his experience with protesters' extensive harassment of the people and companies involved in building his new clinic. Protesters called one company executive's mother at her nursing home and went to another executive's house early in the morning and shined lights in the front window while blasting loud music. Protesters also staged anti-abortion demonstrations outside of the homes of three senior-level contractors every weekend for a year.

Marshall Cook is the primary doctor at the clinic he owns. The protesters who regularly harass Marshall also harass the postal employee when she delivers mail to the clinic. The protesters scream and yell at the postal employee and occasionally have blocked her from delivering mail to the clinic. Marshall made it clear that he considers the targeting of the postal employee a way to target him individually because the clinic is so closely associated with him. Miriam Dixon similarly connected protests against her waste disposal company as attacks on her because she was eventually dragged into a prolonged legal battle over waste management due to the protests and was the face of the clinic during the dispute.

In fact, anyone or anything associated with a provider is a possible secondary target. Several providers explained how protesters picketed providers' churches because of their work. Others told stories of an unrelated employer being targeted. For instance, Kris Neuhaus began her career working for a major university in her state and performing abortions at a local clinic as a side job. Protesters harassed the president of the university for employing Kris, even though she did not perform abortions at the university. The medical director of the university was "totally supportive," but Kris eventually left the university job, in part because of this pressure.

Protesters targeting Elizabeth Moll went a step further in their secondary targeting. When Elizabeth was looking to open a clinic, she found a building she was interested in renting. Protesters then targeted her *potential* landlords:

> We contacted the realtor, the realtor was pro-life and refused to meet with us, so we contacted the owner, and the owner was more than happy to meet with us. They were actually going to lease us the building, but the night after we went to visit the building it was vandalized. Somebody wrote in red paint "Wake" across the front of the building, so I don't know if that was a wake for the babies, the owners, or me. They were a little eighty-five-year-old couple. There were candlelight vigils at their home until they withdrew the offer. It was in a matter of three days they decided they had to pull out because they were worried about their safety.

## Mistaken Targets

In their quest to target providers, protesters sometimes make mistakes and target the wrong person. While providers laughed when telling some of these stories because the protesters seem foolish during their missteps, providers also recognized the serious and unfortunate result of the mistake—a completely unrelated person is inadvertently harassed or harmed.

For security reasons related to anti-abortion violence, Warren Hern owns multiple properties in the area of town where he lives. The protesters who target Hern wound up targeting someone living in one of those houses under the impression that it was Hern:

> I bought two houses adjacent to me so that anti-abortion fanatics could not acquire them. The anti-abortion people have a reputation of, on numerous occasions, a house goes up for sale across the street from a clinic and they go buy it. Because I like to sit and play the piano in the middle of the night in the summertime with the window open, I don't want someone to blow me away like Dr. Slepian, shoot me in the back, while I am playing the piano. I can't guarantee it won't happen, but if somebody that I know is living there, it's less likely to happen than with somebody I don't know. So I own the properties at great expense, and I'm deeply in debt for this. It's a major problem for me. But at one time my nurse was living in one of the houses with her kids so she could be close to my office when she is on call. It was under my name, so they thought that's where I live. They came and gave her one of these flyers, and she gave it to me. My address is concealed, so they didn't know exactly where I live.

Similarly, sometimes people completely removed from the abortion care field are mistakenly dragged into the protesters' harassment. Elizabeth Moll explained how, earlier in the year we interviewed her, a mistake by protesters resulted in someone else being targeted. "We had moved from a house into a condo. They initially picketed this house that had just been sold to somebody else because the woman there worked for a hospital and was wearing scrubs and it took them a little while to figure out I wasn't there." Ellen James had the same experience. Months after she moved, the protesters picketed her old house. When one of Ellen's old neighbors yelled at the protesters that Ellen no longer lived there, the protesters began verbally harassing Ellen's neighbor with anti-gay epithets.

Sometimes protesters' mistakes come from confusion over names. Mark Goldstein, a medical professional at an East Midwest clinic, works part-time at a hospital where one of the doctors has the same name. "He's a pretty big-shot guy. Nice guy, but I felt bad because his name—our name—was on anti-abortion posters, and some people did ask him if he worked here. So it was kind of a weird thing." Maggie Sims had the opposite problem—the protesters originally had the wrong name for her. As a result, someone else suffered:

At first they addressed me by a name that is not my own, and I don't know what that name is, but it wasn't mine. They were confused about who I was. There was a doctor who lives in another state almost a thousand miles away who complained to the owner of the clinic where I worked that she was getting harassing calls and she doesn't even provide abortions and she lives far away. For some reason they thought I was her.

Marietta Spring was bewildered by the protesters' mistaken attempts to target her. A few years before we interviewed Marietta, protesters sent postcards to people who lived in Marietta's home neighborhood, in a Pacific West state halfway across the country from the West Midwest state where she provides abortion care. During our interview with her, Marietta pulled out a "neighborhood alert" that purports to display her picture and explained, "It's so funny this neighborhood alert, it's not even me. They got me confused with someone else. I feel sorry for that person." She showed us another postcard and remarked, "This is also pretty funny, since it's not me." The same woman's picture was on the postcard. "I don't know her by name, but my wife and my son are volunteers for an organization. The organization had this other woman's picture on their website, and maybe my name was on it by mistake or something, so the protesters just thought, 'Well, that's her.'"

Sometimes mistaken targets can suffer extreme acts of violence. In the 1980s, Charles Slattery shared office space with a family physician. Protesters tried to target Charles with butyric acid. Butyric acid is a powerfully noxious chemical, and very small amounts can pollute an entire building. The protesters who targeted Charles mistakenly attacked the side of the building where the other physician worked.

"The protesters just didn't know, and I just felt terrible about that. He obviously had nothing to do with it." Charles believed the mistaken attack on his officemate was triggered by a public remark that Charles made to a newspaper about the general issue of abortion protesting. "I made the comment that I don't apologize for what I do, and I'm very proud of what I do, so I think that ticked them off."

Kris Neuhaus had a similar experience but with an arson. "They actually were successful at burning down an entire internal medicine clinic where I used to work, which was right next to our clinic. Our clinic looked like a house, so I think they were so dumb they just burned the one that looked like a clinic." Kris remembered the doctor whose internal medicine clinic was burned down commenting in the newspaper the next day, "I'm against abortion, so the irony is they burnt down my building and I'm even anti-choice."

## Conclusion

Almost anyone associated with a provider can be a secondary target as protesters go to great lengths to make the provider feel threatened, intimidated, and isolated. In fact, even people not associated with a provider can be secondary targets because protesters often make mistakes and target the wrong person.

This chapter and the three that precede it paint a chilling picture of abortion providers' lived experiences. Providers, their families, and their neighbors are terrorized at work, at home, and elsewhere in their communities. They are threatened, assaulted, stalked, picketed, vandalized, harassed, and murdered. Their personal information is abused to ensure that they and the people they love are intimidated and live in fear, all because they provide a medical service that over a million women per year access and that about one in three American women will undergo.

Largely missing from these stories of the where, how, and who of targeted harassment are the stories of how targeted harassment affects abortion providers. The next two chapters explore this and will show that, although very few providers are deterred from abortion provision because of it, targeted harassment affects abortion providers' lives in profound ways.

# 5

# Providers' Reactions to Targeted Harassment

You just accept it as your normal, and somebody else has no idea that it's even close to being normal. There's no other area of medicine that has to deal with this type of harassment. What's sad is the things that have become my normal are not normal.

—SAMANTHA NEWSOM

If you want to put forth your ideas and parade around in front of a clinic, that's fine, but leave me alone at my house on a Sunday.

—KEVIN BOHANNON

ABORTION PROVIDERS' REACTIONS TO the targeted harassment detailed in the previous chapters vary immensely. For instance, the simple act of a protester discovering a provider's name can cause deep emotional turmoil for the provider. When the protester then calls the provider by name at work, the provider feels that her privacy has been violated. She fears that this one act might mean that some violent protester will harm her. As a result, the provider takes precautions. Perhaps she tries to hide her identity through both a disguise and by erasing her presence online. Perhaps she also takes different routes to work each day and considers investing in a bulletproof vest or gun. In other words, the protester's single act of using the provider's name changes the provider's life.

For other providers, almost nothing seems to rattle them. Protesters may shout the provider's name, address, and other personal information about her children. They may demonstrate outside of the provider's home or other place of business. They may have even threatened the provider in some way. Yet the provider believes this is what is "normal" for people in this field. The provider further rationalizes that there have been murders of abortion providers but that these murders are not common. With this attitude, the provider takes no extra precautions and is not bothered by what she experiences.

Of course, between these two extremes are many reactions and responses to targeted harassment. This chapter and the one that follows finish the first portion of this book by looking first at how abortion providers react to and then at how they respond in an effort to prevent or protect themselves from targeted harassment.

Including these two chapters in the book was a hard decision. On the one hand, consistent with one of the main goals of this book, we and the providers we interviewed want to inform the public about targeted harassment and convey how seriously it affects abortion providers' lives. Dustin Menendez expressed this sentiment forcefully: "Let them know, let them know that I am frightened. I feel physically threatened."

Carolyn Barrick also insisted that people know how she has been affected. During our interview with Carolyn, in the midst of explaining how terrified she was after receiving a death threat the previous year, she developed acute chest pain. After taking a short break from the interview, she said, "You can put that in. Seriously, put that in. I never have anxiety attacks like that, like maybe twice a year." Before the interview, she had not had anxiety-induced chest pain in over ten months. She said, "The only reason the chest pain is important is because it only happens when I'm really stressed out. As someone who has these anxiety issues at times, it would be really important to me, if you think it's relevant, that I developed the chest pain when we were talking because I was so stressed out." As Dustin and Carolyn make clear, providers' emotional responses to targeted harassment are a very important part of their experiences.

On the other hand, including information about the effects of targeted harassment risks encouraging anti-abortion protesters to take more extreme action. After all, if extreme targeted harassment leads to providers experiencing intense fear and serious distress, then maybe protesters will feel that they are successfully terrorizing providers to the point where they may stop working. This risk has led to what Carol Mason, a professor who has studied far-right extremism in the anti-abortion movement, has called an "unofficial policy of silence" regarding targeted harassment. According to Mason, most accounts of anti-abortion harassment and violence do "not publicize the day-to-day effects of anti-abortion harassment and violence for fear of giving their opponents satisfaction, encouragement, and media attention."[1] The providers we interviewed were acutely aware of this possibility and took it very seriously.

While we understand the complexities of this issue and appreciate that others may feel differently, we have nonetheless elected to include these chapters because of their importance in telling the complete story of targeted harassment. Moreover, we agree with Mason, who has argued that silence around these issues has the twin effects of isolating providers from one another by keeping some abortion providers in the dark about their profession and muffling the voices of the people who provide care on a daily basis.[2] Lisa Harris, an academic obstetrician-gynecologist who has also studied this silence, has similarly found that it contributes to "the ongoing targeting of providers for harassment and violence." The harassment and violence reinforce the silence, and "the cycle continues."[3]

We discussed this risk with all of the providers when obtaining their consent to be interviewed, and each elected to proceed with it in mind. They hoped that sharing their stories about the effects of targeted harassment would make the public more willing to condemn these acts and work to make them a relic of the past. The providers were committed to telling their stories, even the parts of their stories that reveal the serious effects that targeted harassment has on their lives, so these reactions are included here.

## Emotional Responses

Emotional responses to traumatic events like being targeted by extremists can be complex. For instance, when Marietta Spring received harassing postcards at home, in a different state from where she worked, she experienced multiple conflicting emotions. On the one hand, she called the postcards "harmless" and said "what else is new?" On the other hand, she also called them "disgusting" and "gross," concluding that "in a way it's a big deal." Marietta's emotional responses also varied over time. As she explained about the ways she is targeted on the Internet:

> I go up and down with it, and right now I'm in the phase of "I need to remind myself not to look and not to get caught up in that stuff," because it's so ugly and it's destructive and it's not helpful at all. It's like being an alcoholic, sometimes I slip and I have a drink. I take a look and it's really not a good thing. It's a never-ending process of dealing with it.

These complexities appear in the wide range of emotional responses explored below. Like Marietta, the same provider may express both fear and stoicism, and these reactions might morph over time. What is evident, though, from these varied, changing, and seemingly contradictory responses is that dealing with targeted harassment can be extremely difficult on providers and that providers have a multitude of ways of coping with these serious acts of intimidation.

*Fear*

Fear is one of the most common emotional responses to targeted harassment. Many providers expressed a generalized fear, not tied to any particular instance of harassment. For instance, Amanda Williams worked at a clinic that was the target of many extreme acts of vandalism. She also worked closely with Dr. Tiller and acutely and personally felt the effects of his assassination. She described being followed home from work by the president of a national anti-abortion organization:

> I remember one day I'd come home from work and left my vehicle on the driveway because I was going to come back out to run an errand. I hardly ever did that. Usually I opened the garage door and pulled in. I remember being there in the kitchen and seeing him come down the street and park in front of the house and start taking a picture. I thought, "Oh my gosh." I totally didn't see him following me home, but obviously he had been.

After describing this incident and the other ways she and her colleagues have been targeted, Amanda revealed her general fear about her line of work. "I suppose if I wanted to be really honest, I'd have to say I was scared sometimes, not knowing what I was going to find at home or at the clinic."

Other providers connected their sense of fear to a particular incident. After Carolyn Barrick received a death threat at home, she was "just terrified, just terrified." She and her family did not sleep at home that night because of the threat. "You're lying in a hotel room and you're just thinking, 'Jesus, am I really going to die?'" Over the course of the next week when she was home, every time she opened the blinds on her windows, she was "afraid someone would be standing there." At this point in our interview with her, Carolyn had the acute chest pain described earlier in this chapter. After she recovered, Carolyn said that the protester who she suspects made the death threat still protests at her clinic. "He still scares me and makes me mad when I see him today."

Warren Hern shared his reaction to a terrifying experience when an anti-abortion extremist followed him as he drove through town:

> I pulled out of here to this intersection, and this particularly threatening protester was behind me with his truck. It scared the shit out of me. I took a turn and he followed me, and I turned and he followed me, and I turned and he followed me. I had to take evasive action. So I went to the top of one street and turned again, but he had to wait for traffic. I accelerated, hit the top of the hill, and went down and turned right onto another street and back up the other way. I lost him. I was shaking.

When protesters dig up and disseminate providers' personal information, providers feel a particular sense of fear related to the invasion of their privacy. Protesters regularly shout at Lenora Polanco, a longtime medical professional for a West South Central clinic, whenever she is at her clinic. They have taken their harassment a step further by notifying everyone in Lenora's subdivision of her address and profession. Lenora explained how this new tactic of spreading her personal information affected her: "I was scared a little bit, because they know exactly where you live."

Lowell Taylor, who has suffered a lifetime of targeting by some of the most extreme members of the anti-abortion movement, was particularly fearful about protesters' use of his children's names and birthdays as well as his address and other personal information. "Sure it feels threatening. It has to. It impacts everything about you. Your family, your marriage, and so forth."

Home protests invoke a unique sense of fear, which Samantha Newsom explained:

It felt vulnerable, because now it was a little more personal than happening where you worked. Not that they didn't call out my name at work and mention my children as I left work in the parking lot as forms of intimidation. Always with the attempt to have you feel intimidated. I felt more vulnerable because it was at home and who do they know and that felt icky. I had been in abortion services for fourteen years before they came to my house, so it wasn't like it dissuaded me from what I was choosing to do, but now it was affecting my family in a way that it hadn't and that was hard.

For some providers, knowing information about one or more of the protesters made them fearful. Bruce Steir was "next on the list" that the police found after arresting a violent anti-abortion extremist somewhere else in the country. Because Bruce knew this extremist's particular history of violence, he became "a little concerned" for his safety. Similarly, having seen a particular protester's "really threatening" website, Albert Tall explained that it is "really frightening" when that protester demonstrates outside of his house, which occurs on a regular basis.

In contrast, not knowing a particular protester can also invoke fear. Catherine Thompson, a longtime clinic volunteer and escort in a West South Central state, talked about the unknown protesters:

The ones that I do worry the most about are the older people who I don't recognize, the ones who don't seem to be fraternizing with the other people. They're not handing out pamphlets. They're just kind of standing off by themselves. Those are the ones that I've always been the most concerned about because you don't know what those people are capable of doing.

Providers expressed fear in chilling ways when talking about how the murders of other providers affected them. In particular, providers spoke passionately about how deeply the 1998 murder of Dr. Barnett Slepian in his Buffalo home and the 2009 murder of Dr. George Tiller in his Wichita church still resonate with them. Mathew Whitley, who has been working in this field for decades and has endured almost countless demonstrations outside of his private medical practice and his home, described a very common reaction to Dr. Slepian's murder:

> There was no face-to-face confrontation. It was totally a person in the privacy of his home, in the company of his family. Someone just out there somewhere shooting through a window in the home. There's no protection for that. If someone is out there across the street in some hideaway room and can see me in my house and can just shoot me and take my life like that, there's just no protection for that. Boy, that really touched something because while I could get police escorts, and while I could get legal rulings to keep the protesters away from the front of my office and clinic, there's nothing to really protect against what happened to Slepian. So that, boy, that was the most intimidating of all the ones that I've seen.

Providers explained feeling similar deep-seated distress following Dr. Tiller's murder. Warren Hern said, "I cannot assume that I am safe. George told the people at the Lutheran church, you don't have to do security, they're not going to bother me here." But, as Hern further explained, "they put a bullet in his head, right there in the lobby." Peggy Gifford expressed a sentiment echoed by many providers after his murder: "I had a gut feeling, like they're coming for us, and I think everyone felt that way. He was such a good person and caring doctor that everyone felt that pain." Likewise, Ruth Hicks put into words the unique sense of fear Dr. Tiller's assassination spurred: "The Tiller incident was probably the most frightening for me because of where it happened—not on clinic grounds. Which is really what concerns me more than here at the clinic—everywhere else I'm circulating."

## Other Strong Emotions

Besides fear, abortion providers also experienced other strong emotions as a result of targeted harassment. Many of the providers were angry that they had to live with targeted harassment, particularly when protesters appeared at their homes. For instance, Sandra Whitley, Mathew Whitley's wife, explained her reaction the first time protesters demonstrated in front of their house: "I wanted to leave, but I didn't want to confront them because I was so angry that I didn't want them to see my anger, and I didn't want them to know how angry I really was. I finally decided to go on out anyhow, and I do remember mumbling to myself, in fact they probably heard me say, 'I wish I had a gun.'"

Others reported being furious when the protesters started talking about their family. Gail Weaver explained how she felt when the protesters talked about her daughter as she walked from her car into the clinic: "I was steaming mad. Oh, I was really hot. 'You can say what you want to me, but don't you ever bring my daughter into this.'" Gail was so mad that she was shaking and her voice was quivering. "It took me forever to calm down. I was really livid."

Some providers who did not feel fearful nonetheless felt aggravated or anxious about the harassment. Staci Hagler said that even though the protesters now know her hometown and publicize it on their website, she does not necessarily fear for her life. "But I always feel like there's something standing right behind me. So I probably don't feel as comfortable in my own home as I should because I know other places they've gone to the people's house." Maggie Sims explained feeling nervous after she received calls from protesters on the landline of the hotel room where she was staying. "The thought that someone who really didn't like me knew exactly where I was made me very nervous because some of these people are not nice."

Some providers expressed feeling disbelief that they had to put up with targeted harassment as part of their job. Reflecting on protesters who harass her and the clinic's patients, Tracey Carter said, "It's unreal. It is so unreal. Life is so precious and they stand out there and protest, but they're kind of taking life when they're doing harm to others deliberately." Jennifer Moore Conrow, a clinic administrator in New Jersey, was "stunned" when she received hate mail at home for the first time. "Theoretically I understood that eventually this could happen, but the reality of somebody taking the time to figure out who I am and where I live and then send this to me, it was like I had been punched in the stomach. It was like all the breath was gone. I was in absolute shock."

Other providers felt frustrated and concerned when their private information was no longer private and was in the hands of people who might use it to do them harm. Irene Gengler expressed this sentiment after receiving letters at home with personal information included in them. She felt "vulnerable" and explained, "I was concerned how they had found me because my phone number isn't listed and I didn't think my address was public."

### Concern for Others

While many providers' reactions concern their own lives, providers who are targeted also experience deep concern for others. They are concerned for their family's safety, their patients' mental health, their clinic colleagues' well-being, their other coworkers' peace of mind, and their neighbors' quiet enjoyment of their homes. Rebecca Lane summed up this response when she explained how she reacted to Dr. Slepian's murder. She quickly transitioned from talking about its effects on her to her concern, as the executive director of the clinic, about its impact on others:

> That really shook me up. I felt such a sense of overwhelming dread. I felt it was inevitable something was going to happen to one of my staff or one of my volunteers. It was so overwhelming, and I couldn't talk about it with my friends because they would never understand. I couldn't talk about it with my family because they would worry. Couldn't talk about it with a single member of my staff. There was nobody I could talk to because I didn't want them to worry and I didn't want to freak them out either.

Almost three-quarters of the providers we interviewed expressed this concern for others in response to being targeted, often saying that they felt this concern more deeply than their concern for themselves.

Many providers were most concerned about the effect anti-abortion protest and harassment has on their patients. A recent study of patients at abortion clinics echoes this concern. The study found that 53% of women who saw, heard, or were stopped by protesters were upset by them.[4] For Dr. P., this is his chief concern. "My patients are harassed from the moment they get out of their cars until they finally get in the clinic."

Providers also expressed concern about how patients are affected by the heightened security at the clinics. Because of the targeted harassment of abortion providers, and physical acts of violence against providers in particular, some clinics have instituted seemingly extreme security measures, as described in more detail in the next chapter. These security measures can have a real downside for patients, as John Steele described:

> This is a real issue for our patients. The check-in process is through bulletproof glass and without other people to accompany them or anything. So even if you have someone who is really sick, for example, we've had patients who have really bad abscesses that come in for care and want their sister to walk in with them. Well, we prevent that from happening because then you start having their brother or their uncle and it's hard to control the security of nonpatients. So it's a very uninviting waiting room, but it's what we need to do to protect our own security.

A recent study of patient experiences at clinics also pointed to this policy as a problem for patients. The study found that "[f]or several respondents, being separated from her companions made the abortion more difficult."[5]

Providers also frequently expressed concern about their own families. After someone was arrested for plotting to assassinate the people who worked at Ruth Hicks's clinic just a few months before we interviewed her, Ruth expressed strong concern for her family:

> I have three young children at home, and I never know what someone is going to do, especially with the recent incident. I was on maternity leave when the person who was planning to attack our clinic shot their firearm in the hotel room, and so that kind of concerns me to the point where I had thought do I need to keep doing this? Do I need to keep coming to this clinic as a provider? Everyone has their reason, but I have two infants at home now.

Similarly, after receiving a death threat against her entire family, Carolyn Barrick thought about her child. "Jesus, is somebody going to hurt my child? Nobody's ever deliberately targeted children of abortion providers, but that doesn't mean they won't start." When we interviewed Carolyn, about a year after the death threat, she was still affected. "I'm very concerned about being out with my kids and being approached."

Many providers, particularly those who are in a position of authority where they work, explained their concern for their staff. After asking Rachel Friedman whether she has ever felt threatened, Rachel did not respond by talking about herself. Rather, she answered, "Obviously the safety and security of my staff is paramount to me. So I spend a lot of time doing whatever I can to make them feel safe." As the public face of the clinic, Rachel believes she is responsible for shielding everyone else who works there.

Miriam Dixon described a similar reaction when, following a state investigation into an aspect of the clinic's operations, a major anti-abortion website posted the names of several doctors who worked at her clinic:

> It was like my doctors had a target on their backs. And I couldn't convey how scary that was to anybody. On some levels I feel protective, aka also guilty, that the doctors have to go through this. So I tried to do what I could to kind of coach them and help them. I actually had a staff person drop them off at the investigation hearing and pick them up because I didn't want them to be walking in the streets, because I didn't know who would be between their parking place and the building. It's kind of insane to me that they had to do that.

Providers' concern for their coworkers extends beyond just their coworkers at the clinic. Staci Hagler explained her worry that protesters will demonstrate at her part-time job that has nothing to do with abortion, like other people at her clinic have experienced. "So at my other job I actually have the protesters' pictures in the back, and it says do not give them any information. I do that just for the safety of my coworkers. We're a family business, and I don't think protest would be very good to have there."

Providers also worry how targeted harassment affects their neighbors and others in the community. Ryan Christopher was protested at two different apartments and eventually "moved out of respect for the building and the neighbors." Thomas Andrews lives across from a park where young children play. When protesters demonstrate outside of his house, he does not feel it affects him much but does feel bad for the parents who bring their children to the park.

### Long-Term Effects

Providers also explained how targeted harassment can have long-term consequences. For instance, Sadie Hay suspects that she developed Crohn's disease from the stress she felt being targeted for so many years. The condition, which Sadie explained happens to people under a lot of stress, was so serious that her gastroenterologist told her, "I have never seen it that bad."

The long-term effects can also be psychological. Months after we interviewed her, Carolyn Barrick sent us an e-mail that she left her job at the abortion clinic for professional development reasons and not because of the harassment she faced. Carolyn said that a friend told her that since leaving the abortion clinic, she looks more relaxed and stress-free than she has in years. Her friend's statement made Carolyn angry "because helping women control their own bodies and reproductive futures should not be stress-producing or subject you to so much hostility." Nonetheless, she is happy in her new job because of her professional advancement as well as the fact that "no one yells at me when I walk into the office. It's a huge change."

Miriam Dixon expressed these long-term effects in terms of her self-identity. The targeted harassment has deeply affected her, which, to Miriam, "is their ultimate victory." She second-guesses herself now, is less confident, and is not the optimistic person she once was. "I'm very conscious that it's affected me this way. I'm getting a little bit like, 'Who is this person?'"

A common long-term consequence of being targeted is developing a sense of paranoia. Of course, just like anyone, bad things can happen to abortion providers that have nothing to do with anti-abortion targeted harassment. However, because of the fear caused by targeted harassment, sometimes abortion providers are quick to believe that anti-abortion protesters are behind other, perhaps unrelated, negative occurrences in their lives. As John Steele puts it, abortion providers

PROVIDERS' REACTIONS TO TARGETED HARASSMENT

are "living in fear all the time." John analogized his experience to racism:

> You start to suspect lots of things around you. Like, why did some-body leave me such a short tip, is it because I'm black? People think about that stuff more than it really occurs sometimes. So a couple of times, some strange messages have been left on my work phone. I reported them to security. I had no idea what was going on. They investigated. I was worried if it was somebody trying to send me some coded message about revelation or death or something like that. It turned out it was somebody drunk who had the wrong number. You just sort of wonder what's going on. You hear a strange sound or you see a car kind of loitering in front of your house, and you wonder a little bit about that. Nothing's panned out, but you don't know. It's definitely not something I felt in my prior job.

Kristina Romero acknowledged feeling this way. "Sometimes I over-react to things. You'll see them at the restaurant or something, and you react when they're just eating. But you think, 'Are they following me? Why are they here?' It gets into your head, it gets into your heart. It gets to be really hard to take."

Targeted harassment also affects providers' relationships. Warren Hern was one of several providers who explained how targeted harass-ment cost him a relationship. "I was married before, and they bothered my wife. The harassment had a lot to do with ending our marriage." He continued, "She was a nurse who worked at an abortion clinic when we met. She totally agreed with what I'm doing, but she wasn't prepared for the kind of harassment that I was having. It was too much for her."

Providers also described the economic effects of targeted harassment. At Dustin Menendez's private practice, some of his patients left once they saw the anti-abortion protesters outside. "It affects me economi-cally, the protesters out there. The patients see the protesters, and then they don't want to be associated with me."

Sometimes targeted harassment can also affect providers' job oppor-tunities. Lucy Brown fears that she has not obtained outside part-time jobs because of what the protesters have posted about her online. "You Google my name and it's just like 'Oh my God.'" As a medical student,

Patricia Yang, now a physician at a clinic in a Middle Atlantic state, did not consider applying to residency programs "too far south" out of a concern for harassment in that region of the country. For the same reason, she has also limited where she might move later in her career. For example, after her husband saw a documentary about violent anti-abortion activists in Missouri, he told her, "We're never moving to Missouri."

## Comparison to Military or Police

Many providers spoke of their experiences dealing with targeted harassment as akin to the sort of trauma police or members of the military suffer. This was a surprising response at first as the providers are all medical or administrative personnel working in offices. Yet they feel that their lives are similar to those who are trained to work on battlefields and crime scenes.

Some providers feel like they are constantly at war. Kristina Romero explained it succinctly and directly: "It's almost like you're in war all the time, and you're in battle mode." Jennifer Young described her experiences dealing with and responding to protesters' targeted harassment tactics as being like "that old comic *Spy vs. Spy*, where they keep trying to outdo each other," a reference that several other providers made as well. Warren Hern attended Dr. Tiller's funeral and was under intense protection that day, which reinforced a long-held belief for him: "It's a totally fanatical, vicious outfit. This is one of the things I have said from the very beginning, that our adversaries are at war with us. They will stop at nothing, up to and including assassination."

For some providers, this comparison provides comfort and a sense that they are working toward a noble cause. Marshall Cook made this point in explaining why he is not bothered by the harassment he faces. "I feel we have a job to do. It's a job we believe in. It's the same as a soldier in the field, a cop on the beat, the fireman going into a building. It's something we do for the better good."

But for other providers, this comparison invokes a particular sense of emotional damage that is more commonly understood to be associated with war. Donald Yates explained that he is "inured" to the violence that has happened in the past, saying that he feels "the same way as when you get the fatality reports from Afghanistan." Kris Neuhaus had a similar reaction to her good friend and colleague Dr. Tiller being murdered. Kris explained that she felt something akin to post-traumatic stress disorder. "I don't feel anything. I'm like those guys that are coming back from Iraq, most of them. They saw a lot of shitty stuff and they just don't deal with it, and that's the way I am."

### Normalization, Fatalism, and Brushing It Off

Kristina Romero expressed a reaction to being targeted that was different from the others already described in this chapter. For her, "it gets to be normal after a while. It's like you're used to this insanity. Other people have to remind you that this is not normal. That living like this, dealing with these things day in and day out, it's not normal. Normal people don't do this." This common coping mechanism—feeling that targeted harassment does not faze her much at all—stands in stark contrast to the many providers who expressed fear, anger, or other strong emotions in the face of targeted harassment.

Other providers agreed with Kristina and shared that they had become desensitized to something that can be perceived as normal within their field. Patricia Yang became so "used to it" that she became "anesthetized" to being targeted. Tami Madison explained feeling similarly but was critical of this feeling. She said that she has become "desensitized" to the on-site harassment, though not to the off-site harassment, such as the regular home protests. "I guess it could be related to domestic violence. When you're exposed to it all the time, you can say 'Oh, well, it's not that bad.' When it really is that bad. Just because you've been exposed to it for so often for so long doesn't mean it's any less worse than the first time it felt so terrible."

Others attributed their lack of a reaction to targeted harassment to a sense of fatalism. Thomas Andrews put it bluntly: "If they want to shoot me in the head, they will. There's nothing I can do about it." Anthony Ward was also very candid about the possibility that something terrible may happen to him:

Years and years ago I thought about it and said to my wife, "One of these days I might not come home. I might get killed." I'm not going to wear a vest. I'm not hiding from anybody. If I get killed, I get killed. It's just the way it is. So I don't worry about it. I lose no sleep over the threats. In other words, I'm not afraid. I don't drive up to work wondering, "Who is here? Who is not here?" I just park. To me, it's part of my life. You get up in the morning, you brush your teeth, you go to the bathroom. On a Friday, I'm coming up here, I expect to see the protesters. Just a part of what I do. If you're a pilot, birds are going to fly to hit your plane. Might take you down.

This fatalism can be comforting to providers. As Joanne Hartzell, a longtime clinic administrator in a South Atlantic state, stated pithily in explaining why she does not worry, "We're a target with some, but there are nutheads out there everywhere." Robert Burton also finds this way of thinking "reassuring." He explained, "A lot of these terrorist guys screw up, but a good terrorist is going to get their job done. It's actually reassuring once you realize that you can't do anything about it. So you can go on with your life."

For some providers, this sense of fatalism is connected to the prior murders of abortion providers, many of whom were close to the people we interviewed. Dr. P. expressed this sentiment very clearly with respect to Dr. Tiller's death: "There's not a lot I can do about it. They shot Tiller in the head, he was wearing a vest. How are you going to stop that? How do you anticipate that? How do you complain about that? You can't. I just don't think about it." Dr. P. had similar thoughts about Dr. Slepian's murder: "Again, the guy who killed Dr. Slepian up in New York, who was a sniper and shot him in his kitchen. How can you prevent that?"

Approaching targeted harassment with a calculated rationality about risk similarly helps providers cope with protesters' tactics. Mildred Randolph described her calculus:

Well, how do you assess risk? Risk has two components, right? It's what are the chances and then what's the impact? The impact would be very bad, but the chances are very low, so the ultimate risk is fairly low. I think on the basis of historical data that administrators don't get hit. I think I have a very common-sense attitude about what really are the risks. The risk is much greater driving to work and being hit by a bus.

Rebecca Lane explained how she learned from a board member about making the same kind of risk assessment. The board member helped

Rebecca and her staff respond to the harassment by walking them through the thought process. "What are the real risks? What are the solutions to all the different risks? How do you balance them? We set up a lot of deterrents, but we didn't go overboard and create additional costs that weren't really going to make a difference."

Part of some providers' risk calculation is the possible effects on their family. For some providers without children, this fact alone makes them feel that they have less reason for concern. John Steele explained that his response would be very different if he had a family. "I don't have kids. I don't have a family at home. That would be very troubling to me, if I felt like I was personally singled out and if I had people I was worried about. That would be a different thing." Tami Madison, who also does not have children, put herself in the shoes of other providers who do. "I am not as concerned about my safety as other people might be. Other people have families, have kids. I understand why they wouldn't want to take as big a risk."

A deep commitment to their job can also give providers a reason for not reacting to being targeted. Marsha Banks, a longtime clinic administrator who has worked in Middle Atlantic and South Atlantic states and has experienced multiple bombings and personal attacks, said, "None of it ever scared me. I feel so passionate about it that it doesn't scare me at all."

Finally, some providers do not react to being targeted because they simply refuse to believe that something bad will happen to them. Sometimes providers are fully aware that they are in denial, while others give explanations for their lack of reaction that sound like denial, even if they do not characterize it that way. For example, even though doctors and other clinic workers were killed in the 1990s, Sadie Hay said, "I think that we were in denial. I really do. Yeah, we felt horrible about it, but we were never scared. I think my family was scared for me, but I wasn't." Similarly, even though his name has appeared on hit lists, his home has been shot at, and he has been stalked by some of the most violent members of the anti-abortion movement, Lowell Taylor explained that he is not concerned. "The human mind is capable of suppressing things of this type. Tomorrow will be a better day."

One common manifestation of this denial is providers' insistence that, though terrible things happen, they only happen to others. Despite experiencing severe forms of targeted harassment, including a nation-ally televised death threat, being followed repeatedly, and her mother being confronted in her nursing home, Sarah Haupt voiced a common response among providers who were not doctors: "I never felt like I was the primary target. Administrators are easier to replace. Doctors are much harder to replace, so that was my logic anyway." Marietta Spring is convinced that she is not on the radar of anti-abortion protesters in the same way as others, even though she has been targeted on-site, at home, and professionally. In thinking of her own risk, she compared herself to Dr. Tiller. "He really was such a target. I mean, he was tar-geted for years on so many levels that I am not at all. I can't really com-pare. So I think the likelihood is pretty small, really."

## Secondary Reactions

Reacting to targeted harassment is not solely the province of those who are targeted. Many providers shared stories of people close to them hav-ing different reactions to the targeted harassment the providers faced.

### Family Members

Providers' family members can have the same variety of reactions that providers have. Providers commonly described family members who were seriously concerned for the provider's safety. After Peggy Gifford became a high-profile target of anti-abortion harassment, her husband expressed his deep concern. "My husband hadn't really gotten his mind around that fear of being in our home. He hadn't before thought about if you stand at the sink, there are nine windows. That kind of stuff hadn't occurred to him." Mark Goldstein similarly explained, "My par-ents and my wife's parents were a little freaked out. They were worried we were going to get shot."

A provider's child can have serious emotional reactions to protest-ers' tactics. Marshall Cook's young son was so scared after protesters appeared at their house that he had nightmares about the protesters for a long time afterward. Rachel Friedman said that her daughter "had a really hard time" with the harassment. She "grew up being completely petrified" of the protesters, who spray-painted "Murderer" in their home driveway and left scary cards and dead animals in the family's mailbox. "I can remember so many fights over 'I don't want you to do this. Find another job.'"

Family members who were most concerned by the harassment sometimes urged the provider to stop. When she was first protested at home, Tami Madison received "a little pressure" from her sisters to stop working at the clinic. Bruce Steir's family was also concerned. "My family wasn't pleased with my continuing to do it. They were protective of me, but I felt that there was a need for abortion providers and there were few and far between willing to travel to the places I would go."

On the flipside, protesters' targeting can sometimes make family members more supportive of the provider. Calvin Litwin explained how targeted harassment transformed his daughter. Originally, his daughter was ambivalent about abortion as she would shy away from using the term "pro-choice" and would always insist that she would "have the baby" if she ever found herself pregnant. However, after a national anti-abortion group organized a large-scale demonstration against Calvin, his daughter changed. "She went on the other side of the fence, and she became a vehement pro-choice individual and realized what was going on. It just took seeing it with her own eyes to have a better understanding of it. She supported me every step of the way."

Sometimes providers are more affected by their family members' reactions than the actual targeted harassment. For instance, after she received hate mail at her home for the first time, Jennifer Moore Conrow was most upset by her grandmother's reaction. "I called my grandmother and she cried, and that was probably the thing that really pissed me off the most. Because I'm not okay with hearing my grandmother cry." According to Jennifer, her grandmother reacted so strongly because she was concerned that, with an anti-abortion protester clearly knowing Jennifer's home address, someone would come to Jennifer's house and hurt her.

### Community Members

If part of the goal of demonstrating at providers' homes and disclosing personal information about providers to their community is to motivate the neighbors to pressure the provider to stop, protesters who engage in these activities seem to be missing their mark. Providers reported

overwhelmingly positive responses from their communities and feelings of support from neighbors, rather than hostility.

Sadie Hay's story was typical. Sadie described living in a very conservative community. After telling us how protesters sent cards to all of
her neighbors with details about Sadie and her job, she explained that
her neighbors became very angry because Sadie's name was on the postcards. Several of Sadie's neighbors called her in response to the cards
saying, "This is not right. They shouldn't do that. They're making you
a target." Sadie was "always surprised" by her neighbors' overwhelming
support. "I never had anybody say, 'You need to stop working there' or
'Why are you working there?'"

Cynthia Kendrick believes that her neighbors' supportive response
stems from a feeling that the community should stick together in the
face of an outside intrusion. When protesters demonstrated outside of
Cynthia's house, the neighbors were very supportive, even though her
neighbors were not usually very social with one another. "They didn't
like their turf being violated. Nobody ever knows how the neighbors
are going to respond, but almost always the neighbors are against the
outsiders who are coming in to cause trouble."

Support from neighbors can be a pleasant surprise to providers,
especially those who did not previously know their neighbors. Before
protesters came to Mathew Whitley's house, he did not know how his
neighbors felt about him and his work. Their response was, as Mathew
described it, "refreshing." Mathew's neighbors rallied around him and
kept the neighborhood peaceful. "They were the neighbors I'd never
talked to, but they knew who I was, and they were there confronting
these folks. I took that to mean that they thought I was a good neighbor at least."

Providers' neighbors have shown their support in interesting ways.
Some providers' neighbors were so supportive that they reacted to the
targeted harassment by sending donations on the provider's behalf.
After anti-abortion demonstrations in Lewis Turk's and Paul Fortin's
neighborhoods, both sets of neighbors donated money to their clinics "in honor of" the protesters. Similarly, after a local newspaper ran
Hern's full-page ad showing a copy of the death threat he had received,
the community responded almost immediately. "By seven in the morning the day it was published, I was getting dozens and dozens and

dozens of phone calls of support. People were sending me money. It was amazing."

Some neighbors directly communicated support to the provider. Anthony Ward's neighbors wrote him letters saying, "Keep up the fight." Tami Madison's neighbors grew frustrated with one protester who picketed and leafleted throughout her neighborhood on a regular basis. One neighbor came to Tami's house and told her, "We're all in agreement that we don't want him here." Even one of Tami's neighbors who was against abortion told Tami that he strongly opposed the protester's harassing tactics. Tami's neighbors banded together and wrote a letter back to the protester that said, "Thank you for unifying our neighborhood. We're all in agreement that we don't want you here."

Lauren Henry's neighbors took a different course of action. Lauren's neighbors were vigilant in looking out for her, and one neighbor in particular tried to protect Lauren when protesters demonstrated at her house. "My neighbor was a state trooper and would always just immediately take his German Shepherd and go over to my house to make sure nobody came up on the property." Lauren's other neighbors called the police, who responded and convinced the protesters to leave.

Despite these common outpourings of support, some providers wondered whether the home protests engendered silent opposition. After describing her neighbors' support when protesters staged demonstrations outside of her house, Samantha Newsom acknowledged that she might not have heard from her neighbors who had a negative reaction. "There may have been, but I didn't hear them." Mark Goldstein lives in what he called a "pretty conservative" neighborhood with two Catholic churches near his house. When abortion opponents protested at Mark's house, several neighbors called him to voice their support, but Mark did notice that he never heard from the "more conservative churchgoing" people who lived in his neighborhood. "They probably weren't happy. The people I heard from were more like my kind of people, more liberal thinking."

*Actions Against Protesters*

While almost all of the providers described trying not to let their emotions get the best of them by taking retaliatory action against protesters, other people, especially family members, sometimes find it harder to hold back.

The simplest response that some people choose is engaging protesters in one way or another, such as a community coming together to convey to the protesters through letters or words that the protesters are not welcome, as described above. Some people are more aggressive though. Marshall Cook described how his wife gets upset when the protesters harass him. "She gives them the finger and tells them to shut up. Get a job or something. I keep telling her 'don't play into it.' That's her though."

Providers' children have at times recognized protesters as an unwelcome presence and played games with the protesters who demonstrate outside of their homes. Thomas Andrews explained that his kids "kind of have fun" with the lead protester who regularly pickets their house. "They think he's a joke. One time I wasn't there and from their bedroom window they made all sorts of weird screeching sounds and every time he would turn around they would stop." Mark Goldstein's sons also responded to the protesters who demonstrated outside of Mark's house. One of his young sons was outside yelling, "Get out of here!" Mark recalled, "That was kind of cute actually."

Finally, several people grew so frustrated with home protest that they resorted to an interesting retaliatory technique—spraying the protesters with water. Cynthia Kendrick relayed one story about her husband after their home had been protested. "He felt like our space was being invaded." He took this invasion of privacy so seriously that Cynthia feared he would be arrested. "He wanted to take a baseball bat out and go swinging at them, but he ended up getting the water hose out and spraying them when they came here a couple of times." Milton Correll and Calvin Litwin shared similar stories about their neighbors' responses to home protests. As Calvin explained, "The neighbors would turn their sprinklers on them."

## Conclusion

Though providers' individual reactions vary tremendously, anti-abortion terrorism seriously affects their lives. Even the providers who brush it off and feel that being targeted is a normal part of their lives and profession raise the possibility that they have been so traumatized by the harassment that they can no longer react emotionally to it. By this measure, the protesters' targeting has its desired effect.

However, as discussed in the last chapter of this book, by another measure the protesters are not effective at all, because only a very small number of providers leave the field due to targeting. Instead, providers have developed countless strategies to deal with the harassment—both to prevent it from occurring in the first place and to protect themselves if it does occur. These strategies, detailed in the next chapter, help providers push forward, despite the harassment and terrorism, in their quest to provide women with the healthcare they seek.

# 6

## Prevention and Protection

For us, it's very normal to be aware of our surroundings, know where the nearest exit is, know where you park, look around, see who is walking around, who is standing around. Make sure that you don't come in or out of the building by yourself. Don't always take the same route home. Take different routes when you drive around. I had to learn how to be more aware and how to walk around with this feeling that I have to constantly be watching my back when I talk in public about what I do. Who is listening? What are their reactions? Learn how to read people's facial expressions—even if you're talking in a restaurant and you're at your own table with your peers, people around you are listening and you have to be aware of that too. So yes, it does change your life.

—PENNY SANTIAGO

If anybody told me when I was in medical school that I would go to work armed and with a bulletproof vest, I would have thought they were nuts. But I do have a bulletproof vest, and I do go to clinics armed these days.

—KEVIN BOHANNON

TARGETED HARASSMENT NOT ONLY has serious emotional effects on abortion providers but also causes them to make concrete changes in their lives in an effort to prevent being terrorized and to protect themselves if they are.

In the midst of explaining their own personal ways to cope with and prevent targeted harassment, the focus of the rest of this chapter, some providers also discussed at length the variety of measures their clinics take to prevent targeted harassment and protect providers. For example, the owner of the building where Howard Stephens works has cameras both inside and outside the building. He also installed speakers on the outside of the building so that he can yell at the protesters when needed. Rachel Friedman's clinic has a policy that no one can be in the building alone at night. "Everyone knows that people come in together, and they leave together." For packages received in the mail, Sarah Haupt's clinic had a policy of "don't touch anything." Sarah explained, "I don't care if it's a potted plant. If it looks like a package from UPS or FedEx, we'll know if we're expecting something, so don't you touch it."

A key aspect of clinic protection is security guards. Samantha Newsom's clinic hired a security guard after discovering that an anti-abortion activist planned to kill multiple clinic employees. According to Samantha, the guard has "been wonderful for both the patients and the providers" because, at the very least, the security person makes the protesters feel like someone is watching them. "It hasn't changed much what they do, but I think we feel better about it." Clinics also use security guards to personally escort providers when needed. Peggy Gifford works at two clinics in two states that are far from where she lives. She flies to those states, and when she arrives at the airport, the clinics arrange for an armed guard to drive her from the airport to the clinic and then back to the airport when she leaves.

Cameras, safety policies, mail precautions, guards, drivers—the options for clinics to protect their providers from targeted harassment run the gamut of security measures. However, the focus of this chapter is on the specific actions that individual providers take to prevent and protect themselves from targeted harassment. These range from a general increased vigilance to various shifts in the provider's routine to carrying a gun and wearing a bulletproof vest.

## General Vigilance

Recently, one of the most vocal and threatening protesters outside of Staci Hagler's clinic yelled directly at Staci. This was not an uncommon experience in itself, but this time, the protester told Staci to "go back to" her hometown, using the specific name of the town. That was the first time the protester indicated she knew this much about Staci.

The fact that this protester, and presumably others, knew Staci's hometown changed Staci's life. "I feel like now I really just watch my back. I pay a lot more attention to my surroundings. Like when I leave, I'll look at my car for anything." She is not necessarily in fear for her life but said, "I always feel like there's something standing right behind me." She now feels "very uncomfortable" in her hometown. "I have to look everywhere to make sure I don't see them."

Staci's hypervigilance affects others as well. Staci lives with her mother, who now closes the blinds whenever Staci is home. When Staci goes to work, her mother expects a phone call when Staci arrives. "If I don't call, she calls me, asking, 'Are you there yet?' She freaks out." Staci has also taken precautions at the restaurant where she works part-time. She has shown her coworkers a picture of the protesters and cautioned them against giving out any information about her. "They all should know you're not supposed to tell anyone where someone works." Staci worries that the teenagers who work at the restaurant might stumble one day and inadvertently reveal that she works there by saying something like, "Oh yeah, she's not here today."

Staci's increased sense of vigilance, though foreign to most people's everyday experiences, is a common part of many providers' lives. For some providers, this increased awareness is a way to avoid or prevent problems. As Florence Davis described, "you just don't want to put yourself in a situation where something could happen." This type of vigilance changes how providers go about even minute aspects of day-to-day living.

Diane Dell attributed her increased awareness to Dr. Tiller's murder. After he was murdered, Diane was much more cautious and aware of her surroundings. "I always look around," Diane said. For example, the clinic where Diane works is across the street from a hospital. As Diane describes it, the space in between the two buildings is "a sniper's paradise because there are all these little places that people could stand." Diane explained further, "Every single time I get out of my car I do this thing where I look around to see who is there. I just check it out." She does not do anything like this when parking elsewhere. "I just do it at work. I always do it at work. I'm not saying that I'm feeling fearful, but it's something that I've had to do. I just do it because there could be somebody there."

Abortion providers are particularly careful with their cars in ways most medical providers do not need to be. Because their cars are usually accessible to protesters during the workday, abortion providers take precautions when they get into their cars after work. For instance, ever since protesters put nails in her tire, each time Tonya Villa approaches her car she routinely checks all four of her tires for nails. Marsha Banks has a similar concern. "When I remember and if I'm not too tired, I'll check my car because it wouldn't take very much for them to come in and take air out of my tire or put sugar in my tank."

Once in their car, some providers take even more precautions. Jennifer Young explained, "Most people just drive home. I never just drive home." Because of the risk of being followed, Jennifer said, "When I'm leaving a clinic, I always watch my rear. I look around at all the cars in the parking lot. I make sure I check out who they are and what they look like. When I drive away, I see if anyone else turns the corner and follows me."

As part of increasing their everyday awareness, many providers also make sure that they can identify the person who is targeting them. For instance, Tracey Carter tries to ensure that she can identify individual protesters if she is ever called upon to do so. She explained that she always pays attention to what they wear. "I'm always looking and trying to describe what they look like. That's my way of life." Various law enforcement officials similarly told Maggie Sims that she "should be able to identify these people because you should know if these people are following you or if they are around."

Taking their vigilance about identifying protesters one step further, some providers track protesters. Providers' tracking systems can include computer databases, photo books, and lists of license plates. Carolyn Barrick would not explain her system in detail but assured us that she has "very sophisticated" ways of knowing who is protesting. "I'll leave it at that. We make it a point to know who our protesters are. I can tell you, we keep a list. We have descriptions of their cars, we have a description of their person, and we get their names."

Providers use these tracking systems for two main reasons. First, providers track protesters so that they can identify known protesters who concern them. For instance, Diane Dell explained that a particular protester served jail time for committing a violent crime against someone who worked at her clinic. The protester was released from prison a year or two before we interviewed Diane. Since then, she and the clinic make sure that everyone who works at the clinic can identify him. "We do have pictures of him at the security desk, and I always show pictures to the escorts."

Second, providers track protesters so that they know when a new protester arrives. In describing what she called her "counterintelligence process," Mildred Randolph explained that she is not concerned about "the folks that show up every day because they have a place in the community. They are not the shooters. Rather, it's the new people in our community, the strangers, who are going to come in and do something dangerous." Because of the way she and her clinic track protesters, Mildred said that she has "confidence that we know when somebody new is out there."

Providers' vigilance in tracking protesters also extends to the Internet. Melinda Birkland explained the "close eye" that she keeps on anti-abortion Internet sites. Melinda is particularly concerned about her online life because she participates in various activities with her children. "I want to make sure that I'm aware if there's going to be any issues." Tami Madison has found her personal information on disturbing websites that display gruesome images, contain cryptic texts, and incite violence against abortion providers. To keep track, Tami searches Google for her name to see what anti-abortion extremists are saying about her.

Some providers have taken surprising precautions in other aspects of their lives. For instance, when Ryan Christopher died, his family was worried that the protesters who continuously hounded him while he was alive would appear at his funeral. One of Ryan's family members explained, "You want to believe that people wouldn't do that and then you see stuff like the Westboro Baptist Church and you realize that people are just oblivious in their hate." Ryan's family arranged for a local police officer to watch the funeral and informed the funeral director to be on the lookout for suspicious people.

This kind of increased vigilance can have unfortunate consequences. Albert Tall explained that the US Marshals Service visited his clinic and warned against suspicious packages. "The next week I get a box. No return address. It came from Mailboxes Etc., addressed to me, and it was wrapped in brown paper and it was oily." The marshals had specifically warned Albert's clinic to be on the lookout for boxes with oily residue. "So I cleared the office and called the bomb squad, and they came, and they opened the package. Unfortunately my cousin, who bakes me knish bread all the time, shipped it to my office. She called up the next day and she said, 'Did you get the package I sent?' I said, 'You won't believe this . . . .'" Though Albert laughed while retelling this incident, he also recognized its serious undertones and how this experience reflects what it means to live a life of constant vigilance. As Albert concluded, "It just disrupts your day because everything's suspicious."

### Alter Routine

Rodney Smith is a big proponent of altering his routine as much as possible to avoid targeting. Rodney sadly recalled talking with Dr. Tiller about this issue before Dr. Tiller was assassinated in his church. "George and I used to have these debates. He would do everything randomly, except go to church. That's the one place. I told him, 'You can't be predictable, George.' I said do something else, don't go every week. But he just wasn't going to do that." Making deliberate changes to their daily routine, like Rodney discussed with Dr. Tiller, is another way abortion providers can mitigate targeted harassment. Providers make adjustments to the way they would normally go about their day or even deliberately avoid having a routine at all.

Many providers explained the ways that they change their work routines in response to targeted harassment, starting with the simple act of parking at work. After Maggie Sims received threats on the phone at the hotel where she was staying, she started parking her car in "strange parking lots," where she meets people who then drive her to the clinic.

Once providers park their cars, they sometimes change their behavior so that they can simply enter the clinic in safety. Kevin Bohannon has an armed "security team" escort him in and out of the clinic. "I call them just before I get there, tell them I'm coming, they are in the parking lot and stand next to the parking place that's designated for me. They're both armed, and they escort me in the back door, and then when I'm ready to leave, the opposite."

Providers who do not drive to work shared similar stories. Charles Slattery lives close to the clinic where he works, so he likes to walk to work. "I always felt walking was good for your mind and your body, so I walk." When Charles's clinic supervisor found out that he walked to work, she pleaded with him to stop so that anti-abortion protesters could not identify and target him. Charles did not want to give up walking altogether, so he made a deal with the clinic. On the biggest protest days, his wife drops him off at the clinic or he takes the car himself; on other days, he still walks.

Marshall Cook took perhaps the most drastic measures with his arrival routine. For years, Marshall flew to work at a clinic about a thousand miles from where he lives. Protesters had somehow figured out his destination airport, met him there, and followed him to the car rental location. The protesters stood behind Marshall and took his picture. "The lady at the car rental desk said, 'Oh, your friends are here to greet you.' I said, 'They're not my friends, please call security.'" The targeting did not stop at the airport as the protesters followed Marshall to his hotel, called him in the middle of the night on his hotel phone line, and demonstrated outside of the hotel. In order to avoid this recurring, Marshall began to fly into an airport about one hundred miles from the clinic so that protesters at the clinic where he worked would not know where or when he was arriving.

Once at the clinic, some providers change their routine to avoid protesters or to ensure their safety if protesters reach them. Tracey Carter said that she and her coworkers "walk in pairs when we come to the center. If we take out garbage, we go together. If it's dark out, we go together." Similarly wary at work, Ruth Hicks stopped eating her lunch outside. "I can't sit outside. I don't want to sit outside. We have a little picnic table. I used to sit outside all the time and eat lunch. I don't do it anymore." Ruth has also stopped leaving the clinic for lunch, explaining that she would prefer to eat inside where no one shouts at her while she eats.

Another tactic that providers use is varying their schedules from day to day. Tami Madison explained that it is important to be unpredictable, so she does not arrive at or leave from the office at the same time every day. At one of the clinics where Jennifer Young worked, everyone altered their schedules in order to avoid the harassment. "If we were starting surgery at eight o'clock, we were there at five o'clock. And when they saw we were there at five o'clock, they were there at four o'clock. So then we had to be there at three o'clock."

Jennifer also did something to avoid harassment that many providers do—she took different routes to and from work as much as possible. When Jennifer left work, she would check her car for any sign of tampering. "Then, I drove wacky ways to get home. I never took the same way twice in a row. And it was a direct shot home, so it was really weird to drive like this." For her, what would under normal circumstances be a fifteen-minute commute turned into a forty-minute drive. Even Charles Slattery, the walker discussed earlier, mixes up his commute. Now, on the days he does walk to work, he takes different routes. "Which I don't mind, you like to see different streets."

Some providers even rotate the cars they take to work. Peggy Gifford does this, and Ruth Hicks has thought about doing the same. "I've thought many times to switch out my car with my husband or do something so that my car is not easily identifiable as the same car that's here every single time." Even the security guard who picks up Lowell Taylor from the airport "changes vehicles periodically to throw them off."

Targeted harassment forces many providers to alter their home lives as well. For instance, because Albert Tall, his wife, and his children feel intimidated when the protesters demonstrate outside of their house, he and his family often leave if they know protesters are coming. If his family is caught inside when the protesters arrive, Albert closes the shades so that his family does not see them. While Albert is content to just drive right through the demonstration, his wife "doesn't want to be seen," so she stays in their house until the protesters leave.

For some providers, simply closing the window shades as Albert described makes them feel safer. Carolyn Barrick captured the rationale, saying that she keeps the curtains and blinds closed because every time she opens the blinds, she is "afraid somebody would be standing there." Dr. Slepian's murder had a very particular impact in this regard. Stephanie McGoldrick clearly made this connection. She bought her house because of its large, beautiful windows but now feels like she has to cover them every night. She adopted this behavior because of Dr. Slepian's murder. "I mean, he had a house with exposed forest in the back of the windows," just like the area around Stephanie's house.

Providers also change their routines outside the home. When out and about, Warren Hern does his best to keep his wife and son "out of the public eye" because he does not want them to suffer at the hands of anti-abortion demonstrators. When Lowell Taylor and his wife have an evening out, they take separate cars and meet at the destination.

## Protect Identity

Some providers respond to the threat of being terrorized by working hard to hide various aspects of their identity. One of the primary ways that providers try to protect their identity is by hiding their home address, which Diane Dell feels is very important. "My address is more personal. They could actually come to my house."

John Steele tries to hide his address by using a post office box for his personal mail. This tactic helps make him anonymous; however, he called this "the single most annoying little thing in my life because you can't use a PO box for everything. Just the other day, I saw that one bank that I have won't let you use a PO box." As a strategy to similarly conceal her home address from protesters, Peggy Gifford registered her car to her private practice. After protesters demonstrated outside his house, Kevin Bohannon reacted by working with his local county to make sure that his home address was no longer public:

> It turns out that here in my county, if you go to the county website, every piece of property is listed with its owner's name and address and various other things, with a couple of interesting exceptions. Police officers aren't listed, and judges aren't listed. But virtually everybody else is. I was told that you can request that your name be removed from that site. I called and talked to a very nice woman on the phone at the property appraiser's office, who it turns out had been a former patient of mine, who was very supportive of me and had heard some of the stuff on the news, and so she said she would do what she needed to do to get me off the list. If I ever sell the house and have a house somewhere else, I'm going to put the house in some kind of a trust name or something and not have my name on the property appraiser's website.

Some providers take similar care with their phone numbers. Aware of the protesters' tactics, Milton Correll listed his phone number under his wife's name. Milton believes this simple step makes it more difficult for protesters to find out his phone number. "If someone knows us and has a legitimate reason to get to us, they know my wife's name." Kevin Bohannon uses only a cell phone because it is not a listed number. "If somebody wants to find me, all they can find is my office phone in the phone book."

Providers also take measures to conceal other sorts of personal information. Inez Navarro uses a service through Reputation.com that helps protect her identity online. Her husband has also developed an expertise with online privacy. "He has ensured that all of our information is pretty much locked down. He has us all scrubbed everywhere online that he can. And Google Alerts notifies us if anything ever comes up." Peggy Gifford also registered with Reputation.com to protect her online identity. Beyond that, when Peggy travels to other states to perform abortions, she stays at hotels using a pseudonym. Patricia Yang uses her husband's identity to protect her information. Her home's utilities are listed in her husband's name, and she shares Twitter and Facebook accounts with him, using an account listed just under his name.

Because protesters sometimes bring abortion providers' children into their harassment tactics, providers also take measures to hide their kids' identities in ways that other parents would not think of doing. Providers sometimes refrain from talking about their children and make sure there is no public information connecting them to their children. For instance, Gail Weaver does not put bumper stickers on her car about her daughter's activities and accomplishments that most other parents would be proud to feature. Even though she wants to show support for her daughter, Gail does not want the protesters to find out more information about her family than they already know. "You want to show your pride, but you can't do anything because I'm afraid it will narrow down where we live."

Several providers detailed how they handle one aspect of protecting their identities—making sure that the protesters do not learn what they look like. Teresa Spellman makes sure not to wear scrubs on her way into the clinic so that protesters cannot identify her as a doctor. She sometimes wears sunglasses or a hat to make it more difficult for protesters to identify her. She explained that she does this because she knows there are "crazy people" affiliated with the protesters. If the protesters do not know what she looks like, they cannot post identifying information about her online that extremists could then use to harm her.

Other providers take similar measures to avoid being targeted, such as Ruth Hicks, who also does not wear scrubs and frequently changes her hair. Calvin Litwin drives himself to the clinic where he works. "I keep a hat in my car, because one of their intimidation techniques is to video you. So they'll have their video camera and I just put something in front of my face so that they can't video me." Roberta Keller also uses hats to shield herself. "I wear a lot of hats, so that if I walk in I can pull a hat over my face because I really don't want my image on the Internet." It helps that she lives in a cold climate. "It's not uncommon for people to wear a hat and scarf, so I tend to like to wear them."

The simplest way for some providers to hide their identity is by posing as a patient or a patient's supporter. Peggy Gifford explained how she tried to trick protesters into thinking she was a patient. "Being of reproductive age and being female, for the first year or more that I worked here, I just came in like a patient and acted like a patient and got escorted in and that was that." She continued, "That got a little harder when I was nine months pregnant, but it was winter and I could wear a heavy coat." Ruth Hicks does the same. She enters the clinic where she works through the main entrance, not the employee entrance. "When I do that, it appears like I'm somebody that's coming to the building and that I'm not a provider." Thomas Andrews finds it "helpful" to be confused as a patient or patient's support person. Sometimes, if new protesters appear at the clinic, the escorts will assist Thomas when entering the clinic. "It's sort of like a red herring thinking I was a patient or helping a patient. So they'll escort me in like they would any other patient or men with patients."

Some providers use their race to conceal their identities and confuse the protesters. Daniel Martin takes advantages of protesters' "perceptions on the basis of race and gender, as an African American man" to avoid harassment. He uses the protesters' racism against them by dressing in sweatpants and wearing headphones when walking into the clinic. "It seems like they don't recognize me as the provider"; instead, because they assume an African American man entering the clinic dressed this way could not possibly be a doctor, they think he is accompanying a patient.

Ruth Hicks knows that race can work to her advantage as well. Her last name is Hicks, but, as she explained, "I don't look like a Hicks." She takes comfort in knowing that if a protester found out that one of the abortion providers at the clinic was named "Ruth Hicks," the protester might not think that Ruth was that person because of the perceived mismatch between her last name and her race. She appreciates being able to use her race to "fly under the radar" in this way.

Many providers go so far as to wear disguises to and from work each day. For example, after she became concerned that someone was following her on her way out of the clinic, Maggie Sims began to wear a Halloween mask whenever she entered or left the clinic. "So I put on my mask and drove to the clinic, but sort of warily. I did tend to feel pretty safe in my mask." She explained further, "People were always trying to get pictures of me as I was going in and out of the clinic with their cell phones. That gave me the willies, and with the mask I could look them straight in the eye, so that was nice."

Providers also protect their identity by remaining silent about their work as abortion providers. Marshall Cook described this as "a big issue among abortion providers, to be open or not about what you do. When you're in a nonwork situation. On vacation, traveling, going out socially. Some people don't let people know what they do."[1]

Many providers handle this situation by using a euphemism for their line of work. Victoria Gates uses one particular phrase that many others use. "I just say 'women's health.' And for those who get it, they know that abortion falls under that umbrella." Victoria uses this term to describe her work for safety reasons. "I don't know who is in that room, so it's more a protective armor or gear or what have you." Victoria worries that if she's out somewhere in a group of new people and identifies herself as an abortion provider, "I kind of leave myself vulnerable if I tell the group, 'Okay, I'm leaving.' And then I go walking off to my car, and one individual has overheard me saying where I work, and they hear all the discussion and the dialogue going on, and they can follow me. Follow me to my car, follow me to my home." She blames extremists for making her uncomfortable with something almost everyone else takes for granted—talking openly about her job.

Others are vague in different ways about what they do or where they work. When asked, Ruth Hicks says she works at "a clinic," without providing any more specifics. "I don't tell people in our community where I work at all just because of the fact that I don't want them treating my children differently." She has only told a small number of neighbors where she works and has asked them not to share that information because of her safety concerns.

Roberta Keller sometimes does not even tell people that she is a doctor. She worries that someone she is talking with or someone overhearing a conversation might take her information or picture and post it online. Connecting her concerns to past violence, she said that as an abortion provider you have to "try to keep your mouth shut because if you're outspoken like Dr. Tiller they find ways to shut you up."

Providers are silenced not only in their day-to-day interactions with other people but also in the broader political and social context of abortion. Charles Slattery's office was bombed after he publicly said that he was proud of his work and would not apologize for it. "My wife, needless to say, almost wrung my neck about making a comment like that. And I've since refrained from doing that." Miriam Dixon similarly avoided a medical board hearing concerning one of her employees because of safety concerns. She wanted to be present to support the employee, but she did not want to be any more visible than she had to be. She worried that a high-profile anti-abortion protester who had targeted her previously would attend the hearing. "I didn't want to run into him. And it's not because I'm embarrassed, but it has to do with security."

Robert Burton has also reduced his public profile. When the US Marshals Service was assigned to protect Robert because he was at serious risk of being targeted, the marshals recommended that he "no longer have a public presence. In other words, stop writing letters to the editor, stop doing this, stop doing that." Robert explained why he followed this advice:

It certainly sounded reasonable. In retrospect, George Tiller was so out there and he confronted people who confronted him, and we all respected him, thought he was just wonderful, and he was a great role model and then he gets killed. What's the message there, right? Could he have not been so public and still have lived? You have people like [another outspoken abortion provider]. I'm sure he carries around three guns with him. I'm not ready to carry around three guns.

Hiding their identities puts abortion providers in a difficult position as healthcare providers in a stigmatized field. On the one hand, providers protect their identities in all the ways detailed here because they want to avoid becoming a target. As Carolyn Barrick, who recently dealt with a death threat against her and her family, explained, "If you're public, you put a big—not target, because I'm hoping no one's ever going to kill us. Isn't that a remarkable sentence? Isn't that a great friggin' sentence? But the fact is they go after people who are public."

On the other hand, hiding their identities can create serious issues. Roberta Keller, for instance, is concerned that working to protect her identity sends the wrong message. "I'm proud of what I do, and yet if you'd look at my behavior, you might interpret that as someone who is not proud. And, you know, it's interesting how that pans out because in trying to protect my ability to live a free life, I have to act like someone who has done something wrong or criminal."

Providers' need to protect their identities can also prevent them from working on the political issues that affect their lives. Mark Goldstein lamented that he "used to be tougher" and "more outspoken" about abortion and his role in providing abortion care, but he has stopped telling people where he works. "There are just some unusual and some-times scary responses." Tami Madison understands these concerns and the conflict it creates, but she believes that being silent contributes to the shame and negativity around abortion:

> I don't think less of the providers who won't speak out. But I think whatever they can do, they should do. Whatever they feel comfort-able doing. Whether it's telling their hairdresser what they do for a living. Or telling a patient their name, even. Something even that simple. I think whatever they feel like they can do they should try and do to just contribute to the end of that stigma. But I understand why everyone can't speak out that way.

Providers also lamented that concealing their personal information can create barriers with patients. At first, to protect her identity, Lucy Brown did not use her name when answering the clinic's phone, but then she realized that "we need to say our names" in order to connect with the people calling. Patricia Yang was similarly concerned about barriers with patients. At her practice, for safety reasons, family-planning providers are not listed in the online "find a provider" section. Patricia feels this is a problem. "It sometimes makes it more difficult for our routine GYN patients to find us because they can't find information about our office."

## Modifying Homes and Offices

Mildred Randolph is a clinic executive who is responsible for several clinics and has thought deeply about how choices related to location, architecture, and layout can prevent providers from being targeted. She explained that one of the clinics she works with kept looking for property until it found space on a medical campus that had private streets. Because of this layout, protesters have to stand far from the clinic whenever they demonstrate, far enough away that one doctor told Mildred that the protesters were "really not an issue at all." Mildred drew from this experience that "physical separation is the best thing you can do."

Another clinic Mildred works with has had two locations. At the first location, the blacktop in front of the clinic was surrounded by a giant fence. "We actually had curtains above the fence." The fence and curtains combined to form "a twenty-foot tall enclosure and we would pull the curtains closed when we were open and pull them back and tie them down when we weren't." As a result, a game of "spy versus spy" emerged between the clinic and the protesters. In response to the clinic's fence and curtains, the protesters used even taller ladders and, in response to the protesters, the clinic would erect an even taller obstacle.

The clinic designed the layout of its new location specifically with protesters' tactics in mind. Mildred explained, "We put a gap between the sidewalk and where our fence is. It's our property, and they're not supposed to be on it. It's hot rocks. And the heat just pops off of it. So if you ever stand out there—it's not so bad in the morning, but by one in the afternoon it is toasty out there, and so that's where they are. And it's kind of nice." In the winter, "it sucks out there" where the protesters stand because "the wind comes screaming right down that street." This layout was an intentional way to "minimize the attractiveness" of being at the clinic to target patients and providers.

Providers use these types of strategic planning decisions about physical space as yet another way to deal with the threat of harassment and violence. In this way, providers like Mildred think about and act on concerns that are different from those of other healthcare providers with respect to physical space. Architecture scholar Lori Brown has studied these "spatial experiences" of abortion clinics and notes the important ways that clinic layout, design, and placement, both external and internal, can affect security. Her research has suggested many ways that clinics can improve their security while offering patient-focused care.[2]

Often this strategy starts with the very basic question of where to locate an office. Many providers echoed Mildred's belief that choosing the right location for their office or clinic was important. For instance, one of Miriam Dixon's clinics is located in a strip mall with an Applebee's restaurant in front, which makes it difficult for protesters to have any effect. "It looks like they're protesting Applebee's because Applebee's is out on the street, and we're in a medical area behind a supermarket, so it doesn't really work."

The threat of targeted harassment also influences where providers choose their homes. Since purchasing the abortion facility she currently owns, Rachel Friedman has always lived in locations with a gate and armed security. "I've always chosen that because of my work." On the other hand, Kris Neuhaus took "the opposite tactic of what a lot of people do" and decided to live in a rough neighborhood so that protesters "were scared to even go there." Kris explained, "There was regular gunfire in that neighborhood, as well as meth labs and other problems. So it was a neighborhood that a lot of the protesters weren't too excited to go to."

Providers take other approaches to home protection aside from living in a gated or unwelcoming location. Marshall Cook lives almost an hour from his clinic so that he has the "barrier of distance" between his home and the clinic's protesters. Taking the opposite strategy, Miriam Dixon moved from a conservative rural area into the more liberal town where her clinic is located. "I wanted to live in the progressive hippie neighborhood really badly. I didn't want to feel worried about neighbors not being safe."

Warren Hern has combined different approaches to protect himself from protesters. First, he lives somewhere that is very difficult to find. In describing where he lives, he told us, "You're smart people, and you can read maps and stuff. If I give you both very clear instructions, it would be a challenge for you to find my house. I have lots of people getting lost coming through." In addition to living in a hard-to-find location, Hern bought the two houses next to his so that he knows exactly who his neighbors are.

After choosing their homes or offices, providers give careful thought to the layout and design of each.[3] In particular, the layout of the exterior of the clinic is very important. For instance, Milton Correll described the layout of the parking lots at two different clinics where he works. The parking lots intentionally have features designed to protect him from the protesters, such as a fence that fully encloses one of the lots and a back door that leads to a private parking lot. With this layout, "they can't get at you."

Stephen Tate also made layout decisions based on personal security concerns. Stephen performs abortions at various clinics but has an office within a suite of offices in a big hospital. Originally, his office was positioned right inside the suite door. His secretary pointed out that "someone could easily come from the hall into my office." The hospital agreed to reposition Stephen's office door within the suite, which "made that office a little safer."

Howard Stephens described layout minutiae that make a difference at one of the clinics where he works. The driveway there runs between two long buildings to the back parking lot. Patients and clinic workers access the clinic directly from this back parking lot, without having to go to the front of the building. Because the parking lot is not accessible from public property, the only way that the protesters can access the patients and providers would be to trespass—driving or walking from the public street into the driveway and down to the back parking lot. As a result, after patients and clinic workers drive down the driveway, they can park, exit their car, and walk into the building "completely out of visual sight of the protesters on the street." While protesters still target Howard when he is driving across the sidewalk to get onto clinic property, "it's only for a few seconds."

If the layout of the clinic site is initially imperfect, providers often incur great expense to try to improve it. Warren Hern knows this all too well. In the past, medical tenants in the building across from Hern's clinic used the same parking lot. Fearful that protesters could rent offices in that building, use the parking lot for anti-abortion demonstrations, and interfere with access to his office, Hern took the extreme measure of buying that building. As Hern described the decision:

> I did it for security, not as a business investment. It's a white elephant. Because I wanted to be able to control this parking lot and assure that there were no anti-abortion people next door. People all over the country failed to do that, and they got run out of business. They got sent out on the street. You cannot let that happen.

Another common way that providers alter their clinics and offices is by installing bulletproof materials. Several providers described installing bulletproof glass after the murders in Brookline and Boston, Massachusetts, where John Salvi entered clinics in both locations and shot the receptionists. Lisa Brink, an administrator at a clinic in a South Atlantic state, described the connection:

> I mean, seriously, my father called me on the phone as soon as it hit the news and asked, "Do you really want to work there?" I said, "Yeah, I really want to work there." And he wasn't saying give up or give in, but he was scared for his daughter's safety, and that's when we got bulletproof glass. We've always reacted to what has been happening with the violence.

Hern also installed bulletproof glass after a violent incident at his own clinic in which someone fired multiple bullets through the front window while the building was occupied. "We never found out who did it. I put in bulletproof windows, which are up there now. All the windows in the front and back are high-impact plastic."

While it offers added security, bulletproof glass is not always ideal for a medical setting. In particular, the check-in process for patients can become difficult. Rachel Friedman explained some of the changes that her clinic made in response to anti-abortion violence and elaborated on some of the consequences of these changes:

> You know how you go to a medical office, and they have a window that slides open and slides back and then they shut it after you register. And you usually see somebody with a really beautiful smile and warm eyes to make you feel comfortable. But we couldn't do that anymore because now we had to put up bulletproof glass. We had to add some locks and a buzzer system so that people could come in and you'd have to swipe to be able to get in if you're a staff member. It really began to change. Not just what we physically put into place for security, but the impact that it had on patients. Now, when you have bulletproof glass, you can't just talk in a low comforting voice, you have to be able to say [in a loud voice] "Hi! Do you have an appointment with us today?!" And then they whisper and you can't hear them, and you have to say, "Can you speak a little louder, because we have bulletproof glass!"
>
> It's just such a shame that the customer service quality and the way that we used to be able to provide it has changed so drastically. It's kind of cold, not only emotionally if someone is struggling with this perhaps, but also the constant reminder that your safety is not a hundred percent. These are the factors we have to take into consideration.

A 2012 interview-based study of patients at abortion clinics echoes Rachel's impression, finding that the safety precautions clinics take to prevent targeted harassment can increase patients' "feelings of stigma, secrecy, and isolation [and] make the experience more upsetting."[4] Not only is bulletproof glass sometimes an impediment to good patient care, but it is also not perfectly effective. Kristina Romero discussed her clinic's struggles with protecting its employees from bullets. When we interviewed her in her clinic's large conference room, she pointed to the huge windows that surround the room:

> So that's bullet-resistant glass, but that's not a bullet-resistant wall, so what are you going to do? Jump up in the air and stand up here

[in front of the glass]? You start playing these silly games, thinking what are you going to do? That's not bullet-resistant glass in front of the receptionist. But that is a bullet-resistant mantrap right there [in the front entrance area]. So that's not bullet-resistant, that little thing around there [near the door]. You do different things, but it's really a false sense of security.

Some providers consider the same precautions when thinking about the safety of their homes. When protesters disseminated flyers with her home address on them, Tami Madison responded by taking the street number off the front of her house. "It was not easy to do because it was securely glued to the front of my house. So I kind of just ripped that off." When the protesters then warned that they would demonstrate outside of her house, Tami had to improve her home security system. One of the protesters then threatened to ring Tami's doorbell and trespass on her property, so Tami put "No Trespassing" signs around her property. "I didn't want there to be any question that he didn't have permission to be here."

## Community Outreach

Another strategy that providers employ to prevent or minimize targeted harassment is reaching out to neighbors and other community members. Providers do this because, as Tami Madison put it, "most communities do not want terrorism."

Most of the stories of community outreach came from providers who talked with people in their neighborhood in advance of or in response to protesters demonstrating outside of their homes. After finding out that protesters were going to stage a demonstration at her home, Stephanie McGoldrick wrote a letter to her neighbors and then followed up with a visit. As a result of her efforts, her neighbors were "totally supportive" after the home demonstrations began.

Peggy Gifford also reached out to her neighbors before any protesters appeared at her house but used a different approach. While Peggy has not yet been protested at home, nor have protesters threatened to do so, she is nonetheless preparing for it to happen because other providers in her area have experienced home picketing. Rather than reveal to her neighbors that she is an abortion provider and that people might show up in the neighborhood to protest her, Peggy's strategy has been "to be a really cool neighbor" so that "when the signs show up, it's like 'Why are they at Peggy's house?'" She explained that her natural instincts would be to come home from work and relax at the end of the day by herself. "That's how I was in my old neighborhood. But I plan on living in my new neighborhood forever." Peggy knows that home picketing would disrupt her neighbors' lives, so she wants to blunt the possible effects by preemptively establishing relationships with them instead of keeping to herself.

Ellen James's community outreach took the form of a fundraiser for her clinics. After seeing protesters picket Ellen's house, one of her neighbors donated a large sum of money to Ellen's clinics. Ellen turned that donation into the start of a unique "pledge-a-picket" campaign. Many clinics across the United States have organized "pledge-a-picket" campaigns that raise money for the clinic based on the number of protesters who appear at the clinic on a particular day. Ellen's campaign is different as it is based on protesters showing up "anywhere but a health center because, again, health centers are a norm." With this campaign, the clinics not only raise large sums of money but also educate the community about the off-site targeted harassment that abortion providers suffer.

Providers sometimes reach out to their children's schools. After protesters showed up at Todd Stave's daughter's middle school, he feared that they would reappear and visit his older son's high school. Todd went to both schools and assured the administration that the specific people protesting had no known history of violence. Nonetheless, Todd warned the high school principal that the protesters would probably show up at the high school as well and gave the principal advice on how to handle the situation if they did. Based on experiences like Todd's and other providers she knew, Samantha Newsom anticipated that protesters would protest at her children's school. "I approached the school where my children went, just to ask for the community's awareness and protection, so that if they needed anything, they would let me know."

## Guns

Most medical professionals do not, as a result of their job, face the difficult question of whether to own and carry a gun for protection. Abortion providers, however, do; and they are split on the issue. Because of their work, some feel safer owning and carrying a weapon, while others, despite the risks, think it is not worthwhile.

Working at an abortion clinic can make people consider owning a gun even if they never thought about it before. Ruth Hicks explained that she began to seriously debate whether to purchase a gun when she and her colleagues were nearly attacked. "I've thought about carrying a firearm in my home, which I never really thought about until I started working here and there was almost a serious violent attack." After that close call, Ruth's husband asked her, "Do you think we need to have a gun somewhere?" Julie Burkhart reported that, because of her profession and the targeted harassment she has faced, she has had intense pressure from friends and family to obtain a concealed weapon permit. Julie, who already keeps a gun at her home, acquiesced to these pleas and was in the process of obtaining the permit when we interviewed her.

Providers have varying comfort levels with handling the weapons they own. Some providers carry their weapons all the time. Kris Neuhaus always carried her gun to work and was very public about it. She reasoned, "If somebody had shot at us, we would have certainly been a nuisance in return. It was like a MAD policy—Mutually Assured Destruction. We had always felt like we had to think on their level and respond that way." Kevin Bohannon has owned a gun "for years." He carries it with him when he walks from his car into the clinic where he works even though he knows that when he walks out in the open "anybody with a rifle who is a good shot could easily kill me." Kevin "would have no qualms" using his weapon to defend himself and his loved ones.

Other providers own guns but are less comfortable with them. Constance Phillips keeps her weapons at home and said that she never wants to resort to them but that one particular protester who constantly harasses her worries her. "He's the first person who has ever made me think he may become violent and that I need to know where the weapons are in the house." Donald Yates purchased a gun because of security concerns related to being an abortion provider and used to carry the gun, but has stopped. "It's never there when you need it. Particularly in this kind of situation. Unless you have it in your hand, cocked, and you're looking around, if they're there to get you, they're going to get you." He now keeps his gun in the desk drawer in his office.

On the other hand, many providers insisted that, despite the risks of their profession, they could not own or carry a gun. Dr. P. voiced two common reasons that some providers choose not to resort to a firearm. First, he joked about his lack of comfort doing so. He said, "Carry a gun? I'd probably shoot myself." He laughed and concluded, "No, no, no" on the point. But second, he explained that doing so would be futile. "Again, the guy who killed Barnett Slepian in Buffalo, he was a sniper who shot Slepian in his home. How can you prevent that? That could happen to a senator. Anybody. You're not going to prevent that."

Others also considered owning a gun but decided against it. Peggy Gifford had a visceral reaction to the issue: "I am not one for guns. I feel like I would use a gun if I had a gun, and I don't necessarily think my life would be saved. I don't correlate that to personal safety. I'm just not really a weapons girl." Sherry Bruner had the opposite explanation for why she decided against a gun. "You can't have a gun if you don't intend to aim it at somebody and fire it, and I don't think I can do that."

## Bulletproof Vests

Similar considerations arise with the question of whether to wear a bulletproof vest for protection. For some providers, wearing a bulletproof vest gives them the peace of mind that they need to continue performing their job. Lowell Taylor has been wearing a vest off and on for almost twenty years. He started wearing it when a known violent member of the anti-abortion movement, who would later murder another doctor, threatened him in person at his clinic and fired multiple bullets into his house. Lowell wore the vest for several years following those incidents but stopped in the early 2000s when "things seemed to quiet down." However, following Dr. Tiller's murder, the FBI approached Lowell and recommended that he wear a vest again. As a result, whenever he travels to work, he wears a vest because "the FBI says to." Lowell also believes it is the right thing to do. "I get worried about some of the people around here. There are some strange characters that lurk at the front gate. I don't know what they're capable of."

Tami Madison also related wearing a bulletproof vest to Dr. Tiller's murder. She started wearing one soon after he was assassinated, as did some of the doctors who work at her clinic:

That's a personal decision that every doctor who is affected has to make for themselves. I'm here sometimes by myself and leave by myself, so that went into part of my decision. It's not something that we talk about as much because I guess you don't want them to know when you're wearing it and when you're not, but I wear it when I feel more threatened or more vulnerable. So it may not be all the time, but since then I do wear it and I didn't before.

Tami considered purchasing vests for her entire staff, but it was too expensive. Ultimately, Tami knows that in her line of work she has to be this vigilant, but at the same time, she wishes things were different. "You want to live in a society where you're not terrorized, and sometimes to cope you just have to be free and live freely and try somehow to not let that get to you. But unfortunately, in the work we're in, there are threats, and you have to incorporate that kind of looking over your shoulder mentality into your daily lifestyle."

For some providers, wearing a vest seems futile, so they decide against it. Rebecca Lane said that she never considered it seriously. "What was I going to do, wear it all the time?" Ruth Hicks was similarly dismissive when her clinic asked her if she wanted a vest following a failed violent attack. "The attacker was going to aim for the head, so the vest wouldn't help me unless I'm wearing a helmet too, so I said no."

Some providers decide against wearing a vest because they believe doing so is unnecessary. Believing he might be at some risk, Mark Goldstein wore a vest "for a while" when he was going "in and out of work." However, he eventually stopped wearing it. He stopped because he thought it was "overkill," since he did not think he was actually in danger, and it was itchy. Mildred Randolph voiced a similar concern. She owns a vest but has worn it only once. "I felt goofy. I felt overprotective and I've never worn it since, so it's sitting in a drawer upstairs."

Finally, some providers explained that they refuse to wear a vest because they believe that doing so would give protesters too much emotional power over them. Donald Yates said that, even though one of the clinic directors where he worked repeatedly suggested that he wear a vest, he never could bring himself to do so. "I'd feel like more of a victim if I had to put on a bulletproof vest every time I go in and out of the office and in and out of the house." Tamara Cocci also explained that she does not wear a vest because it would make her focus on being "fearful and dysfunctional."

## Conclusion

The strategies covered in this chapter can be very helpful in blunting the effects of targeted harassment. Providers dealing with targeting for the first time or even anticipating that it may happen in the future could survey these strategies for tools to address their own situations. But these self-help strategies alone are not enough, nor should the onus of preventing or minimizing targeting be solely or primarily on the provider herself or himself. Rather, law and society should be proactive in addressing the various threats posed by anti-abortion terrorism. The remainder of this book looks at how this already happens and how both law and society can do a better job of making abortion providers safer.

# 7

## Six Stories of Law and Targeted Harassment

*I felt like I had to go back to ninth-grade civics class and figure out how is it that government really works? Who is it that I need to talk with? Where do we begin?*
—CYNTHIA KENDRICK

PROVIDERS' INTERACTIONS WITH LAW are as diverse and varied as their experiences with harassment and protest. As the providers interviewed for this book recognized, law can take many forms. For instance, when people think of law, they often think of laws that are "on the books" or, in other words, laws that are passed by elected officials. These laws include state and federal statutes, local ordinances, and even national and state constitutions.

But law is more than just what is "on the books." It also includes people like police, lawyers, judges, and others who enact and enforce the law. In addition, the providers interviewed for this book recognized the close connection between law and politics. In talking about law, they discussed running for elected office, working with elected officials on a matter of concern, testifying before a legislative body regarding a particular area of expertise, and lobbying to influence the legislative process.[1]

This chapter and the chapters that follow use the term "law" in this broad sense so as to adequately capture individual providers' varied and unique experiences. As these chapters show, providers often turn to law to help solve their problems with targeted harassment. Sometimes law responds as the providers had hoped and is helpful in addressing the situation. Other times, providers experience roadblocks, such as an unsympathetic local police force or a law that does not cover the particular harassment they face. Still other times, providers experience law itself as a form of harassment and protest. The next three chapters explore these assorted experiences and paint a picture of the legal landscape providers face in dealing with targeted harassment.

This exploration of law and its response to targeted harassment begins the same way as the previous portion of the book began—with a selection of full stories of providers' experiences with targeted harassment and law. All of these stories contribute to the important take-away from this part of the book: law can be improved to better address abortion providers' experiences with targeted harassment. These stories begin the exploration of what that improvement should look like.

### Calvin Litwin

Calvin Litwin is a physician who has been providing abortion care since the 1970s, both in the Mountain West state where he now lives and works and in a Pacific West state where he used to work. Calvin has his own obstetrics and gynecology practice separate from the clinic where he provides abortions.

Calvin's first experience with targeted harassment came in the early 2000s when he started working at the clinic that currently employs him. When Calvin started working there, he noticed that anti-abortion protesters visited the clinic every day that abortions are performed. At first, these protesters did not know Calvin, so he was able to slip into the office anonymously. However, they eventually discovered Calvin's identity and home address and began targeting him at his home.

The first demonstration at Calvin's house occurred when he was away on vacation. Apparently unaware that Calvin was away, a group of thirty to forty protesters staged a demonstration in front of his house with signs that the neighbors later described to Calvin as "inappropriate for young children," including signs with arrows pointed toward Calvin's house that depicted dismembered babies and said "Abortionist." While in front of Calvin's house, the protesters yelled "baby killer!" and made references to the Holocaust. The protesters also marched their signs around the neighborhood and put flyers about Calvin in his neighbors' mailboxes.

Following this first demonstration, the protesters targeted Calvin's home in this manner every Saturday for the next year. At first, Calvin and his wife reacted to the protest by hiding in their house and waiting for the protesters to leave. Eventually, however, Calvin realized that the best approach was to simply leave his house so that the protesters could not harass him.

The weekly protest at Calvin's house was initially more disturbing for Calvin's neighbors than for him. Calvin's neighbors feared the anti-abortion demonstrators invading their community, and they often called the police. Despite these initial fears, the neighbors eventually became Calvin's supportive allies, a development that Calvin greatly appreciates. For instance, the home protests started during an election year. One neighbor printed yard signs, at the neighbor's own expense, to post around the neighborhood alongside the campaign yard signs. The neighbor's signs read, "We support our friend and neighbor Calvin Litwin and a woman's right to choose." Calvin was touched by the gesture. "To come home from work and see all those signs in people's yards was very heartfelt." Calvin's neighbors also sent him supportive letters with sentiments such as, "I don't really know you, but I support you and I'm sorry that you're going through this. We need people like you."

In the face of the home picketing, Calvin also greatly appreciates the support he has received from his local police force. During the first protest at Calvin's house, the police responded immediately to Calvin's neighbors' calls and were very helpful in keeping order. When Calvin himself called the police during subsequent protests, the police response was also very helpful.

In particular, the police ensured the protesters' behavior conformed to the local residential picketing ordinance. In Calvin's words,[2] the residential picketing ordinance prohibits picketing outside of a particular residence unless that picketing follows certain requirements. Specifically, the law requires that protesters "go a block one way and a block the other way and then back around. They cannot stop." The law also states that "signs had to be of a certain size. They couldn't be these big signs, and they couldn't have permanent signs on their cars."

Calvin is thankful that the ordinance is in place and that his local police force has been effective in "protecting and serving" the community. Because of efforts by Calvin and others, the police force is well educated about the anti-abortion protesters' tactics and the severity of their targeted protest. As a result, the police are extremely responsive when working with Calvin. Nonetheless, Calvin was clear that the ordinance and effective policing do not completely solve the problem. Until the police arrive, the protesters push the limits of the ordinance and "do whatever they damn well please."

From these experiences, Calvin has developed a very positive personal relationship with the local sheriff and the members of his police force. For example, after the home protests started, the sheriff urged Calvin to purchase a gun and then granted Calvin's emergency application for a concealed weapon permit. The murders of other abortion providers weigh on Calvin. "It's a little scary. I mean, but that's why I carry a weapon."

Another time, Calvin woke in the middle of the night during a snowstorm. He put on his glasses, looked out the window, and realized there was a car flashing lights in his driveway. Calvin grabbed his gun, went downstairs, and heard someone ringing his doorbell. As soon as Calvin looked outside, he realized it was the police. Calvin opened the door, and the sheriff said, "Dr. Litwin, your garage door is open, and I felt like it was better to wake you and have you close it than worry about you because I don't want anything to happen to you."

The sheriff has also acted preemptively to help Calvin with the demonstrations at Calvin's house. In one instance, when Calvin's community learned that the protesters were planning a massive anti-abortion demonstration outside of Calvin's home that would attract out-of-state protesters, the sheriff held neighborhood meetings at Calvin's home to discuss how the community should safely respond to the event. The neighborhood decided not to engage with the protesters; instead, Calvin's daughter held a barbeque for neighbors on the day of the protest. The sheriff also stationed five or six squad cars at Calvin's home. When the mass of protesters arrived, the police successfully kept order and ensured that the protesters followed the town's ordinance.

The sheriff is supportive despite Calvin's and the sheriff's differing political beliefs—the sheriff is a Republican and Calvin is a Democrat. The politics of abortion has not become an issue between them because, as Calvin perceives it, "the sheriff wants to protect his citizens, and he wants peace and doesn't want anybody being hurt." This "all business" approach has, according to Calvin, limited the frequency of the home protests. While protesters initially targeted his house every weekend for a year, they now limit their home pickets to certain holidays.

By contrast, Calvin's experience with targeted harassment and police response at work has been entirely different from his experience at home. Calvin works in a town several miles from his hometown and under the jurisdiction of a different police force. While Calvin feels safe in his home community as a result of his positive interactions with the police, he has had very negative experiences with the police force that he interacts with at work.

When Calvin arrives at work in the morning, the protesters regularly bombard him with a variety of incendiary comments, including "baby killer," "quit killing babies," and "God won't forgive you." They have even shouted that Calvin will "turn out like" one of the previous providers at the clinic, who died several years ago, or the clinic's past security guard, who is also deceased. In addition, the protesters throw themselves at Calvin's car and record video of him driving into the driveway.

The police response at the clinic has not been helpful. The police regularly tell the clinic directors that they will station officers at the clinic during protests; however, the police do not follow through with these promises. For example, on the morning we interviewed Calvin, there was a demonstration outside the clinic. When Calvin's coworker arrived, she saw an officer outside the clinic; however, when Calvin arrived a short while later, the officer had left, even though the demonstration was ongoing. As Calvin describes it, the police are unreliable and often fail to make an appearance.

Even when the police do appear, they frequently fail to enforce the law governing clinic protest. Calvin's clinic is covered by a "buffer zone" law. This type of law, discussed in more depth in the next chapter, establishes a fixed zone around an abortion clinic within which interaction with clinic patients and providers is restricted. The protesters regularly violate the law by standing well within that zone and harassing Calvin and other clinic employees as they enter. Despite the protesters' disregard of the buffer zone, the police do not reprimand the protesters or enforce the law. In fact, a protester once infringed upon the buffer zone by approaching patients and touching them as they entered the clinic. Because the local police failed to respond, the clinic called the federal Department of Justice, which responded to the incident. Calvin lamented, "You can get federal people to come out and do something about it, but you can't get the local."

Calvin also expressed frustration with the way the police responded to a threat he received at his private medical practice. Protesters routinely send postcards to Calvin's home, throughout his neighborhood, and to his medical practice. Usually the postcards say things such as "Jesus saves" and "Jesus loves." However, Calvin received one particular postcard at his private medical practice that said "You could end up dead." To Calvin, this postcard was "semi-threatening," so he called the local police. The police went to Calvin's office, took a copy of the postcard, and told Calvin that his office needs to improve its security. Calvin never heard anything else from the police, and nothing came of this incident.

Calvin believes that the police where he works are unresponsive because they personally hold anti-abortion beliefs. In contrast to the police force that covers his home community, Calvin feels judged by the police where he works. He believes that the politics of abortion prevent the police from responding appropriately. Calvin also thinks the police where he works feel that they have more important business than responding to his concerns and that "until something bad happens to us, they're not going to do anything." Ultimately, this worries Calvin because "that's what we're trying to prevent!"

## Tami Madison

Tami Madison has been a clinic director in a Middle Atlantic state for over a decade. In the early 2000s, she moved her clinic to a new part of town, and protesters appeared immediately. Looking to ensure the safe operation of the clinic in its new location, Tami organized a meeting with the local police at the new clinic site, the state police who were responsible for the old clinic site, and the FBI. At this meeting, the clinic representatives and the law enforcement personnel discussed the aggressive protesting that had begun at the new location, particularly the protesters' picketing in the public alley that runs between the clinic's entrance and the clinic's parking lot. The police explained that, according to a local ordinance, individuals need a permit to protest. However, because of the narrowness of the alley, the police would not issue permits in this instance because protesting would interfere with traffic.

Over the next several months, protesters regularly demonstrated in the narrow alley between the clinic building and its parking lot. With sometimes large numbers of loud protesters in such a small space, Tami felt intimidated walking across the alley from the parking lot to the building's entrance. The protesters did not have permits and sometimes trespassed onto private property, and as a result the police frequently arrested the protesters. As a witness to some of these events, Tami testified in court at the trespass hearings.

Because of this intimidating environment outside the building, the clinic administration met with the mayor. The mayor showed an understanding of the issues associated with clinic protest and the possible risk of violence. He increased police presence at the clinic, but protesters continued to aggressively picket in the narrow alley.

Following several repeated arrests for not having a protest permit, a group of protesters filed a federal lawsuit against the city. The protesters claimed that the permit ordinance was an unconstitutional restriction of their freedom of speech. Ultimately, as a result of this challenge, a federal judge found that the manner in which the city applied the permit requirement against the protesters was unconstitutional and that the protesters did not need a permit to protest on the alley's public walkways.

Nonetheless, the local police still determined that it would be unlawful for the protesters to protest in the narrow alley. Because the alley was an active street that actually had, contrary to the judge's order, no sidewalks or public walkways, walking in the street violated local traffic safety laws. As a result, the police issued traffic citations to the protesters, who then challenged the citations in court. As part of these court proceedings, the protesters subpoenaed Tami and sought important clinic documents from her. These subpoenas concerned Tami. To her, the confidentiality of the clinic and clinic staff was placed at risk. Moreover, in dealing with the numerous subpoenas that compelled both confidential information and her physical attendance at various hearings, Tami believed the protesters were using the legal process to harass her, the clinic, and its staff.

Until this point, Tami's experiences with harassment were confined to the clinic and the legal process. However, this changed one fall day, as Tami described:

> I live right on a main street corner at a traffic light. When I drove by on my way home I thought I saw one of the protesters talking to a neighbor. And you think you're seeing things. It was like twilight, it wasn't fully bright out, but I thought, "Nah, that couldn't have been him." And then I looked at my door, and I saw this little orange piece of paper sticking out of my door. At that second I just knew what it was. My gut dropped. I'm like, "They found me."

The flyer included very personal information about Tami. It started, "Dear neighbors of Tami Madison" and listed Tami's home address. It continued, "You may have seen this attractive young lady in her red Honda, thinking that she's going to a respectable job, when in fact she's killing babies." The flyer listed a phone number that purported to be Tami's and instructed recipients to call and convince Tami not to work at the clinic.

This incident made Tami "a little hysterical." She contacted the local police, who came to her house and took a report. Certain protesters admitted their involvement in distributing the flyers but were not charged with any crime. Without a local law in Tami's hometown against this type of harassment, the police told Tami that there was nothing they could do other than tell the protesters not to trespass.

The flyers reached Tami's home within a year after one particularly worrisome protester had begun to appear at the protests at Tami's clinic. This protester maintains an anti-abortion website, where he regularly posts inflammatory anti-abortion newsletters. He also mails these newsletters to prisoners who are incarcerated for committing violent crimes against abortion providers, such as murder or bombing clinics. In his newsletter he notes that he believes in the use of violence to stop abortion, though he expresses doubt as to whether he can actually carry it out. When this protester discovered Tami's address, he printed it and other personal information about Tami in his newsletter. The protester regularly mailed Tami copies of his newsletters and later told her, "I didn't want you to think I was talking about you behind your back."

In response to these personal attacks, Tami explained that she "had to start living differently." Tami's reaction was rooted in her awareness of the history of violence against abortion providers. "I just felt uncomfortable in my own house from that point on, and it continues to this day, really, where if I can't see outside, like at night, I want to make sure that my shades are closed. I just feel like I can't be exposed because of some of the doctors that have been shot in their homes."

At the same time that the harassment followed Tami home, protesters initiated a second federal lawsuit against the city. This suit claimed that the police violated the protesters' First Amendment rights by issuing citations to them for protesting in the street. This second lawsuit settled before trial, and the protesters each received a lump sum from the city as part of the settlement. In exchange, the city and the protesters agreed on specific zones in the alley behind the clinic where the protesters could demonstrate. They also agreed to create a makeshift crosswalk between the parking lot and the clinic door for patients to use to access the clinic. The protesters could walk across that crosswalk when picketing but had to vacate the crosswalk whenever a patient or a staff person needed to use it.

Following the settlement agreement, the protests at the clinic became even more personal. The protesters used their settlement money to, as they told clinic personnel while taunting them, "buy a lot of private investigators" to discover the names and other personal information of every person who worked there. Focusing specifically on Tami, one of the protesters told Tami that she was going to change her schedule to mirror Tami's personal schedule so that she would be at the clinic every time that Tami worked. To Tami, "it felt like stalking. It felt like harassment. And it was definitely disturbing." Overall, Tami felt that she and her coworkers "were clearly working in a culture of terror. It was all about harassment and intimidation."

In particular, the protester who writes the newsletter for violent anti-abortion prisoners increased his targeting of Tami. He not only appeared at the clinic more frequently but also told clinic staff that if Tami "didn't come out and talk to him that he was going to make a home visit." Fearing he would follow through with his threat and demonstrate at her home, Tami put "No Trespassing" signs around her property and increased her home security. This protester and others did indeed start picketing Tami's home, and they have continued to do so on a regular basis ever since.

Following the settlement of the second lawsuit, the protests at the clinic not only became more personal but also grew larger. When walking from the parking lot into the building, the clinic staff and patients had to dodge the people demonstrating outside the clinic. Even though the demonstrators were supposed to withdraw from the makeshift crosswalk between the parking lot and the clinic, "that wasn't really happening. The protesters were reaching their hands across and touching us as we walked through it." In a brainstorming session about how to cope with the protesters' aggressive actions, a clinic volunteer came up with a novel idea. "I have some tarps at home. Why don't I bring them in and we'll try using tarps to create a wall so that patients won't get touched while walking in the clinic."

The clinic volunteers adopted this idea and began to carry the tarps along the side of the crosswalk to help escort patients and providers from the parking lot to the clinic entrance. The tarps infuriated the protesters, who responded by bringing a third federal lawsuit. This time, the protesters sued not only the city but also the clinic and Tami personally. The protesters claimed that by using the tarps to shield patients as they entered the clinic, the clinic and Tami conspired with the city to thwart the protesters' access to patients and providers and therefore deprive the protesters of their First Amendment right to freedom of speech. Being sued as an individual felt very frightening and personal for Tami. "I wasn't served by a constable or someone from the court that would normally serve papers. I was served by one of the protesters who worked at the court part-time."

Because the protesters claimed that Tami and the clinic conspired with the city to deprive them of their constitutional right to free speech, the clinic and Tami were wary of their interactions with the police out of fear that such contact could be seen as proof of the conspiracy. For instance, Tami described an incident in which the protester with the newsletter drove from the clinic to Tami's neighborhood in a truck that contained large orange barrels that looked as if they contained gasoline. Tami reported the incident to the FBI rather than her local police "because unfortunately what's happened with this last lawsuit is that it's pretty much just stopped all communication with the local police department because of this conspiracy charge." Going forward, Tami said, "We'll call the local police if we feel there's an immediate concern, but the city solicitor has told us that there won't be any arrests unless there's a threat to life or person." So far, that threshold has not been met, so the solicitor has not allowed the police department to press any charges. Overall, because of the conspiracy lawsuit, Tami finds that "it's just really complicated to communicate with the police these days."

Through the course of the three lawsuits as well as her testimony before the local magistrate in the protesters' criminal cases, Tami felt the protesters used the legal system, and the pretrial discovery process in particular, as a way to target her. Despite Tami's lawyers' efforts to limit what the protesters could find out about her, Tami said the depositions were grueling and that the protesters' lawyer repeatedly sought irrelevant information about her personal life. "I just felt like they were out to get me," Tami recalled.

When the protesters' lawyers sought sensitive clinic records, such as the floor plans and the building surveillance footage, Tami worried, "How do I know they're not going to use them to decide where to put a bomb? So it's that kind of threat that I felt when I was subpoenaed to hand over that information." Tami felt trapped. The protesters' lawyers asked questions that were very broad and could compromise her own security as well as the security of her clinic and its personnel, but she also felt that the legal process compelled her to answer most of them. In one of the first depositions, the attorney for the protesters had a list of names of people he believed worked at the clinic. "He wanted to go down that list and verify with me who was working at the clinic. And I just don't see any purpose of that, other than to use that information to harass and intimidate."

The courts finally resolved the third lawsuit in Tami's favor. Tami was fortunate to have access to legal counsel, who represented her on a pro bono basis. She might not have been able to afford to fight these legal battles against the protesters without these attorneys. Tami feels that the protesters have a "mafia-type mentality" and that their goal is to scare her from being an abortion provider through whatever means they can—on-site harassment, home picketing, using the legal process to target her, and more.

Despite this mentality, Tami insists that they will not succeed because she will continue her work despite what they do to her and despite law enforcement's less-than-ideal response. "For me, what it goes back to is just being so committed to the work that we do. And that without abortion providers, there is no choice. We're the ones that make choice an option for women, whereas they wouldn't have it if there were no providers. That's what keeps me going and keeps me working here."

## Paul Fortin

Paul Fortin is an obstetrician-gynecologist who lives and works in an East Midwest state. He works with a private medical practice that is affiliated with a large city hospital but has also worked at two different abortion clinics in the same city. He has been involved with abortion provision since he was a resident in medical school over fifteen years ago.

Anti-abortion protesters first targeted Paul at his home about a year and a half before we interviewed him:

> It was a Saturday morning, and my young kid said, "Hey Dad, there's a parade outside of the house." And I'm like, "What the hell?" So I look outside of the house; it's all the same people who protest at the clinic. And they have their signs, and it's all written down. My name. And there must have been thirty or forty of them. On our side of the street, on the other side of the street, across the street. I got my wife and kids out of the house because it's hard to explain that to small children.

Paul believes that the protesters from the clinic found out where he lives either by following him home or through the state medical board, from which it is fairly easy to discover a doctor's home address.

This group of protesters demonstrated outside of Paul's home on Saturday mornings another "six or eight times" over the course of a year. They also mailed letters to all of Paul's neighbors. The letters stated that Paul was a murderer who lived in their community.

During the first several home protests, Paul believed he did not have the support of the local police. The day before the first demonstration, protesters informed the police that they were going to demonstrate at Paul's home. The police did not reach out to Paul to inform him that they were coming. Rather, the police later told Paul that they did not want to let anybody know about the protest ahead of time because they worried that doing so would escalate the situation. Paul admitted that perhaps if he, his family, and his coworkers had advance notice of the protest, they would have counterorganized and that the situation could have escalated. Nonetheless, Paul still felt that being informed would have been useful for his family's peace of mind.

When protesters demonstrated outside of Paul's house a second time, they yelled to Paul, "We're going to get you. We're going to teach you a lesson. We're going to tell your family, and we're going to come after them." After hearing this, Paul called the police and told them that the protesters who were picketing at his house were threatening him. The police did not respond, so Paul called again thirty minutes later. He said, "Look, I'm going to go to my garage and I'm going to get an axe. And I'm going to go out and I'm going to tell these people to get off my property, and it's going to get ugly. So either you can come or you cannot come, but this is what I'm going to do." After this second phone call, the police appeared but did nothing to stop the protesters. "The police just stood there and watched them. Some of them stood there and talked to them, almost friendly. But I mean, I figure we call the police, we call the FBI, what else can we do? We're very powerless with these people."

This frustration with the police surfaced repeatedly during the home demonstrations. "The cops came. I walked out. I talked to them at the car. They didn't make the protesters take the signs down, nothing. They just said, 'Hey, it looks like it's a peaceful demonstration.' So it's really infuriating because it's as if I have no rights."

According to Paul, the police feigned sympathy and interest in helping him, but the protests "just kept happening and kept happening and kept happening." Because law enforcement would not respond, Paul felt forced to take his own measures. While Paul strongly believed that law enforcement should be involved and continued to pressure the police and city officials as well, he also began to monitor the protesters himself. When the protesters were picketing at his house, Paul went outside to write down their license plates, their descriptions, and anything else he could about them. He used that information to put pressure on the police to act. "Every time the cops came out they said I needed a paper trail. I'd go up and I'd spend an hour talking to the police, and writing a complaint. It would get filed, but the next week the protesters were back at my house."

Eventually, after Paul repeatedly pressured the city's lead prosecutor, city officials told Paul they would station a marked squad car outside of his house. The prosecutor said there had been enough occurrences to warrant doing so and to arrest the protesters if they refused to comply with police orders to remain civil. What Paul did not know was that even before the prosecutor committed to putting a marked car outside Paul's house, an unmarked police car had been there every Saturday. "They were there. I don't know if just they drove by or they got tipped off."

As a result of the new visible police presence, at the time we interviewed him, protesters had not returned to picket Paul's house. "From what I've heard, their organization was warned that they need to watch it because the next time they come back they'll be arrested." Paul admitted that he did not know precisely on what grounds the police would have arrested the protesters. The city where he lives does not have an ordinance that prohibits or restricts residential picketing, so Paul interpreted the warning as a somewhat empty threat. As a result of Paul's situation, local politicians have expressed support for changing the ordinance, but that has not yet happened.

In addition to his experiences at home, Paul has been targeted at the clinic where he works. "I would drive in to the clinic and my name would be on the sign, 'Fortin is a killer' or 'murderer.' And they would yell at me and they would videotape me. There's a gas station at that corner where they wait for me and my car to come through."

The most threatening incident occurred one Saturday morning sometime in the year before we interviewed Paul when about forty protesters were at the clinic. The group carried their usual signs, but a new sign displayed Paul's picture in crosshairs. "I was just shocked that that was legal. I just can't see how that's fair." Paul contacted the FBI about the targeted protest, particularly in light of the sign with the crosshairs. "They said it's perfectly legal. The protesters could do that, and they could do worse." The FBI told Paul that as long as the protesters were not standing in one location, were not trespassing, were not touching him, and were not violent, "they're well within their rights."

Because of the home picketing and threats at work, Paul would like to obtain a restraining order against the protesters. "I know who three or four of them are, they're regulars, and they're not ashamed of it." However, legal fees for obtaining a restraining order are costly. A clinic that Paul knows of spent between $50,000 and $75,000 on legal fees just to obtain an order that a protester stand farther away from the clinic. Paul lamented, "I don't have that kind of money."

The demonstrations outside of Paul's home and the targeted protests at the clinic have had a lasting effect on Paul. He has worn a bulletproof vest ever since Dr. Tiller was murdered and carries a baseball bat in his car because of the ways he has been targeted. "It's kind of sad that you've got to put on a bulletproof vest to walk into work, but these people are crazy."

Not only does Paul wear a bulletproof vest and keep a bat in his car, but he also lives in a constant state of awareness. At home, even though the demonstrations appear to have stopped, when Paul awakes on Saturday mornings, he looks out his window. "You live in fear of these people, because you never know who's going to be here. They're real crazy. Who is going to come after me? But I get up and I look through the bedroom window and hear a car door slam, somewhere between eight and eight forty-five, and I feel like I'm a prisoner in my own home looking out to see." Even when he is away from his home and where he works, Paul says that he always looks over his shoulder and surveys his surroundings. He has a cell phone on him at all times with 911 on speed dial, and he is cautious about broadcasting his job. "I always thought I'd be a little more vocal about the cause, but I just feel like it would be putting my family at undue risk."

## Elizabeth Moll

Elizabeth Moll is a physician who has worked in family medicine since the mid-1980s. Though she is trained in abortion care and thought about becoming an abortion provider in the past, she exclusively focused her practice on family medicine in a Midwest state until recently when she tried to expand her practice to include abortion.

Abortion-related protest is not new to Elizabeth or her community. A doctor who used to provide abortions in that community had been subject to severe harassment for decades. After this doctor stopped providing abortions, nobody immediately stepped up to provide abortion care in the community, forcing women to drive three to five hours to find an abortion provider. Because Elizabeth saw the community's desperate need for someone to provide basic access to abortion care, she began to consider whether she should try to fill the void. Elizabeth hoped that she could expand her practice to include abortion a few days a week while still focusing on family medicine the other days of the week.

Because of her community's past issues with extreme abortion-related harassment, Elizabeth anticipated that anti-abortion protest would likely be an issue for her. As one way to deal with it, Elizabeth thought that she could post signs on the parking lot entrances explicitly warning people not to trespass on her practice's private property. Elizabeth hoped that hanging these signs around the property would effectively warn protesters that she would not take any unlawful protesting lightly.

Because she rented her office space, Elizabeth discussed the possible protest issues with her landlord and assured him that she was committed to protecting the property. Elizabeth let her landlord know that she purchased the equipment to provide abortion services, hoped to start the procedures within a few months, and, given the anti-abortion climate in the town, wanted to put up "No Trespassing" signs that she would purchase. Unfortunately for Elizabeth, talking with her landlord had two undesired effects: making her the target of protest and a lawsuit.

Immediately after Elizabeth told her landlord of her plan to start providing abortions, anti-abortion protesters began demonstrating outside of her office. The protests started one Saturday morning when two prominent anti-abortion groups staged a large rally. Concerned about this demonstration and the possibility that it might escalate into the extreme harassment the community had seen before, the local police reached out to and eventually worked with agents from the federal Bureau of Alcohol, Tobacco, Firearms and Explosives to assist Elizabeth with security. The two agencies trained Elizabeth and her staff about what threats they should take seriously, what types of packages to look for, and how to track letters and other types of communication.

Following that first rally, protesters began staging demonstrations at random times. During these demonstrations, protesters stood at the corner of the parking lot on public property by the street and carried "big, generic anti-abortion signs." Elizabeth and her staff did not know when or how many protesters would appear, so they warned all of their patients that there might be protesters trying to disrupt the office. Although Elizabeth was not yet providing abortion care, these demonstrations disrupted her practice because many patients called before their appointments to see if there were protesters and, if so, sought to reschedule their appointments.

Protesters also began targeting Elizabeth outside of her practice. In preparation for becoming an abortion provider, Elizabeth trained in a city a few hours away. Protesters from her home area followed her to her training site and staged anti-abortion demonstrations there that were targeted at her. At this other site, the protesters yelled "specific threats" at Elizabeth. To get through the protesters, Elizabeth entered the clinic with an armed guard.

Protesters also began picketing Elizabeth and her family off-site. One of the most difficult days for Elizabeth was the day that protesters appeared at the condo where she lives. To the best of Elizabeth's knowledge, they protested there only once when she was home alone. Forty to fifty people staged a demonstration on the main road in front of the driveway to her development:

> It's quite a ways from where I park the car to getting into my door. They were yelling and it was pretty anxiety-provoking because you begin to think their rhetoric is such that they're never going to let abortion back in this area, and it felt like I was very exposed. I didn't think there was going to be any violence, but I just didn't really know for sure at that point. So I kept all of the shades down and went to the basement where there were thick walls. I just kind of hid for four hours while they were there. I just wasn't feeling real safe there for a while.

Elizabeth's contact at the FBI eventually showed up, though not until an hour after the protest ended. He helped her assess her security, which made her feel "safe again."

Others also felt the brunt of the protest. Elizabeth's god-brother lives in a farmhouse that Elizabeth owns. Protesters discovered that Elizabeth is the owner, and they demonstrated outside of the farmhouse several times, apparently thinking that Elizabeth lived there. However, because of where the farmhouse is located, the protesters actually had to stand closer to the neighbors' houses while they were protesting. Elizabeth explained that the neighbors "were somewhat more harassed by these guys" than she or her god-brother.

Protesters also targeted members of Elizabeth's staff. One of the most vocal protesters followed a staff member while she was going to pick up her children at day care. Another staff member returned home to find her neighborhood and yard "plastered" with "Wanted" posters of her. With each incident, the local police were very responsive, though they said there was little they could do because they "considered this a free speech issue and not a harassment issue."

Elizabeth believes that the police responsiveness was due in part to the history of severe abortion-related harassment in the community. They treated Elizabeth's and her staff's calls seriously and always appeared when called. They also frequently stationed a patrol car to observe Elizabeth's office. Because Elizabeth felt that law enforcement was truly committed to her safety, she felt comfortable with her decision to bring abortion care back to her community.

Elizabeth's plans were also affected by a different form of anti-abortion harassment. When the protesters first appeared at her office, Elizabeth did not initially understand how they had learned of her plans and why they had started protesting. She was not yet providing abortion care and had not publicly announced her intention to do so. But she soon made the connection—her landlord is a close friend of a prominent figure in the anti-abortion movement. Elizabeth suspected that immediately following her conversation with her landlord about the "No Trespassing" signs, her landlord informed the local anti-abortion groups of her intentions.

Elizabeth's suspicion was soon confirmed. Not long after the protests started, Elizabeth's landlord initiated a lawsuit against her, claiming that she was creating a public nuisance. The theory of the landlord's case was that because there were protesters outside of the office and those protesters were creating a disturbance, Elizabeth was negatively affecting the landlord's business. The landlord claimed that as a result of the anti-abortion demonstrations, he was unable to rent any open space in the building and that other tenants were thinking of leaving or not renewing their leases.

The lawsuit was an expensive battle for Elizabeth to fight, and she soon reached the conclusion that expanding her practice in that location to include abortion care was no longer a viable option. Elizabeth decided not to look for different space either because her state passed a new law more strictly regulating abortion clinics' physical space, which would have been very difficult and expensive for Elizabeth to comply with. The lawsuit quickly went away once Elizabeth made this decision, and the protests stopped as well. Elizabeth believes that her landlord helped coordinate the protests at her office; since the lawsuit disappeared, there has not been another protest at the building.

Despite her decision not to perform abortions at her medical practice, Elizabeth continues to fight legal battles associated with being targeted. At the same time the protests started at her office, Elizabeth received many anti-abortion letters at work. The office developed a protocol for handling such letters. Any time the office received a letter that was remotely threatening, the office manager called the police department and an officer responded by visiting Elizabeth's office and looking at the letter.

One letter in particular concerned Elizabeth's staff. A well-known local anti-abortion protester who frequently protested at Elizabeth's office sent a letter that read, as Elizabeth recalled, "You'll always have to look over your shoulder. You'll have to look under your car, never knowing if it's going to get blown up." Elizabeth's office manager called their police contact, who was concerned enough to call the FBI. The FBI did not believe the letter was a direct threat to Elizabeth, so the agency did not investigate the letter.

However, lawyers from the Department of Justice believed that the letter was threatening enough to pursue an action under the Freedom of Access to Clinic Entrances Act (FACE), the federal law that prohibits, among other things, threats against abortion providers.[3] The department brought a civil lawsuit against the protester and sought an injunction prohibiting the protester from contacting or coming near Elizabeth. The lawsuit also sought monetary damages.

During the lawsuit, Elizabeth worked closely with the lawyers from the Department of Justice. She met with two attorneys in particular who were part of a federal task force dedicated to responding to threats against abortion clinics and providers. The attorneys were extremely helpful to Elizabeth throughout the litigation. Nonetheless, the federal judge assigned to the case ultimately ruled against Elizabeth, finding that the letter did not constitute a direct threat and was constitutionally protected free speech. When we spoke with Elizabeth, the Department of Justice was appealing that decision.

Despite this ruling and her landlord's lawsuit that thwarted her planned abortion practice in her current location, Elizabeth believes that her efforts were a worthwhile venture. With another abortion provider opening a clinic in her area, Elizabeth is content that she was possibly "the lightning rod to get services here" because, to her, it was never about being a hero. "I just wanted to get services here for people because it's really hard for a lot of women to go three, three and a half hours away."

## Stephanie McGoldrick

Stephanie McGoldrick is a physician who provided abortions for several years in an East Midwest state but eventually moved to the Middle Atlantic region, where she lived in one state while performing abortions in another. Before Stephanie started her position on the East Coast, one of her friends suggested she wear a disguise to protect herself from anti-abortion harassment. Since she did not have much experience with anti-abortion harassment where she previously worked, Stephanie was taken aback by this suggestion. Nonetheless, she thought, "A reason to put on a wig, why not?"

What Stephanie initially thought was a cute joke eventually became a necessary and routine part of her job. Even though Stephanie's new coworkers told her that there would be only "a few protesters," she followed her friend's advice when she drove to the clinic for her first day of work. Before she arrived at the clinic, she pulled over to a rest stop and put on a disguise in the bathroom. She cloaked herself in a long black wig with long bangs, big black sunglasses, and a black trench coat with a hood. To Stephanie, she "looked like Elvira."

Looking back, Stephanie described it as a "fortuitous accident" that she followed her friend's advice. As it turned out, her office's warning about "a few protesters" did not prepare Stephanie for what she would endure:

> They didn't tell me that the protesters were domestic terrorists, which is what I consider them. Protesters are one thing. These guys were more than protesters, so I was a little pissed at my office for not realistically portraying what I was getting into because once I started looking into them online, I was horrified. It was pretty scary.

Clinic administrators apparently agreed because they gave Stephanie a bulletproof vest when she showed up for work the first day. She wore it under her "Elvira" disguise every single day that she worked there.

Although Stephanie never spoke to them, after only two weeks protesters "started hurling personal information" at her. They began calling Stephanie by her name. They told her to go back to the specific Midwest state where she used to live. They knew she had a son and yelled at her, "You have a son. You didn't kill your son."

Though deeply personal, these initial interactions did not have a particularly strong effect on Stephanie until one night, a few weeks into her new position, when she was leaving work. Stephanie left late and walked down the block to the parking lot where she had parked her car. As she approached her parking spot, she recognized one protester. "He was sitting in his car in the alley next to the parking lot waiting for me at seven at night—and they started protesting at eight in the morning—and then he followed me out of the alley." At first, Stephanie thought, "this guy is a freak, he's just crazy." However, as she thought about it more, she became troubled. "He's also probably seventy-five years old, which means if he gets pancreatic cancer, he has nothing to lose. That's what bothered me—that he had nothing to lose and he seemed so obsessed."

After this incident, Stephanie talked with her coworkers, who then warned her about this particular protester, the same protester who targeted Tami Madison through the newsletter that he posts online and sends to violent anti-abortion prisoners. Stephanie's coworkers warned her that this particular protester was "scary" and "nasty."

This protester and several of his associates regularly targeted Stephanie. Because of her disguise, they called her "black widow." They continued to talk about her son and repeatedly told her to go back to the Midwest. Protesters also threatened Stephanie by telling her she "would be hurt." A week before Stephanie's birthday, protesters yelled at her, "If you don't go back by your birthday, we're going to send you somewhere."

One morning, protesters at the clinic handed Stephanie a letter that warned her that if she did not stop providing abortions, they would demonstrate outside her house that coming Sunday. Stephanie's coworkers told her that these protesters had picketed the homes of a provider who worked at the clinic before Stephanie as well as that provider's girlfriend.

Stephanie felt threatened and took the letter seriously. Stephanie lives in a big house that sits atop a long driveway in a remote wooded suburban neighborhood where the homes are far apart. She reached out to the National Abortion Federation, who advised her to put "No Trespassing" signs around the perimeter of her property. They also told her not to ignore "the little stuff" and to be vigilant because of the history of violence associated with anti-abortion protest. Following this advice, Stephanie put "No Trespassing" signs on her property, bought long curtains to close at night, and installed outdoor lighting around her property.

In anticipation of the home protest, Stephanie also went to her neighbors' houses to warn them of what might be coming. She said to her neighbors, "This is what's going on, and I just want to let you know ahead of time. I'm not trying to cause any trouble, and I appreciate whatever good feelings or thoughts or support you have." Though her neighbors reacted positively to Stephanie's visit and were supportive of her, she thought going door to door to warn her neighbors of the home protest was "not a pleasant experience," especially since this was her introduction to many of them.

Stephanie also reached out to her local government for support. Every week in Stephanie's town, the mayor opens her office for residents to visit and express their concerns. Stephanie took advantage of this opportunity and visited the mayor to raise the issue of the upcoming protest. In response, the mayor was sympathetic. She told Stephanie,

"We can't stop them from coming out, but we are not going to tolerate any kind of foolishness from these people."

As a result of Stephanie's efforts, when protesters arrived at her house on Sunday, there were police stationed nearby. This first home protest was, according to Stephanie, relatively tame. "There weren't many protesters—about five or six people." The protesters walked around the street with pickets. They also set up a table with pamphlets. The next week, when Stephanie went into work in her disguise as she always did, the protester with the newsletter who seemed to organize the home protest complained to Stephanie that her neighbors were not very welcoming.

Stephanie's initial success with her local law enforcement was short-lived. After the first home protest, the police told Stephanie that the protesters "acted really nice and they were really old-looking," so they were "no big deal." The police decided they would no longer come to Stephanie's house during the protests because there was no real threat. If Stephanie wanted help, according to the police, she should hire a private security guard. Their only promise to help was a generic "If there is any problem, give us a call."

As she learned more about the protesters' histories, Stephanie became even more disappointed in her local police department's refusal to assist her. Stephanie remained vigilant and wore her disguise and bulletproof vest to work every day. To the best of Stephanie's knowledge, the protesters had never seen Stephanie without her disguise, so she took comfort in knowing that part of her identity was still hidden. She also took other precautions, like being extremely cautious when out in her neighborhood. For instance, Stephanie once enjoyed going on walks where she lives, but she stopped walking once the protesters targeted her at home.

Not long after the home protests began, as Stephanie was driving home from running errands, she turned her car into her long, steep driveway. As she rounded the bend, Stephanie saw, at the top of the hill next to her house, the protester who writes the newsletter along with one other regular protester. They were far from the public street and were very clearly on Stephanie's property looking closely at her home.

Seeing these two protesters next to her house invoked a "fight or flight" reaction in Stephanie. She became "shaky and jittery" but decided to "fight." She accelerated her car and drove right past them—without her disguise—and pulled her car into the garage. "I was really shaky. I would say it wasn't just angry, I was scared. For some reason it just triggers a fear response. I was scared, and I was really angry." Fortunately for Stephanie, because the protesters had never seen her before, they did not seem to realize that she was the one driving the car that passed right by them. In fact, Stephanie had short hair at the time, so the next time she went to work, the protesters said to her, "We met your son."

As soon as she entered her house, Stephanie called the police and told them the protesters were trespassing. The police arrived, and the two protesters turned around and went back down the driveway. After the protesters left, the police told Stephanie they would talk to the protesters but would not pursue trespassing or other charges.

Stephanie felt frustrated with the lack of police response: "I don't have much protection, the police aren't coming out, the FBI can't do anything until they shoot me, and the only thing I have are these 'No Trespassing' signs and these guys don't care about the signs." Not content to let this incident slide, Stephanie went to the police station the following day to file her own trespass complaint against the two protesters.

Because of Stephanie's persistence, the city issued citations to both protesters, which they contested in court. Attorneys from a nearby law firm partnered with a women's rights organization to represent Stephanie on a pro bono basis for the trespass hearing, which took place in local traffic court. The hearing presented a difficult conflict for Stephanie. She knew that, as a witness, she would have to testify about the incident. But she also knew that if she testified in open court, the protesters would discover her identity, which she feared would open herself up to even more harassment. After discussing these concerns with her attorneys, the attorneys petitioned the court to allow Stephanie to wear her full disguise while testifying. The court agreed and allowed Stephanie to testify in disguise.

The hearing turned into another opportunity for the protesters to harass Stephanie. The protesters brought dolls and small plastic babies to the court, which they displayed during their hearing. They questioned Stephanie's credentials and her background. One of the protesters' associates stationed herself outside the courthouse and tried to take a picture of Stephanie. When the police saw this protester outside of the courthouse, they told her she was loitering and had to leave.

Ultimately, the judge convicted the two protesters of trespass and fined them both several hundred dollars. Stephanie was happy about the conviction. "It made me feel like the next time they do something bad, there'll be some history, and it'll look worse." However, the conviction did not alleviate all of her fears. "I kind of expected something else to happen. I didn't expect they would stop." When asked if the conviction gave her comfort in her day-to-day life, she replied, "Not particularly. Not in terms of the woods in the back and the lights at night. I didn't start walking again. For a while I was wondering if they were going to try to be worse because of retribution."

That something worse came in the next edition of the protester's newsletter. The protester published Stephanie's name, address, and phone number in the edition, but did not stop there; he also published a picture of Stephanie in her disguise with, as Stephanie remembers it, this accompanying comment: "Nothing will stop her but a bullet in the head." He mailed this edition of the newsletter not only to his regular list of violent anti-abortion inmates across the country while posting it online, but he also mailed it to Stephanie and all of her neighbors. To Stephanie, "that was just scary. It was all scary before, but that was a hard thing."

This threat had two effects. First, one of Stephanie's colleagues contacted the Department of Justice, and the department brought a civil FACE action against the protester. The FACE complaint focused on the threat, but it was helpful that the two protesters had been convicted of trespassing on Stephanie's property. The complaint turned into a full-blown trial against the protester, and the judge ultimately ruled that he had violated FACE. As a result, the judge ordered the protester to remove the threat from the Internet, enjoined him from issuing similar threats in the future, and fined him pursuant to the statute. For a short period of time the protester took down his entire website, but it eventually reappeared.

Second, after the newsletter threat, Stephanie began to look for another job because she decided she was "not sure this is worth it." When she found another job, she stopped providing abortion care. Stephanie laments this result but knows that it was the right thing for her. Looking back, she questions the efficacy of FACE if, as she perceived her situation, a provider has to quit for the Department of Justice to bring a case. "What good is a law that doesn't take effect until after you quit?"

## David Crowther

David Crowther, an obstetrician-gynecologist who has performed abortions in four different Middle Atlantic, West South Central, and Mountain West states, has a story unlike the others featured in this chapter, because he was targeted in his professional life for his role in teaching abortion to new physicians. David is currently a professor at an academic hospital, where he provides abortions and teaches abortion care to medical students and residents. In the position he held immediately before this one, David was the director of an obstetrics and gynecology residency program at a hospital in a Mountain West state. This residency program offered opt-out abortion training for residents.[4]

The hospital where David worked was a joint venture between a Catholic hospital and the county public hospital system. Under this merged program, the county hospital system sponsored the residency program and employed some of the residents, while the Catholic hospital employed the rest. Because the hospitals did not offer all of the training that the residents needed, many of the residents' training rotations took place off-site. For example, because of the religious dictates of the Catholic hospital, the program did not offer on-site abortion training. Instead, the residents trained at one of the nearby abortion clinics. This arrangement predated David's tenure at the hospital, and when David started, the nuns at the Catholic hospital explained that they did not object as long as he abided by the religious requirements of the institution.

One of David's responsibilities as the director of the residency program was to prepare the necessary paperwork for the independent accreditation of the residency program. As part of this accreditation process, David prepared and updated all of the affiliation agreements with the various off-site locations where his residents trained. When David presented the affiliation agreements to the hospital's director of education, she signed off on all of them except for the agreement with the abortion clinic. Instead, she wrote a note on the document indicating that she refused to sign for moral reasons.

Because the director of education refused to approve the affiliation agreement, the county board of supervisors, functioning at that time as the interim hospital board during a period of transition for the hospital, asked David to attend one of its meetings to discuss the need for abortion training. At this meeting, however, the chair of the board did not let David speak and ultimately asked David to leave. David was frustrated that he was not allowed to defend his program but became even more aggravated when he later learned the reason. A local anti-abortion group had talked with the chair of the board and had convinced him that abortion training was not a real requirement for residency program accreditation and that David would lie in trying to convince the board otherwise.

After David left the meeting, the CEO of the hospital, who was also David's friend, met David outside. The CEO was upset at what occurred in the meeting and what it meant for the hospital. He said to David, "You've got to stop sending the residents to the abortion clinic now." In that moment, David responded, "Okay."

The next day, after the CEO had a chance to cool down, David approached him and explained that if the hospital stopped sending the residents to the abortion clinic, they would be out of compliance with the obstetrics and gynecology residency program's independent accreditation requirements. Nonetheless, as a result of the board of supervisors' commands, the hospital halted the residents' abortion care training, and the board instructed David not to notify the accreditation committee of this change. David notified the accreditation committee anyway because he, as well as the attorneys he consulted about this issue, believed he had an obligation to do so.

This controversy ultimately threatened David's job. The board of supervisors approached the private company that employed David and told the company to fire him. The company refused, stating that David had a contract and had done nothing to warrant being fired.

The board of supervisors did not let up. Instead, it hired a private attorney to investigate David. Shortly thereafter, the board again approached David's private employer, this time raising a number of allegations against David that supposedly justified his termination, including a sexual harassment claim. David's employer hired an outside firm to conduct an independent investigation, which found no evidence to support any of the allegations. During the investigation, David was put on leave for six weeks.

Before David could return to work, however, even more allegations arose. One of the vocal anti-abortion faculty members at the hospital where David worked copied charts of some of David's abortion patients and claimed the abortions were illegal. Based on these new allegations, county prosecutors opened an investigation. Like the investigation by the outside firm, the county prosecutors' investigation revealed that David had done nothing wrong.

During the battle over the residents' abortion care training, David's routine reappointment for hospital privileges came before the board of supervisors. The medical staff agreed to reappoint David, but the board of supervisors, still running the hospital on an interim basis, refused. Instead, the board sent the reappointment paperwork back to the medical staff and told them to conduct yet another investigation of David. The board claimed that David had intimidated everyone at the hospital during the previous investigations, so it needed another investigation. The medical staff opened this new investigation but concluded that there was no reason to refuse David hospital privileges because no one alleged medical incompetency or anything else that would call into question David's ability to practice medicine.

The board continued to target David. This time, it turned its attention to David's family as a way to convince David's employer to fire him. The board's private attorney learned that some hospital employees had conducted business with David's wife's private company. The board argued that the hospital's conflict of interest policy prohibited this and, therefore, David should be fired. Even though the hospital's conflict of interest policy said nothing about this issue, the board of supervisors voted to remove David from his position at the hospital based on this claimed conflict of interest. However, the private company that employed David again refused to fire him, maintaining that it would not be legally justifiable to do so because he had done nothing wrong. Nonetheless, the board withheld part of David's salary from the payments it made to the private company.

During this fight over David's position, the board required him to transfer the sponsorship of the residency program from the county hospital system to the Catholic hospital. As a result of the board's directive, David wrote to the accreditation committee and explained that he had been instructed to request a transfer of the sponsorship. Aware of some of the issues at the hospital and having received complaints from some residents about a disruption in their residency training, the accreditation committee warned David that the transfer would not be acceptable. The committee needed assurance from the hospital that it would bear financial responsibility for the program, but despite David's efforts, no one with authority from the hospital would sign the required forms.

By now, David had become wary of the seemingly never-ending investigations and battles that he had to fight just to maintain his job and provide abortion training for his residents. David did not want to leave his job. He loved the work and believed that if he quit, he would lose any claim he might have in a possible lawsuit against the board. Eventually, David and the private company that employed him reached an agreement that allowed David to separate from the company.

While this entire saga was playing out, David's attorney received several threatening phone calls warning David to be careful. In response, the attorney cautioned David to be vigilant, take different routes to and from work every day, and keep the top up on his convertible. David also received multiple threats, including from board members who threatened more unfounded legal actions.

David's search for a new job also became an avenue for harassment. As he began applying for jobs elsewhere, people from the anti-abortion community surrounding David's old hospital started calling and writing to David's potential employers. They tried to convince potential employers that David forced residents to participate in abortion training against their will. They also strongly implied that they would come and demonstrate outside of any hospital that hired David.

Other people were targeted as well. For example, when the CEO of the hospital, one of David's friends, refused to fire David, the board fired the CEO. The board also fired the hospital's chief nursing officer, who had refused to vote to revoke David's hospital privileges. Stretching even further, the board tried to press criminal charges against the president of the medical staff, a former monk, for hiring his own attorney, rather than using the county attorney, to seek advice on whether the medical staff could fire David.

Following his separation from his position, David, refusing to be bullied, took matters into his own hands and filed a lawsuit against the board of supervisors. His suit raised three claims against the defendants: that they improperly interfered with his employment contract with the private company that employed him, that they violated his First Amendment rights because he was fired for speaking up about abortion, and that they violated a provision in the state constitution that protects teachers from being terminated based on religious or political beliefs.

The expense of David's lawsuit almost thwarted it. Initially, David worked with a private attorney who told him that the lawsuit, though likely a winning case, would probably cost hundreds of thousands of dollars because David was going up against the county's numerous attorneys who would try to "bury" David during the litigation process. At that cost, David could not afford to proceed with the lawsuit with his own money. However, a national reproductive rights group became aware of David's situation and decided to represent him along with a large law firm that volunteered its services. Armed with the support of these lawyers, David eventually settled the case for a large sum of money.

Reflecting on the entire experience, David believes that the board of supervisors targeted him because of certain anti-abortion groups' deep influence where he previously worked. David subsequently learned that representatives of a large anti-abortion group had multiple meetings with the board of supervisors to discuss who would replace him.

Although David was ultimately successful in obtaining a favorable settlement, the litigation did not come without costs. The day David filed the lawsuit and the local newspaper published the story, his house was burglarized. The only thing that was taken was his tablet computer, where he kept all of his notes. David suspected that people involved with the board took his tablet to try to find more information about him. David believed this because it was widely known that he took notes on this tablet computer at every meeting or presentation and because more valuable items in his house remained untouched. David called the police, filed a report, and told the police his suspicions. However, the police did not investigate further.

Despite the initial difficulties of the litigation, David was glad that the lawsuit ended the way it did and that he was able to effectively use the litigation process to obtain a settlement. He sees his legal victory as sending an important message to other residency directors who are committed to teaching their residents how to perform abortions. He strongly believes he has done the right thing and "made a difference." There were several times when he thought his career was ruined, but he persisted because he knew that what he was doing was just. To David, abortion is "a religious freedom issue." David is a Methodist, and his church does not proscribe abortion. "The concept of saying, 'My religious belief is just as important as yours'—I have to stand up for that."

## Conclusion

The six stories here highlight ways that providers can experience law. Some of the providers interacted with police and other law enforcement officials, while others interacted with courts and lawyers. All of the providers profiled understood that their experiences as targets of anti-abortion terrorism necessitated legal intervention. Some had positive experiences and felt that the law adequately addressed their situations, while others were left feeling that the legal system had let them down.

In order to better understand these legal interactions and how to improve them so that more providers have the positive experiences described in this chapter, a more systematic analysis of the law is needed. The next two chapters provide this by surveying legal options available to providers and then suggesting ways that law and society can be reformed to better assist providers.

# 8

## Legal Responses to Targeted Harassment

This legislation is about violence—violence against women, violence against doctors, violence against nurses.

—SENATOR EDWARD KENNEDY, discussing the Freedom
of Access to Clinic Entrances Act[1]

I went to the police substation, walked in, and he kept on driving and didn't pull in after me. I walked in, I said, "My name is Constance Phillips, and I worked at the local abortion clinic. I'm being followed by a protester. I came in here because I am frightened." And the officer said, "If you work in a place like that, what do you expect?"

—CONSTANCE PHILLIPS

TWO ABORTION PROVIDERS SUFFER the same forms of targeted harassment—they are both threatened at work, repeatedly followed while leaving at the end of the day, and then picketed by a large crowd outside of their homes every weekend. Although they have been harassed in the same way, based on where they live these two providers could have very different experiences using the law to address this targeting. While they both will be covered by the federal law that prohibits threatening or physically harming abortion providers, one provider might be able to take advantage of an expansive state law against stalking and a local law that regulates or even prohibits home picketing, while the other provider might live somewhere that has neither. This is the nature of the US legal system, and this is what the next two chapters explore.

While the previous chapter related the individual stories of six different abortion providers and their experiences with law, the next two chapters analyze providers' varied interactions with the legal system and then, based on the providers' experiences, suggest reforms that can improve law and society's response to targeted harassment.

In accomplishing this goal, this chapter draws a basic distinction between law and legal tactics. Law, as described in the last chapter, encompasses the various ways the legal system can address a problem. This chapter first discusses the federal, state, and local laws that can assist abortion providers suffering from targeted harassment. Helpful law can specifically address abortion providers and targeted harassment, or help can come from a generally applicable law that is broad enough to cover the forms of targeted harassment discussed in this book. Both specific and general laws can be powerful tools in combating targeted harassment.

After describing these laws, this chapter explores the tactics providers can use to summon law to help their situations. For example, providers often need attorneys or law enforcement to assist them, but both present pitfalls. They can pursue civil lawsuits or criminal charges against protesters. Or if no legal recourse currently exists, they can advocate for political change to try to create it. No one option is a panacea, but all options can be valuable to providers depending on what is happening to them and where they live.

These laws and legal tactics are sometimes beneficial but can often be deficient in protecting providers. These deficiencies have a variety of causes. Sometimes, the law itself is insufficient. For instance, a particular state's law about harassment or stalking may not cover the exact situation that the provider experienced. Other times, the law is sufficient, but the people who implement the law, whether police, lawyers, judges, or other government officials, act in an inadequate way. Like anyone else seeking assistance with the legal system, abortion providers sometimes encounter overwhelmed, incompetent, or slow actors within the system, but they also face an obstacle that most other people do not—officials who are opposed to abortion and refuse to act because of this personal opposition.

The stories and analysis in this chapter and the preceding chapter are the building blocks for what follows in the next chapter—recommendations about how law and society can change to help abortion providers in the face of targeted harassment.

## Laws

Laws in the United States can come from multiple sources—the federal government, state governments, or local governments, such as counties and cities. Generally speaking, in the United States, federal law addresses only a specific set of national issues and is uniform throughout the country, whereas state and local law is almost unlimited in what it can address. State and local law also vary dramatically from place to place. Within these different types of law, abortion providers can gain protection from both specific laws geared toward them or targeted harassment as well as generally applicable criminal and civil laws.[2]

### Laws Specific to Abortion or Targeted Harassment

The most widely applicable and well-known law protecting abortion providers from harassment is the federal Freedom of Access to Clinic Entrances Act, commonly referred to as FACE. Beyond that, there are other laws at the state and local levels that protect providers.

### FACE

The Freedom of Access to Clinic Entrances Act became federal law in 1994. Spurred by a rash of clinic violence and blockades in the late 1980s and early 1990s, including the first murders of abortion providers, FACE was championed as a way to ensure abortion access for patients. Attorney General Janet Reno testified before Congress that Department of Justice lawyers had found the previously existing federal law "inadequate" to protect access to abortion. She urged passage of what she called "essential legislation" that was needed to "secure the rights of women seeking reproductive health services."[3]

However, FACE was not just about protecting women's access to abortions. Legislators and advocates also championed FACE as a way to prevent targeted harassment and violence. Providers and their relatives testified about the importance of legislation to address targeted harassment, and Attorney General Reno testified that the law protects "individuals who provide [reproductive health] services."[4] Senator Edward Kennedy, one of the bill's vocal supporters in the Senate, defended the law by saying that the "legislation is about violence—violence against women, violence against doctors, violence against nurses."[5]

The actual language of the law bears out these dual purposes. The law describes a person who violates it as someone who

> by force or threat of force or by physical obstruction, intentionally injures, intimidates or interferes with or attempts to injure, intimidate or interfere with any person because that person is or has been, or in order to intimidate such person or any other person or any class of persons from, obtaining or providing reproductive health services.

A separate provision of the law also declares that someone violates the law if that person "intentionally damages or destroys the property of a facility, or attempts to do so, because such facility provides reproductive health services." The law defines "reproductive health services" to include "medical, surgical, counseling or referral services relating to the human reproductive system, including services relating to pregnancy or the termination of a pregnancy." It provides for criminal penalties and civil fines based on the severity of the actions as well as the number of offenses committed.[6]

The language of FACE that protects abortion facilities from being damaged or destroyed is easy to understand, but the main provision of FACE, quoted in full above, is difficult to parse. One way to break down the language is to focus on four things: (1) who is protected, (2) what actions are prohibited, (3) how those prohibited actions are carried out, and (4) the reasons behind the actions taken.

**Who**: The law protects two groups of people—those obtaining and those providing reproductive health services. In other words, it protects both patients and providers.

**What**: The law prohibits three actions (as well as attempts to engage in these three actions): (1) restricting the patient's or provider's movement, (2) injuring a patient or provider, and (3) making the patient or provider reasonably fear bodily harm to herself or someone else.

**How**: FACE only applies to actions that are accomplished by force, by threat of force, or by making it difficult, dangerous, or impossible for the patient or provider to enter or leave a facility.

**Why:** The motivation for these actions must be that the patient is obtaining abortion services or that the provider is providing them. The law also covers actions taken to intimidate a person out of obtaining or providing services. In other words, the violator must be motivated to act because of a person's involvement with abortion or to prevent that person from being involved with abortion.

For example, an anti-abortion protester violates FACE if he blocks a patient from entering a clinic by putting his body in front of the patient and refusing to move in an effort to prevent the patient from obtaining an abortion. In contrast, a large number of customers of the business next to the clinic who stand outside that business and inadvertently block a patient from entering the clinic are not violating FACE. Taking action to prevent abortion can violate FACE, while taking action for accidental or other unrelated reasons cannot.

FACE's effect on abortion provision has been profound, though limited. A study by the National Abortion Federation in the immediate aftermath of FACE found that violent protests drastically decreased as a result of the law: "[T]here has been significantly less violence outside clinics and a significant opening of access, with fewer blockades and less picketing."[7]

However, statistics show that FACE has affected only certain types of anti-abortion activity—clinic invasions and blockades. In the seventeen years before FACE, there were 347 reported clinic invasions and 634 clinic blockades, resulting in 33,661 arrests. In the nineteen years after FACE, there were 52 reported clinic invasions and 144 blockades, resulting in 178 arrests. By contrast, other types of anti-abortion activity have continued without the same stark decrease. Notwithstanding FACE, anti-abortion demonstrators have continued to commit crimes such as murder, attempted murder, bombings, arsons, chemical attacks and threats, assaults, death threats, and bomb threats. In fact, reported incidents of some types of anti-abortion criminal activity, such as vandalism, burglary, and stalking, as well as providers' experiences with hate mail, harassing calls, and picketing, have increased since FACE became law.[8]

The experiences of the providers interviewed for this book bear this out. Many expressed great appreciation for what FACE has done to increase abortion access and to decrease abortion blockades. Providers who have been in the abortion field for decades were the most impressed by the positive changes that came from FACE. For example, Dr. P.'s clinic faced terrible obstruction and invasions in the pre-FACE era. When asked about whether FACE made a difference, he thought about it and responded, "I guess that must be what did it because they very seldom came in the office building after FACE. I noticed the difference."

Lowell Taylor attributes FACE's effectiveness to its enforcement. Before FACE, the protesters "came right up to the front door, and you had to have an armed guard to keep them out of the door at times." However, with FACE, there was a "big difference" because the federal agents enforcing the law had "a reason for being there. They had a law. Like it or not, they are going to enforce it."

Though FACE helped in some ways, many providers also criticized the law. Importantly, providers expressed concern that FACE does not reach most of the types of targeted harassment they face in their everyday lives and that are detailed in this book. For the incidents covered by FACE, several complained that the Department of Justice seems to require too much from providers to initiate a FACE complaint. For instance, Stephanie McGoldrick felt that she had to quit before the federal government thought the situation was serious enough to bring a FACE complaint against the protesters. "It's almost like the anti-abortion protesters win and then the government officials bring a case." She also felt that the penalties in the law are not stiff enough, especially for a repeat offender.

Similarly, some providers expressed concern that there is too stringent a definition of what constitutes a threat. Carolyn Barrick and her coworker both felt threatened by protesters in separate incidents, but the federal authorities did not feel that the threats were specific enough to bring a FACE action. "Someone called me and announced we were all going to die. But they didn't say 'I'm going to come to your house by midnight and kill you.'" The federal authorities thought that this was an "implied death threat" that was not enough under FACE.

Elizabeth Moll had a similar experience, but with a federal judge. The judge decided that a note left under Elizabeth's car warning her to look under her car in the future was not a threat because, according to Elizabeth, "free speech trumps safety." Elizabeth worries that biased judges can ignore a useful law like FACE and use the First Amendment as a justification for not enforcing federal law because, where she lives, judges often have strong ties to anti-abortion groups. "It just doesn't feel like you can get any fair consideration here anyway."

Other complaints about FACE were similar to providers' general concerns about law enforcement. Providers described how enforcement of the law varies based on whether individual federal agents take the law seriously. Providers also expressed frustration with how difficult it is to gather evidence of a FACE violation. Clinics do not have the resources to devote to collecting evidence, and if providers call the police to assist, protesters seem to quickly abide by the law as soon as police appear.

### Other Specific Laws

States and localities also have laws on the books that specifically address abortion providers or targeted harassment.[9] Abortion providers who live in these states or localities have tried with varying success to use these laws to help protect against targeted harassment.

For example, several jurisdictions around the country have laws known as "bubble zone" or "buffer zone" laws. These laws create zones around a clinic and generally prohibit people who are not using clinic services from entering the zone. A bubble zone creates a zone around a person entering or exiting a clinic. For instance, in general, an eight-foot bubble zone would make it unlawful for someone to come uninvited within eight feet of a person as he or she moves to or from the clinic. In contrast, a buffer zone is a fixed amount of space around a clinic that only people doing business with the clinic can enter. This type of zone is usually larger than bubble zones, but it does not move with the people who come and go. Bubble and buffer zones do not infringe the First Amendment freedom of speech as long as the laws are not too broad and governments can show that there have been sufficient problems in the past that warrant having this type of protection.[10]

Though largely geared toward general clinic protest,[11] bubble and buffer zones also help providers with targeted harassment by creating a safe space free from on-site targeted harassment.[12] Tamara Cocci said that the buffer zone around her clinic allowed her staff to avoid directly interacting with abortion providers when they enter or exit the build-ing. Similarly, this space makes Patricia Yang feel better about going to work because she knows she can enter the clinic without the protesters being right at the front door and without having to make efforts to force them to move out of her way.

Some jurisdictions also have helpful laws and ordinances cover-ing picketing in front of a house in a residential neighborhood. Mark Goldstein described multiple such laws near his home. In one city near his home, protesters are allowed to demonstrate in residential com-munities as long as they walk back and forth and do not venture onto private property. However, in his hometown, the law prohibits pro-testers only from yelling while engaging in residential picketing. Thus, when Mark told the police about protesters demonstrating in front of his house, at first the police said there was nothing they could do. "The protesters were within their rights. And I said, 'But not only are they out here walking back and forth, they are also yelling out that I'm a baby killer.' They did say, 'Well they're not allowed to do that.'"

Some of the residential picketing laws are very specific. For instance, in Lowell Taylor's city, the local ordinance prohibits protesters from picket-ing a single home and instead requires that they march past two homes on either side. "I live in an old area, and the houses were built on acreage. So if you do two homes on either side, you walk a half mile." In the town where one of Ellen James's doctors lives, any protest with more than seven people requires a permit and protests are allowed only from dusk to dawn.

One state has tried a different approach to protecting providers with a law that hides their identities. California has a statewide law that is part of a program called Safe at Home. Safe at Home was created in 1988 to protect victims of domestic violence. The program allows vic-tims to protect their home address in public state records "through the use of a substitute address, which is used to conceal the participant's actual whereabouts."[13] In 2002, the California legislature expanded the program to include any abortion provider who is "fearful for his or her safety or the safety of his or her family because of his or her affiliation with a reproductive health care services facility."[14]

California lawmakers expanded the law specifically because of tar-geted harassment. The legislature found that keeping providers' home address information confidential is necessary "to prevent potential acts of violence from being committed against providers." The legislature also noted the declining number of abortion providers because of "fear on the part of physicians to enter the reproductive health care field and to provide reproductive health care services." A provider using the program can use the substitute address for all state and local agencies, and the secretary of state, who administers the program, is prohibited from disclosing the provider's real address unless it is required by law or court order.[15]

One provider we interviewed[16] extolled the law's virtues, saying that California providers are "lucky" to have the law at their disposal. This provider, who works in a supervisory role, repeatedly informs others about the law. In particular, "there was an e-mail including the program's information that I passed around to all the docs right after the Tiller assassination." The provider thought some of the paperwork for the program was cumbersome but that ultimately the program was "good for us."

### Generally Applicable Criminal and Civil Law

Given the variety of targeted harassment tactics that abortion providers face, many different generally applicable criminal and civil laws may be helpful to providers. Every state and every locality has different laws, and federal law sometimes overlaps. Knowing about all of the laws that may help providers requires diligence and research, as Catherine Thompson explained in talking about her efforts to fight harassment: "I researched the local ordinances so that I could ask questions. I went online and looked at every one that I thought was relevant." With this knowledge, Catherine feels she is better able to assess whether protesters have crossed a line.

Basic criminal law can help providers. For instance, laws prohibiting assault and battery protect against the threat of or actual harm to another person's body. In some situations, such crimes are easy to prove. When Rodney Smith was assaulted in the Supreme Court, as described in Chapter 1, Supreme Court personnel immediately swarmed the assailant and arrested him. The assailant was convicted and served time in jail for the assault. Debra Fulkerson was also assaulted when she was kicked by a protester wearing steel-toed boots. The police responded, and ultimately the assailant was found guilty of criminal assault.

Sometimes, though, assault is more difficult to prove because the police do not observe the incident or because the anti-abortion assailant claims that the provider was also physically violent. Providers explained that in those situations the police rarely do anything. This happened to Catherine Thompson after an aggressive protester slapped her hand. The protester told the police that Catherine assaulted him, so "nothing ever came of it because it was he said/she said."

Trespass laws can also apply to targeted harassment. Laws against trespass prevent people from intruding on another person's property. Kevin Bohannon had success with his local trespass law. After protesters picketed at his house, Kevin placed metal posts in the ground connected by orange tape around the perimeter of his property and posted "No Trespassing" signs. Even with these precautions, a protester trespassed inside the marked perimeter. While the protesters had previously trespassed on Kevin's property without Kevin involving the police, this time he called because the trespasser was the leader of the protest group. In response to Kevin's accusation, the protester claimed that he was on public property. Kevin showed the officer his property survey, which clearly marked Kevin's property line. The officer looked at the survey and cited the protester for trespassing. Under the applicable trespass law, if the protester trespasses again, he will go to jail. This experience emboldened Kevin. "In the future, if they're on my property, I'll probably cite everybody else just to give them a hard time."

Not all providers are so successful with pursuing trespass charges. When protesters occupied the hallways of Mathew Whitley's private medical office to demonstrate against his providing abortions at another location, Mathew could not convince the police to make any trespass arrests. The officers escorted the protesters out of his office but would not arrest them. Only after the building owner stepped in and also complained did the police eventually arrest a small number of protesters for trespassing. In response, the protesters rented space of their own in the office immediately adjacent to Mathew's office. From that space, they were able to protest Mathew on their own property without trespassing.

Providers sometimes use laws that prohibit stalking, harassment, or invasion of privacy. These laws vary widely from jurisdiction to jurisdiction but generally prevent repeated acts against an individual that could intimidate or create fear.[17] Julie Burkhart benefited from one such law. A particularly aggressive protester repeatedly protested at Julie's house in the months before we talked to her. During these demonstrations, the protester stood outside of Julie's house with other people from his church and held a sign that asked "Where's your church?" Julie believed this was a clear reference to Dr. Tiller's murder and perceived it as a death threat, so she sought a protective order against the protester. The local judge agreed. The judge found that the applicable stalking law prohibited the repeated death threats and granted Julie's motion for a protective order. At the time we talked with Julie, the order was only temporary, but she hoped that it would become permanent because it has been very effective in minimizing her experiences with protesters.

Laws that address the intimidation of or retaliation against witnesses are another possible recourse for providers. These laws could be useful leading up to or following a provider testifying in a proceeding involving anti-abortion protesters. Danielle Figueroa could have benefited from vigorous enforcement of such a law after she testified in court against protesters who allegedly violated a local noise ordinance. After Danielle stated her name in open court for her testimony, the protesters began targeting her directly and personally by using her name and photograph in their demonstrations. The local police department and district attorney's office told Danielle they would look into bringing witness intimidation and witness retaliation charges against the protesters based on the fact that the harassing signs with Danielle's name on them appeared after she went to court, not before. Nonetheless, the district attorney informed Danielle the county was not going to pursue witness retaliation charges. Danielle suspects that the city and county "don't even want to touch it, because they're afraid of a lawsuit" from the protesters, which has happened before. "And who the hell am I? I'm nobody. You get a lawsuit and everybody's backing down."

Various aspects of civil law can also protect providers. Depending on the context, different personal injury claims might apply, such as infliction of emotional distress, interference with contract, invasion of privacy, defamation, and false imprisonment.[18] David Crowther's story, detailed in Chapter 7, is one example of a successful lawsuit for wrongful interference with an employment contract.

Generally applicable permit requirements can also be helpful for abortion providers. When anti-abortion protesters try to target a provider through a public assembly or protest in a street, they may have to obtain a permit if the jurisdiction has a law requiring permits for public assemblies. This happened to protesters who showed up in large numbers at Mathew Whitley's house. A local law required them to obtain a permit to be in the street because the neighborhood had no sidewalks. The permitting process alerted the police to the protest, and in turn they were more responsive to Mathew's and his neighbors' concerns about the protesters.

Permit requirements can help providers to be prepared for a demonstration. According to Ellen James, the best part of the local home picketing law is the permit requirement. "We can phone in advance of any of those weekends that we think they might come out and know if they got a permit."

Providers have also benefited from laws regarding public displays of signs. Amanda Williams was able to take advantage of such a law after protesters targeted her by placing signs on telephone poles around the city where she lives. The signs contained her name, picture, and other personal information. At first, when Amanda complained to the city, officials told her there was nothing they could do about the signs. However, after people living in an affluent part of the city called to complain about the signs, a city representative came to Amanda's clinic and told her about a city ordinance that prohibits signs stapled to telephone poles. The representative told Amanda that "he had gone around and had a crew removing all of the signs that they could find." Amanda praised the city for taking the signs down. "That was the first real help, and it was I think just because the right people called the right people."

## Legal Tactics

The various legal remedies described above may help abortion providers, but only if the provider has a way to use them. This section describes the tactics providers use to implement these legal remedies and their varying degrees of effectiveness.

*Preemptively Talk with Law Enforcement*

Common among many of the providers interviewed was a strategic decision to talk with law enforcement *before* any targeted harassment occurred. Providers who pursue this strategy believe that by talking with and educating the police about the unique issues abortion providers face, the police will be proactive and more responsive in dealing with targeted harassment. Kevin Bohannon said that before he talked with his local police about the risks associated with his job, "they just had no idea that this kind of stuff went on in their vicinity." After he talked with them, they visited his house, looked at his property, and told him they would, in order to "make sure that things were peaceful and quiet," observe his house on days anti-abortion protesters appeared.

Another reason providers preemptively talk with police is to inform them about certain people or events. Carolyn Barrick said that her clinic keeps close tabs on the different protesters, and they regularly share that list with law enforcement. Nellie Wayne contacts her local police when there are holidays or anniversaries approaching that may be significant to protesters.

Providers also preemptively communicate with law enforcement to let them know what type of response would be most helpful to the provider. For instance, one of Howard Stephens's main concerns was keeping a low profile, so when he learned the protesters were going to demonstrate outside of his house, he requested that the police try not to be too disruptive by "coming out there and throwing weight around and harassing the protesters." Howard wanted the police to "keep the peace in the neighborhood" so that Howard could live there without bothering his neighbors. By preemptively talking to the police, Howard was able to inform them not only about the protesters in case anything happened but also that he wanted a low-key police response.

Talking with law enforcement in advance has been a successful strategy for almost all of the providers who used it. This has been true in communities that providers identify as being conservative as well as communities that providers identified as liberal. For instance, Rachel Friedman described living in a liberal area and has had success with the police. Her clinic hired an off-duty police officer to provide security, which helped build a connection with the department. She eventually developed a "nice relationship" with the police chiefs, and they had frequent meetings. "We always kept them posted. When we had an alert, we always communicated." Although the police did not always respond exactly as Rachel wanted, she knew that her clinic was taken seriously and was a priority.

Despite working in an area she described as very conservative, Eva Sager was also successful in cultivating a good relationship with her local police and FBI agents. "I insisted that they come in to talk and see the facilities. I always wanted to make sure they had a computer architectural design of the layout of the building and that they knew the contact people and the security guards as well as my pager and beeper numbers."

Like Eva, some providers have invited the police into their offices and clinics so the police have a better sense of who the providers are, what their work entails, and how to best complement the clinic's own security. John Steele heard that the FBI was willing to do on-site inspections, so he reached out to them. "They did a full inspection of cameras and our ability to lock all our sites." John was also able to link the clinic's internal security to the FBI's database so that they could each cross-reference information about particularly troubling protesters.

Many other providers have used this approach as well. Penny Santiago invited the local police to her clinic for an information session. "We explained the history of abortion harassment and why you take these things very seriously." As part of her general plan to "schmooze" the police to build connections, Rebecca Lane even allowed the local police to use her clinic for SWAT team training. "That helped to continue to build the relationship."

Providers have also benefited from having law enforcement preemptively visit their homes. After he received a letter from a protester telling him that there was going to be a demonstration in front of his home, Thomas Andrews alerted his local chief of police and made sure that he would dispatch officers if there were any problems. Thomas also talked with the FBI, who visited his home. Based on the visit, the FBI gave Thomas advice on security alarms, door locks, curtains, and other safety measures.

Many providers were impressed when law enforcement proactively reached out to them. Law enforcement usually, though not always, reached out in this way following a high-profile incident involving a different abortion provider. Patricia Yang shared a story that many providers experienced. After Dr. Tiller was killed, the FBI and other federal officials approached Patricia's hospital and a local clinic to inform them of the local FBI contact. "They just wanted to make sure that we all were aware of our safety and whom to contact with our issues." Like the other providers, Patricia was comforted by the attention and support the federal government offered her and her colleagues.

### Subsequently Talk with Law Enforcement

In contrast to the almost universally positive experiences providers reported when they preemptively talked with law enforcement, providers' experiences talking with law enforcement *after* they began to be targeted were much more mixed. Providers contact law enforcement after an incident for different reasons: to create an official record of what happened, to help put a stop to the problem, to protect themselves while the incident is ongoing, to have the incident investigated and possibly prosecuted, or to strategize about how to prevent it from happening again in the future.

Perhaps the most comprehensive law enforcement response to targeted harassment came in Maggie Sims's case. Maggie received multiple threatening phone calls where she worked. She and her mother also received letters at their homes, which are in a different state in a different region of the country from where Maggie worked. After she contacted the FBI and the police where she lived, Maggie had a coordinated meeting with two federal marshals, a special agent from the FBI, and a detective and lieutenant from the police force where she and her mother live. According to Maggie, "they were wonderful":

> Everyone was saying anything that ever happens let us know. The US Marshals were trying to provide guidance about what I could do to help prevent problems, what I could do to protect myself. They were happy to answer any questions and gave me their cards and their cell phone. The lieutenant in the local police force was saying, "If you use a cell phone don't ever call 911. This is the number you have to call to get us because you'll get the state police if you call 911." And he asked whether I wanted any special police at my house, did I want

this or that. As far as the US Marshals, they explained what they could do and what their levels of involvement could be depending upon what I needed. They were wonderful, and I felt very supported and very safe. The odd thing is they said always turn on your house alarm, especially when you're home. And they said be more vigilant. That was one of the big messages.

Mathew Whitley also had laudable assistance from law enforcement. Mathew provides abortions at an independent clinic that is not far from the office building where his private practice is located. When Mathew walks from his private practice to the clinic, protesters sometimes wait for him outside and then confront him or follow him to the clinic. "Usually I don't say anything or even acknowledge their presence, but I must tell you, you never can tell when one of these people will be the sacrificial lamb and just decide that they will take out a major operative." For a time when Mathew felt most threatened by this situation, the local police provided him "safe passage" by escorting him from one office to the other. They do not do this anymore, but he was very clear that he felt safer when the police provided this service.

In addition to escorting Mathew, the local police alerted Mathew and his wife Sandra when the protesters planned to start protesting at their house. Sandra recalled that the officer who alerted them "just called out of the blue because she knew that the protesters had been in the area before." When the protesters eventually did picket the Whitleys' house, a local police officer parked across the street. This watchful official eye "meant a lot" to the Whitleys.

While many providers had positive responses from law enforcement, other providers had troubling experiences. These disappointing experiences most often took the form of law enforcement's failure to respond promptly or at all. A few years before we interviewed Rodney Smith, Rodney's clinic suffered a fire. The fire burned for ten hours before the police and firefighters responded. During that time, neighbors of the clinic made four different calls. In response to the first call, the sheriff's deputy "rode around the area and didn't see anything." The police did not respond at all to the next two calls because they thought they had already sent someone. Only after the fourth call did someone respond.

Rodney believes the police were "less aggressive than they should have been, or probably would have been, if it was somebody else."

Other times, law enforcement responded to providers' calls but refused to do anything to help the provider or, in the provider's view, did only the bare minimum. For example, after a protester shot into Lowell Taylor's home at night, Lowell immediately called his local police. The local police called the FBI and other federal authorities; however, the combined law enforcement response was ineffective. The officials asked Lowell simplistic questions like "Well, Doctor, do you know of any enemies that you have from business or anything?" and did nothing more than that. From Lowell's perspective, "there wasn't even an effort."

Another common concern was that law enforcement appeared hostile toward the provider and did not even address the protester. As recounted in Chapter 1, after a particularly threatening protester told Inez Navarro that "no one is going to protect you," Inez called her local police, who laughed at her in response. When Inez explained more about the threats, one of the officers said to her, "Well, you work at the abortion clinic."

Even worse, providers who have been targeted reported being charged with crimes. When protesters picketed outside Todd Stave's child's school, Todd and the police arrived at the school at about the same time. When one of the protesters saw Todd, the protester told the police officer that Todd had been aggressive and assaulted him. Because the protester wanted to press charges, the police officer felt that he had to file the charges against Todd.

It is impossible for providers to know exactly why they received a good or bad response from law enforcement, but a variety of possible factors surfaced in the interviews. One common link among the providers who spoke highly of the law enforcement response was that the provider had, as described in the previous section, preemptively cultivated good relationships with law enforcement.

Providers also linked a good response from law enforcement to police knowledge of high-profile violent incidents. Eva Sager was impressed with the law enforcement response to a death threat that she received immediately following two other providers' murders in her region of the country. Law enforcement officials protected her and even intercepted her mail. Almost two decades later, when Eva was harassed by a neighbor because of her work in abortion care, she felt that the local police officer responded well to the situation because he was aware of the past violence. "He got that. And he understood why this new incident was concerning."

Providers also thought that they received a good police response when police officers seemed to believe that their chief mission was ensuring law and order, regardless of the politics of the abortion issue. Providers expressed this sentiment even in locations that they described as more politically conservative. For example, the local police where Howard Stephens lives were more supportive than Howard had expected based on his assessment of local politics. When he talked with his local police after anti-abortion protesters staged a demonstration outside his home, the police assured Howard that they were going to be vigilant. They said, "We'll get a car over there, and we'll park it there just so that there's a presence to let people know that, you know, no funny stuff. And we're watching. This is going to stay really legal." Since then, the police have been "really responsive." Howard attributed their positive response to the fact that "they want to keep the peace as much as anybody else."

In contrast, providers traced poor law enforcement response to a perception that a particular incident was not worth law enforcement's time or was futile to pursue. For Donald Yates, this was a problem when he repeatedly found drywall screws in his tires. The local police did nothing because they said "you can't catch them" and that "there's nothing they could do about it." Penny Santiago faced a similar response from the police after a protester told her that someone was going to chase her with a hatchet. The police took a report but did nothing else because, as Penny understood it, "unless somebody's bleeding on the ground," the police were not concerned.

Other times, providers believe that law enforcement does not act because the official dealing with the situation is biased against abortion providers. Tamara Cocci's story illustrates this, even though she lives in a state that is generally considered liberal on abortion issues. Tamara was sorely disappointed with the police response to repeated home picketing and protesters who often trespassed on her property. For instance, when Tamara approached a protester's car that was parked halfway in Tamara's driveway, a police officer watching the protest threatened to arrest Tamara. "And I said, 'Why would I be arrested? I'm just trying to find out who this is. Their car is on our driveway. They don't have any right to have their car in the driveway.' And the officer literally threatened me, so that was pretty dismal.'" Tamara believes that her "local police seemed to be not only just consumed by the anti-abortion people's First Amendment rights, but I think were also tacitly against abortion themselves, and just very unsupportive, and so they always say there was nothing they could do." Tamara suspects the police were "more supportive of the protesters."

Law enforcement is sometimes afraid of helping providers because they fear protesters. Sherry Bruner received a death threat, but her local police force would not do anything about it even though Sherry knew who made the threat. "They felt it was enough of a judgment call that they didn't want to do it." She explained that the local police force "has been sued two or three times by these protesters, so they're gun-shy." Lucy Brown's experience was very similar. After Lucy was harassed by a protester who trespassed at the clinic where she works, the chief of police told her, "We can't arrest her." The chief explained further, "We've already spent millions of dollars trying to fight these people in civil court." This worries Lucy, who wonders what extreme act it will take for the police to actually do something.

Some providers connected federal law enforcement response to the politics of the president at the time. Carolyn Barrick explained this simply: "Elections do matter." Carolyn was very pleased with the way law enforcement handled the death threat that her family received. "I cannot say enough about the law enforcement response." She believes federal law enforcement was so helpful "because President Obama, quite clearly, has given direction that the DOJ, and by extension the FBI, has to take those threats seriously." She also feels that her local police were supportive because the governor and mayor are both pro-choice.

By contrast, multiple providers were critical of President George W. Bush and the federal response while he was president. Albert Tall is one of the providers who was critical. He explained how the federal law enforcement response varied when protecting him from protesters violating a court-ordered injunction. "A lot of the activity to protect me changed with the administration. When Bush was in, Republicans weren't as supportive as Clinton was." Marshall Cook agreed, saying "it was pretty gloomy during the Cheney–Bush era."

However, one provider spoke highly of the federal officials under President Bush. Lowell Taylor has felt that the FBI and other federal agencies have been concerned with his safety for a long time, regardless of the president. "I think they realize that this means business. It meant business even under George Bush."

## The US Marshals Service

One law enforcement agency that has been particularly helpful in protecting providers has been the US Marshals Service. Federal marshals are law enforcement officials within the federal Department of Justice whose chief responsibilities are to provide security for the federal courts, to enforce court orders, and to track down fugitives. As part of their security functions, marshals provide personal protection for federal judges, court officers, witnesses, and other people who are threatened when the threats affect the judicial process or other official proceedings.[19]

Prior to the enactment of FACE, federal marshals were occasionally involved with protecting abortion clinics and abortion providers but generally in the context of federal court cases about abortion. For instance, before FACE, Lowell Taylor was a witness in a federal case about a state restriction on abortion. To prepare for his testimony, Lowell flew to the location of the trial to visit the local clinics and assess the impact of the state restriction on those clinics. The marshals were involved in protecting him from the outset. "The marshal service contacted me and said, 'Here are airline tickets. We will call you one hour before you are to report to the airport. We will pick you up and take you to the airport.'" Lowell said, "That was my first introduction to what real picketing and real harassment can be."

Lowell arrived safely at the location of the trial and spent ten days there. Federal marshals were stationed outside of Lowell's hotel door around the clock for these ten days. "We had a little two-way radio, and if I wanted to leave and go get a bite to eat, they had to accompany me everywhere. We traveled in a caravan with a marshal car in front and a marshal car behind me." Lowell concluded, "The protection steeled my nerves to what this profession was all about."

In the mid-1990s, the federal marshals expanded the scope of their protection of abortion providers. This expansion happened partly because of FACE and partly because Attorney General Janet Reno established a federal task force concerned with abortion clinic violence.[20] When needed, federal marshals now provide personal protection to abortion providers as well as investigate threats to providers.

Many providers described their experiences with federal marshals providing round-the-clock protection. Robert Burton received federal marshal protection for about four months after Dr. Slepian was murdered and described his experience in depth. The marshal detail consisted of a rotation of three cars, each with three marshals. Of the nine marshals assigned to him, one set of three was with him at all times. "They lived with me." Robert said that he "loved it, actually." He and his family always had a "warm car to go into," and the car drove "a hundred miles an hour." He also found it comforting to "have three big linebackers near me." Despite the protection, Robert said, "I was also very scared. I was scared for my family. I had a young kid." Robert's son, on the other hand, was "too young to understand" what was going on. "He thought my car was broken because I was being driven everywhere by these big guys. He was going to day care and being dropped off by these federal marshals."

The marshals who protected Robert were "very friendly," and Robert appreciated their work. "Being a federal marshal is a hard job. You're required to spend a certain percentage of your time away from home, and a lot of the work details you get are potentially dangerous, and you're ready to give your life. You'd jump in front of a bullet for someone."

As in Robert's experience, marshal protection has typically followed a high-profile violent incident, such as the murder of an abortion provider. Several of the providers we interviewed were offered protection after Dr. Tiller was murdered. Some of those providers were closely associated with Dr. Tiller or worked in the same part of the country as he did. Others had no association with Dr. Tiller but were high-profile providers with national reputations. Still others were far from the national spotlight and never received an explanation as to why the marshals contacted them.

Many of the people we interviewed who were offered this protection after Dr. Tiller's murder accepted it, though not all did. The marshals contacted Marietta Spring "right away" after Dr. Tiller's murder. Marietta had protection for a "week or so" and felt that, through the protection, the federal government "let everyone know they were doing something, that they care about this." At Dr. Tiller's funeral, federal marshals provided intense security. Warren Hern, a close friend and colleague of Dr. Tiller's, described the scene from his perspective:

> I was surrounded by federal marshals all the way there and all the time I was there. I was very heavily protected. I think you'd have to say I was practically under a presidential level of protection because I got there and I was held in a secure hotel room and all the marshals were around me. I went to have breakfast, they were sitting all around. Took me in an armored car to the funeral, to the place where they had the reception afterwards. There were sixty federal marshals at the funeral. I was told that quite a few of them were there to protect me. They regarded me as the prime target. They were worked up about shoulder-mounted rockets and stuff like that. They thought there was potential for great mayhem, that the anti-abortion people were going to stop at nothing. That if they could take out a couple hundred of us, they would. They would stop at nothing.

David Crowther, on the other hand, turned down the offer of protection after Dr. Tiller's murder. "I said no. Again, what are you going to do? First of all, they're not going to follow you around the rest of your life. And second, if anybody was really trying to cause me physical harm, they'd just wait until the marshal is gone." Although David rejected the protection, he was concerned about what it meant that it was offered to him. "Whether there was any 'We're going to get Crowther' or whether there was just a 'Who should we contact?' I don't know for sure and the marshals didn't say."

Other times, providers were offered marshal protection or assistance as part of a court proceeding or an ongoing investigation into a threat. As part of her FACE trial, Stephanie McGoldrick was given protection while going to and from court. "There was a guy there, and he drove us in the garage. He was a big guy who had been doing this for a while, a really nice guy, big police-type guy."

Almost all of the providers who had experience with marshal protection felt it made them safer. Bruce Steir had protection for "about three years" when he flew to one particular clinic that was having serious trouble with protesters. "The marshals would meet me at the airport. They would take me to the men's room, where I would put on a flak jacket." When the federal marshals drove Bruce to the clinic and then escorted him in, he felt safer. "I walked between them, and they wore shirts or jackets that said 'Federal Marshal,' and I don't think those picketers or snipers would want to shoot a federal marshal." Once in the clinic, the marshals waited for him in the kitchen. Bruce described the marshals as "morose" about the assignment at first. "After a while, though, when they saw that the women were taken care of so well by the nurses and by myself, they turned around and became pro-choice. They even went outside the clinic every once in a while to tell the protesters to stop making so much noise or they'd be arrested."

Even if they felt safer, providers still noted some downsides of marshal protection. For one, the marshals are an ever-present reminder of the dangers associated with being an abortion provider. After multiple abortion providers in Eva Sager's region were shot and the murderer threatened to kill Eva, the federal government told Eva that marshal protection would be in her best interest. She accepted and was grateful for the protection but nonetheless unhappy about what the protection meant:

> I had the marshals just everywhere. They were in my house and outside my house. They were down behind my house and underneath the deck. And it was cold. It was January, and they were in cars in my driveway, and their cars were running. It was noisy and intrusive. There was snow everywhere, and to get our driveway plowed I'd have to get them to move. They did a wonderful job, they were very committed, and it was very comforting that they were there, but they were a constant reminder that I was in a very dangerous situation.

Another downside is the extreme invasion of personal space. To Marietta Spring, "it was really intense." Two marshals followed her everywhere. "It gave me an insight into what it's like to be one of these politicians. You have no privacy whatsoever. They're just right there."

Following Dr. Tiller's murder, Warren Hern lived with a twenty-four-hour armed security detail who drove him around in an armored car. While both he and his wife felt "more secure" and Hern understood that this detail was "necessary," he also found having people with him twenty-four hours a day to be "very disruptive."

All in all though, providers were grateful for the marshal protection and thought it was important. Sarah Haupt captured this sentiment when talking about the marshal protection she received. "It made a statement: the federal government was involved." Bruce Steir similarly explained, "The pro-choice movement was getting more validity by having federal marshals there to protect us and to show that the federal government was really pro-choice, not just saying they were."

### Talking with an Attorney

Using the law to improve a situation often requires consulting with attorneys. Attorneys can inform providers about the law, give advice on how to proceed, and help initiate legal proceedings if that is the desired course of action. Attorneys cannot solve every problem, but they can often be of great assistance.

For abortion providers dealing with targeted harassment, attorneys can sometimes be the key to accessing legal protections. Some clinics have attorneys who assist the clinic with the clinic's legal matters and also assist employees when it comes to targeted harassment issues. For example, Jennifer Young received assistance from her clinic's attorney when a protester sued her for assault, and Rachel Friedman described her clinic's pro bono lawyer as "phenomenal" in providing assistance in dealing with the protesters' targeted harassment.

Other clinics and providers rely on local or national nonprofit legal organizations for assistance. For example, providers we interviewed described receiving help from the American Civil Liberties Union and its local chapters, the Center for Reproductive Rights, the Feminist Majority Foundation, the National Abortion Federation, Planned Parenthood Federation of America, and the Women's Law Project.

However, not every provider has been able to access affordable and competent help from an attorney. Diane Dell described her and her clinic's troubles finding an attorney to assist them with their harassment issues. She complained that one attorney was "useless" and overly consumed with "how much you could recoup and whether it would cost you more than it's worth." Her clinic eventually hired new attorneys to help with clinic matters, including targeted harassment. However, Diane lamented, "The money is really tight and the clinic does not want to contact the attorneys unless it's absolutely necessary, so we don't have anybody who is doing the pro bono work that we would love."

*Lawsuit*

Providers can also try to remedy their situation by filing a lawsuit. Lawsuits must be based on a particular legal claim, such as one of the claims available to abortion providers described earlier in this chapter. Lawsuits can ask for either of two different types of relief—damages or an injunction. A damages award means that someone who has done something wrong must pay money to the wronged person. An injunction is a court order requiring a person or organization to do or stop doing something. Abortion providers have been successful in obtaining both types of relief.

Perhaps the most prominent lawsuit over targeted harassment occurred over the "Wanted" posters, "Deadly Dozen" list, and Nuremberg Files website. As described in Chapters 2 and 3, all three are detailed lists of abortion providers that appeared in the mid- to late-1990s with information inciting violence against the providers involved. Several abortion providers and two clinics sued those responsible for creating these threatening lists, claiming a violation of FACE and the Racketeer Influenced and Corrupt Organizations Act, the federal law against organized criminal activity. After years of litigation and many appeals, the courts agreed with the providers that the protesters had threatened the providers and violated both federal laws. The court awarded the providers monetary damages and issued an injunction. The injunction prohibited the defendants, two anti-abortion groups and a nationwide list of anti-abortion extremists, from making or distributing the posters, the website, or anything similar. The original damages award was over $100 million, but it was reduced on appeal to just over $5 million.[21]

Not every lawsuit involving targeted harassment results in multimillion-dollar verdicts and nationwide injunctions. Smaller-scale lawsuits can also be quite effective.[22] For instance, when a protester established a harassing website about Rachel Friedman, Rachel initiated a lawsuit against the protester and won. As a result of the lawsuit, the judge ordered the protester to cease using the website and pay Rachel over $10,000. Rachel was thrilled with the ultimate outcome: "We really scared this guy. He literally physically left the area over this."

Injunctions can also be effective remedies against targeted harassment, though their effectiveness depends on the scope of the injunction and how well it is enforced. For example, Albert Tall benefited from an injunction that his clinic obtained years before Albert started working there. The injunction prohibited protesters from protesting within five thousand feet of the house of any employee who worked at the clinic. Because the injunction did not specify a particular employee but rather covered any employee working at the clinic, Albert was covered even though he started working at the clinic after the court issued the injunction. For a while, the injunction worked very well, and no protesters bothered Albert at his house.

However, after the clinic changed ownership, protesters appeared at Albert's house. When Albert brought the injunction to the town's attention, a representative from the town questioned whether the injunction was still effective given that the clinic now had new ownership that was not involved with the original court proceedings. To Albert, the town representative gave the impression that he "wasn't spending township money to find out if the injunction still applied, and it just sort of sat there." Because of this complication, Albert now has a difficult time convincing his local police and county attorney to enforce the injunction.

Warren Hern obtained a very specific injunction against one particular protester who repeatedly targeted him. The injunction prohibited the protester from being within one mile of Hern. Overall, Hern finds the injunction "effective" because the protester "seems to be observing it." Moreover, despite how much area the injunction covers, the local law enforcement agencies have been "very helpful and collaborative" in enforcing the injunction. One time, both Hern and the protester were testifying about the same bill at the same time in the state legislature, so they had to be in the vicinity of one another. Even though enforcing the exact specifics of the injunction was impossible, law enforcement nonetheless worked with Hern to make sure he was safe. "We had the cooperation of the state patrol who does security in the state capital. We made it very clear that this guy had to be kept out of the chamber when I was testifying. He couldn't come in there. And he was a dangerous person. They seemed to understand that."

### Criminal Process

When providers want to use the criminal process in response to targeted harassment, they often start by consulting with law enforcement. However, they can sometimes talk directly with the local or federal prosecuting attorney. Usually this is a local prosecutor such as a district attorney for state or local crimes or an assistant US attorney for federal crimes.

Prosecuting attorneys can be very helpful. For instance, as described in the previous chapter, after Paul Fortin contacted his local prosecuting attorney about protesters demonstrating outside of his home, the attorney assisted Paul. The local prosecutor worked with the police to station an officer at Paul's house during pickets, which Paul found helpful.

Sometimes, though, local prosecuting attorneys are subject to influences beyond the provider's control, such as the politics that affected Danielle Figueroa's experience. Initially, Danielle thought the local district attorney was being supportive after a protester verbally harassed her, posted information about her on signs, and pushed a police officer. The district attorney said to Danielle, "Confiscate the signs. Do whatever you gotta do. And we're going to go forward with this. They're going way too far." The protester responded by suing the police officer, claiming a violation of her First Amendment rights. As a result of the lawsuit, the district attorney stopped helping Danielle. A police officer later explained the district attorney's rationale: "The district attorney says we now have to leave this alone. We can't go near it with a ten-foot pole. There are too many lawsuits going on." To Danielle, the district attorney's fear of lawsuits and the resulting lack of support for the clinic now mean that the protesters "can do anything they want."

The providers had almost universally positive experiences with federal prosecutors in the Department of Justice. Stephanie McGoldrick described the assistant US attorneys she worked with as "totally professional" and "happy" that she was pursuing the case. Elizabeth Moll worked with two assistant US attorneys who came to her from Washington, DC. Because they were part of the federal task force concerned with abortion clinic violence, they were "really, really helpful." Providers were positive about federal attorneys regardless of the president, as they spoke about having positive interactions with them during the Clinton, Bush, and Obama presidencies.[23]

*Influencing Policy*

Another option for abortion providers is to advocate to change law or policy on the local, state, and federal levels. This advocacy was key to enacting FACE, as abortion providers and their advocates worked hard in the years leading up to the law's enactment to publicize their stories and bring attention to the issues of clinic blockades and violence. In California, the concerns of abortion providers and their advocates were part of the reason the law protecting the personal information of domestic violence victims was expanded to include abortion providers.

In the city where Cynthia Kendrick works, the city council may never have passed the existing buffer and bubble zone laws without a push from abortion providers. After decades of problems in front of clinics for both patients and providers, Cynthia and other providers from the area testified before the city council about their issues, including targeted harassment. The effort to change the law was successful, and the city passed legislation to protect clinics.

Lobbying politicians can be effective not only in changing the law but also in influencing how government services are allocated. Three days after she received a death threat, Carolyn Barrick had to leave home for a trip to Washington, DC, to meet with her congressional delegation about a different matter. "That was easily the most difficult thing I've ever done. I didn't want to be far away from my family." Despite this feeling, she was able to make the meeting as constructive as possible:

> We were meeting with one of my representatives in Congress, who has always been very helpful. Because the death threat had just happened, I kicked off the conversation mentioning it, and he was obviously very concerned and deeply moved. Within the next two days, he personally called the FBI for my state, and he personally called

the US Marshals for my state and expressed interest in the case. Gave them my name, the whole situation. This helped me feel safer that the FBI in my state and the US Marshals in my state had been told that a member of Congress was personally interested in the case. That was very helpful.

Rachel Friedman has a unique approach to influencing policy around this subject. "Maybe twenty years ago I decided that anybody who wanted a political contribution would have to come to the office on a Saturday to meet with me." When the politicians visit the clinic, they have to "drive through where all the protesters are and get out of their car, get screamed at, see the signs." Rachel believes that by doing this, the politicians will have a clear picture of what Rachel and her coworkers go through and better understand the work that they do. One politician had a very emotional reaction when she took Rachel up on the offer: "Recently, when our new mayor was running for office and came here on a Saturday, she actually came into my office and just burst out in tears because she remembered illegal abortion and she had no idea that women continued to have to go through this harassment."

## Conclusion

Like anyone else in the United States, providers who want legal assistance must resort to a patchwork of local, state, and federal law. The legal strategies available to them vary and can be tailored to their particular situations and their individual goals. Nonetheless, though they have a variety of laws and legal tactics at their fingertips, providers need better and more options. Law is often insufficient, the First Amendment poses unique considerations that often make police and courts wary, and other legal actors sometimes refuse to take sides. Given the severity of targeted anti-abortion harassment and the extreme effects it has on providers' lives, the next chapter explores multiple ways law and society can be reformed to better protect abortion providers.

# 9

---

# Legal Reform

> Most communities do not want terrorism in their neighborhoods, and so I think it's important to focus on that—that it's really not about abortion, it's about extreme harassment and intimidation of people providing a legal service and how it affects the healthcare of women.
>
> —TAMI MADISON

AS THE STORIES IN this book reveal, abortion providers are targeted in a multitude of ways, and providers drastically change their lives as a result. Law can respond effectively but often does not. Are there solutions that law can implement to do a better job of helping providers address targeted harassment? This chapter answers that question in the affirmative and draws on providers' experiences to propose several reforms that could improve the everyday lives of abortion providers.

These reforms are necessary for many reasons. First, and most simply, people should be able to go about lawful activities without being targeted. Opposing, even strongly opposing, what someone else does is one thing; tormenting that person in the ways described in this book is completely different. Stalking people, intimidating them at home, harassing their children at school, sending threatening mail to their offices, physically attacking them when they are out in the community— these activities create an overwhelming sense of fear and insecurity among many providers and are not activities that the general public should consider acceptable. Law should address these actions by proscribing them before the fact and punishing them afterward.

Second, the considerations described in the previous paragraph are even more significant in the context of healthcare. Abortion care is healthcare. Abortion is, as the preface to this book sets forth, a common medical procedure that almost one-third of American women will undergo. Medical professionals working to provide this common and safe procedure should be able to do so with the same dignity, physical safety, and peace of mind as professionals working in any other medical field. Anything less is an affront not only to the providers but also to women's rights, as this procedure is one aspect of common healthcare for a specific segment of the population—women.

Finally, targeted harassment of abortion providers threatens women's access to their constitutional right to terminate a pregnancy. Although almost all of the providers we spoke with continued working through the terror they faced, other providers quit because of the harassment and still other people never enter the field in the first place.[1] With fewer providers, there is less access to safe, legal abortion. With decreased access to safe, legal abortion, an increasing number of women will resort to unsafe, illegal ways of obtaining an abortion. This is the story throughout American history, this is the current story internationally, and this is the story today in places in this country where access is limited.[2] By reforming law to reduce the targeted harassment abortion providers face, this one particular barrier to women's access can be lowered.

Drawing from the providers' experiences, this chapter proposes reforms aimed at various legal actors and entities that could ultimately assist abortion providers when they encounter targeted harassment. It first identifies ways to improve law enforcement's interactions with providers, then proposes legislative improvements, highlights aspects of the judicial process that can improve to assist providers, and finally identifies a necessary shift in the way society thinks about anti-abortion protesters' tactics—that this extreme harassment should be considered anti-abortion terrorism. We derive these reforms directly from the experiences of the providers interviewed in this study.

Like the providers we interviewed, we recognize that law is only one way to address this problem and that the issue of abortion may be too politically and emotionally charged for targeted harassment to ever completely disappear. However, we and the providers we interviewed believe that law can improve the situation dramatically, and these reforms address that sentiment.

## Improving Policing

Many providers told stories of excellent policing that addressed their situation to their satisfaction, but others found that law enforcement did not respond well to requests for help. From these stories, both the good and the bad ones, several ways to improve police response emerge. Some of the things providers talked about were general good police practices, such as not allowing personal bias or politics to affect interactions, responding to concerns quickly and professionally, conducting a full and thorough investigation when necessary, understanding the importance of preventative or proactive policing instead of just reactive policing, delivering a strong message of support from higher levels of law enforcement, and cooperating among different law enforcement agencies without territorial disputes. Providers spoke repeatedly about these general good police practices, and all law enforcement agencies could improve in these areas to help with targeted harassment.

These general good police practices would certainly help providers, just as they would help anyone who interacts with the police. Additionally, providers' experiences with law enforcement can form the basis for more novel improvements that are specific to targeted harassment of abortion providers. With the suggestions detailed below, law enforcement at every level can better protect providers.[3]

### No Tolerance Policies

A common thread among several providers' assessments of the police is that given the nature of targeted harassment, law enforcement should not tolerate even minor violations of the law. We heard several stories of law enforcement ignoring seemingly minor legal infractions, such as trespassing or picketing ordinance violations. For example, Sarah Haupt complained about her local police not enforcing criminal trespass laws when a protester was on the clinic's property. "We know criminal trespass is against the law, so if you have somebody that's on the property, the least the police could do is get them off." Although the police knew that the protester was on private property and was not going to leave, they told Sarah they would not enforce the law because "he says he's not going to hurt anybody."

Jennifer Young explained why routinely ignoring these minor viola-tions is a problem: "I know that minor infractions lead to major infrac-tions. I have seen that slippery slope a million times, and I know it's just a matter of time before horrible things happen." Kristina Romero likens protesters who get away with minor violations to children. "Just like kids, if you keep playing that game, they're just going to keep doing it until you actually do something about it. So the police have just let them run over us and do whatever they want. The police could have changed the dynamics here by stopping the problems at the beginning."

Jennifer's and Kristina's concern is evident in the history of abortion-related violence. Paul Hill, who in 1994 killed two providers in Pensacola, Florida, began as a protester creating minor disturbances at the clinic. A month before Hill murdered Dr. John Britton and clinic escort James Barrett, the FBI refused to arrest him for violations of the Freedom of Access to Clinic Entrances Act (FACE), saying "this is not the time to make an arrest."[4] Scott Roeder vandalized a Kansas City clinic twice in the week before he killed Dr. George Tiller, including the day before the murder. The clinic owner informed the FBI about both incidents and gave them identifying information about Roeder. The FBI took the report, knew who Roeder was, but did not investigate Roeder or work with local law enforcement officials to address the vandalism.[5] Of course, not every crime or seemingly minor violation precedes a major crime like Dr. Tiller's murder, but some have; and allowing pro-testers to repeatedly violate the law risks greater crime because it sends the message that protesters can violate the law with impunity.

Taking all violations seriously not only helps prevent a much bigger problem down the road but also could assist in obtaining legal remedies in the future. Sherry Bruner explained that her employer encourages documenting every infraction and trying to convince the police to pur-sue every violation because it can help convince a court of the need for an injunction in the future. "You make anything stick that can because you may be able to get an injunction against them later. So not neces-sarily going for one great big thing, but nailing all the little stuff as it happens."

The same strategy was helpful in Stephanie McGoldrick's FACE case against an extremist who had threatened her in his online newsletter. Stephanie had previously been successful in pursuing a criminal case

against the protester for trespassing on her property. That prior conviction proved useful in the FACE case against the protester.

Another benefit of taking all violations seriously is that doing so
develops a record that can be used to support future legislative efforts.
Generally speaking, when assessing the constitutionality of laws that
establish bubble and buffer zones near abortion clinics, courts look
at the government's purpose for enacting the law at issue. Courts will
uphold the law against a First Amendment challenge if the court finds
that the law does not burden more speech than necessary to achieve the
government's purpose. The Supreme Court has affirmed that governments have an interest in "ensuring public safety and order, promoting
the free flow of traffic on streets and sidewalks, protecting property
rights, and protecting a woman's freedom to seek pregnancyrelated services." A record of violations can help demonstrate the significance of
the state's reasons for enacting a bubble or buffer zone law as well as
demonstrate that the specific terms of the law are warranted.[6]

Taking all violations seriously is not without its downsides. As highlighted in Chapter 7, a group of protesters sued Tami Madison and her
clinic, claiming that both Tami and the clinic conspired with the police
to deprive them of their First Amendment rights. Tami expressed hesi-
tation about calling the police for every violation she observed because
she feared that the protesters would use all of her interactions with law
enforcement as evidence of the alleged conspiracy. Alan Stewart voiced
a different concern, likening constantly calling the police for minor
infractions to "the boy crying wolf." The risk, in Alan's mind, is that
when something "really big" happens, the police could grow frustrated
or brush off the call, thinking "Oh, it's just the clinic complaining again."
Many providers calculate the risk of frustrating the police each time they
call. Nonetheless, based on the repeated concern from providers and the
history of abortion-related protest escalating into violence, providers'
fears of escalation from uncorrected minor problems is serious enough
that police should respond to all violations, not just the major ones.

*Identifying Providers for Quick Response*

Police can also help by flagging particular providers' addresses for quick
emergency response. Several providers told us how much they appreciated law enforcement doing this for them. For instance, ever since

Kevin Bohannon first had problems with home picketing, law enforcement dispatchers tagged his information in their computer system so that when Kevin calls the police and his name appears, a message indicates to the police "don't waste any time, call the guy who is in charge today and tell him to get his butt over there."

After her family received a death threat, Carolyn Barrick received similar enhanced protection from her local police. The police computer system identifies her address as that of someone who received a death threat in the past. "They know when my address calls, it is the death threat house." Carolyn's neighbors inadvertently tested this system when they noticed one night that Carolyn's kitchen door was open. "They called the police and then they called us, and by the time I went home the police had already shown up. Why? Because our address showed up as 'this is the lady who got the death threat.'" In the end, Carolyn was safe—the open door was the result of an accidental broken lock, not anything malicious—but Carolyn appreciated that the police knew her and that her address triggered this careful response.

Although law enforcement flagged Kevin and Carolyn's addresses after they had problems, other providers have been able to preemptively convince the police to give special attention to their homes. For instance, Inez Navarro and her husband explained to their local police chief that they were concerned about their safety generally because of Inez's job and more specifically because of the harassment that she had experienced at work and others had experienced at home. As a result, the police now check in with Inez and her husband and have flagged their house for extra protection. Inez explained that she knows this is the case because her husband accidentally set off the alarm one day and the police were at her house with a dog in less than a minute.

Regardless of whether the individual provider has yet been targeted, providers should be able to comfortably reach out to their local police department, identify their profession, and receive this added level of protection.

### Stationing an Officer at Home Protests

Law enforcement can also better assist providers by stationing a police officer outside providers' homes when protesters demonstrate there. Home protests are some of the most sensitive and threatening forms of targeted harassment, and they can and have turned into confrontations or criminal activity. With a police presence there, the home picket can be less stressful and dangerous for providers. As Stephanie McGoldrick said, "It would have been nice if the police had come out and had just one guy at least drive by or stand here whenever the protesters were out there."

Many providers described the benefits of having a police officer watch over these demonstrations. Mathew Whitley explained how an officer parked on the street when protesters came to his house. "He never got out to confront them and intimidate, but I think he just wanted to show 'I am an official, I see you, I know what you're doing.' Which meant a lot to us and I think to the neighbors as well."

Paul Fortin's story in Chapter 7 also shows the value of this type of police support. He appreciated that the police were at his house during a home protest because the protesters were "not as vocal" with the police there. The police presence was also "vindication that there was some support among the law, saying that we are here to keep this on our terms." While this kind of support will not prevent home picketing or all of the emotional distress it causes, it can help assure providers that their homes and families are safer at that difficult point in time.

## Improving Communication with Providers

One particular aspect of policing deserves special attention—how providers and law enforcement communicate. Good communication with law enforcement is critically important. Research by the Feminist Majority Foundation has stressed the importance of a good relationship with law enforcement. Their 2014 report on clinic violence found that "[c]linics that rated their experience with local law enforcement as 'poor' or 'fair' were significantly more likely to experience anti-abortion violence and harassment than those who rated local law enforcement 'good' or 'excellent.' "[7] To improve communication with law enforcement, several different reforms are warranted.

### Police Liaison/Task Forces

A dedicated police liaison or task force for abortion clinics and providers is one way to improve communication between law enforcement and providers. Cynthia Kendrick explained that her "clinic has one officer that is the principal responder. It makes a whole lot of difference." She compared her clinic's experience to that of another clinic in the same city where she works and noted that the other clinic had problems with harassment that her clinic did not have, specifically because of the better policing around her clinic.

A police liaison can improve a provider's security in many ways. The liaison can meet the providers and learn the providers' particular concerns so that the provider knows whom to contact in case of trouble. The liaison can also assess the clinic and individual provider's security needs and recommend ways to preemptively address them. When issues arise, a liaison can better respond to the problem because the liaison already knows the providers and the clinic and does not have to be brought up to speed about their needs.

Providers who already have liaisons explained how helpful they are. Albert Tall extolled his liaison's virtues. "I find it reassuring. At least you know that there's somebody out there you can call if you have to and they don't have an agenda. They'll come. You never know what people's agenda is, right?" Rachel Friedman similarly noted the value of having this kind of relationship with a police officer. "They understand our special exposure, and they take our concerns very seriously, and I think that gives us a lot of confidence."

*Providing Information*

Law enforcement can also help by being more proactive about giving helpful information to providers. Many providers complained that during police investigations into incidents involving anti-abortion targeting, the police withheld information that would have made providers feel safer or would have enabled them to better protect themselves.

These complaints often came in the context of an ongoing investigation. Police sometimes fail to communicate with the provider about what they did to investigate an issue or whether they resolved the problem. This is a general policing problem in contexts beyond abortion-related harassment, but it is a particular issue for providers because targeted harassment tends to induce fear of falling victim to an even worse crime. If the police discover that a threat has been alleviated or does not exist, they should immediately communicate that information to the provider to quell the provider's fear.

For instance, after an anti-abortion protester was arrested the night before a planned attack on the providers at Samantha Newsom's clinic, the police conducted a full investigation. To Samantha, just knowing that the investigation was ongoing was not enough to calm her fears that something else might happen. She wanted more information from the police, but they were not forthcoming. "There was so much that they didn't feel like they should share," she explained. The clinic's security director "had to do a lot of asking and requesting that probably should have been automatically communicated for people to feel safe." Without complete information, Samantha and others at the clinic had to guess which precautions to take for their own security.

Carolyn Barrick voiced the same frustration with the investigation after her family received a death threat. She was impressed with the way that law enforcement immediately handled the threat, but her one complaint was how little she was told about the subsequent investigation. Without concrete information from the police, she and her colleagues were left to "pure speculation" about their ongoing level of risk. Tami Madison summarized this same concern, saying that providers would "feel more secure on a day-to-day basis" if they knew what the police were doing in response to complaints about targeted harassment.

Police should also communicate with providers when they know ahead of time that a provider will be targeted. Paul Fortin's local police found out that protesters planned to stage a demonstration outside of his home but did not tell him. "The police said they didn't want to let anybody at the house know because they thought if we knew before, we would counter-organize and it could become violent." However, Paul and his family "thought a heads-up would have been nice" so that they could have adjusted their lives accordingly.

A slightly different aspect of the same concern is that police sometimes tell providers only part of the information about a known event or risk. Lowell Taylor explained this problem well. Soon after Dr. Tiller was murdered, law enforcement strongly recommended to Lowell that he wear a bulletproof vest and carry a handgun. Lowell appreciated that they gave him this information, but he was left to wonder, was there a specific threat made against him? Did the investigation into Dr. Tiller's

killer uncover a connection with Lowell? Were there other people connected with Scott Roeder who wanted to harm Lowell? Without more
information from the police, Lowell was left to speculate on his own,
increasing his level of fear.

*Removing Roadblocks to Preemptively Talking with Police*

Abortion providers frequently mentioned feeling that they can better protect themselves by preemptively talking with law enforcement.
As described at length in the previous chapter, providers preemptively
communicate with law enforcement for a variety of reasons: to educate
police officers about the unique problems abortion providers face, to
inform the police about certain people or events that might cause trouble, to discuss particular responses that might be more or less appropriate, and to strategize about safety protocols. Almost all providers who
talk with police ahead of time expressed a greater sense of safety as a
result.

However, a particular type of lawsuit by anti-abortion protesters
threatens both this preemptive communication and general communication with the police, even for an agency with a liaison or a history of
good communication. Tami Madison's and Rachel Friedman's stories in
particular illustrate this strategy, as Tami's story from Chapter 7 details.
Anti-abortion protesters sued Tami and Rachel, as well as their clinics, alleging that the providers and clinics conspired with the police to
infringe upon the protesters' First Amendment rights.

The theory behind these cases is that when abortion providers communicate with the police, including preemptively talking with the police
about anti-abortion protest and how to protect themselves and their
staff, what they are really doing is working with the police to develop
ways to limit the protesters' freedom of speech. Normally, because the
Constitution protects against *government* infringement of rights, not
*private* infringement, a private individual like Tami or Rachel, or a private entity like their clinics, cannot violate the First Amendment. By
way of example, this rule, called the "state action doctrine," means that
you cannot sue your neighbor for forcing you to refrain from speaking
about your political views while at her dinner party. But you can sue
your city police officers if they force you to do the same while talking
with your friends in the town square. In both of these examples, your

neighbor and your city police officers are restricting your speech, but the Constitution is only concerned about the latter, not the former.

There are many exceptions to this rule, but the important one for these purposes is that private individuals acting in concert with the police to limit free speech can be considered state actors. When this happens, the speaker can sue both the police and the private individual for limiting her free speech rights.[8] This is precisely the claim that anti-abortion protesters brought against Tami and Rachel.

These frivolous lawsuits not only place a wasteful burden on the legal system but are also dangerous for abortion providers. As Tami's and Rachel's stories illustrate, after they and their police departments were sued, law enforcement shied away from helping them. Because of the lawsuits, the police were wary of anything that might possibly appear to be conspiratorial action. Rachel explained this lawsuit as "trying to drive a wedge between the city and the provider." One of Rachel's coworkers agreed. "I think that their lawsuit did what it intended to do in terms of making officers wary about being targets." Because of the unwarranted conspiracy lawsuit, one of the most effective tools in the abortion provider's toolkit to avoid targeted harassment—preemptively talking with law enforcement—was no longer available to Tami, Rachel, or anyone who worked at their clinics.

Judges should be aware that these lawsuits threaten abortion providers' safety and need to keep this important point in mind when navigating these cases. They should develop doctrine and resolve these cases so that abortion providers cross no legal boundaries when they preemptively work with law enforcement to handle the threat of targeted harassment. They also need to firmly punish frivolous lawsuits of this nature with appropriate sanctions. By doing so, law enforcement will not fear consulting with abortion providers about how to best respond to the unique concerns they face, nor will abortion providers fear consulting with law enforcement.

### Providing Clear Guidelines for the Police

Another important lesson from the interviews we conducted is that police are more effective, and abortion providers feel safer, when the law provides clear guidelines about how to handle targeted harassment.

As described in the previous chapter, buffer zones, bubble zones, and home picketing laws are in place in many jurisdictions. Sometimes these laws are geared toward general clinic protest, but they also often address targeted harassment.

Laws or regulations that have clear guidelines for law enforcement give the police specifics about how to respond and give abortion providers a clear sense of how to remain safe. Without specifics, police are left to make judgment calls that can be biased by their own sense of abortion politics or influenced by their own cowardice in the face of claimed constitutional rights. When law enforcement has a clear law with specific guidelines to enforce, these judgment calls are less likely to come into play. Abortion providers likewise feel more secure when the law has predictable rules that they can count on.

Mathew Whitley explained this difference from his experience with his city's buffer zone. Before the buffer zone, the police had a hard time protecting him when he walked into the clinic. "The protesters could follow you right up until the point where you opened the clinic door," but the police could do nothing about it. However, once the city passed a law that created a clear buffer zone around the clinic, the police enforced the law's specifics, which "provided great relief. It was sort of a safety zone, safe landing, once you got to that part." In light of the 2014 Supreme Court decision striking down Massachusetts's thirty-five-foot buffer zone as unconstitutional, jurisdictions looking to enact a new law like the one Mathew found helpful will have to carefully justify and tailor the law. If they do so, a clear boundary for police to enforce should not run afoul of the First Amendment.[9]

Dr. P. had a similar assessment of his experience with law enforcement before and after FACE. Before FACE, law enforcement "really didn't want to be there"; and when they were there, they were never sure exactly what they should do. However, once FACE became law, law enforcement had a clear requirement they could apply. The law says that protesters cannot blockade patients or interfere with clinic access, and, based on Dr. P.'s experience, law enforcement is able to apply this clear law.

Another way that law enforcement could have clearer guidance would be for the US Department of Justice to issue guidelines for handling targeted harassment of abortion providers. The Department of

Justice already has a taskforce dedicated to abortion provider and clinic protection that should do this. Established in 1998, the Task Force on Violence Against Health Care Providers has served various functions over the past decade and a half. It coordinates the federal response to provider and clinic safety, enforces FACE, and meets with relevant parties to discuss safety issues.[10]

One of the task force's other roles is posting information about safety for abortion providers. The task force's website lists fifty-eight different tips for providers and clinics relating to home security, work security, vehicle security, and public transportation and travel.[11] These are valuable tips that many of the providers we talked with implement. The providers particularly appreciated when federal government representatives, whether members of the FBI, federal marshals, or Department of Justice officials, met with them to review these precautions and how they could work in their day-to-day lives.

These tips for providers are invaluable, but the task force should produce similar information for local police departments. Such guidance would help local law enforcement understand the issues related to abortion provider safety, the complications around the First Amendment, the intricacies of FACE, the roles of the different federal officials and how they can work with local officials, and other areas where the task force's expertise could help local law enforcement. Guidelines such as these would help local police enforce appropriate laws to protect providers and clinics.

## Enacting Home Picketing Laws

Laws that restrict or prohibit home picketing improve providers' lives. Stephanie McGoldrick explained that such a law might have prevented her from leaving the field. "It's like if you can deal with it at work or you can deal with it in court, you do. But if you have to live with it every day at home, that makes it harder. To see those people in your space, that makes it harder, even just on your walking path. That makes it harder, to know that they want to come at you like that." Stephanie is not alone. Ellen James said, "I spend lots of hours and days and nights working this tough job, and your home is your place, your home is your sacred space, your home is where you finally get to kind of sink in and live your life." Home picketing makes providers feel personally invaded and threatened, and providers alter their day-to-day lives because of it.

Because home picketing laws are vitally important to many abortion providers' well-being, more jurisdictions should enact such laws. In doing so, however, legislative bodies need to be careful not to infringe on First Amendment rights. Courts in the United States have allowed restrictions on home picketing in certain circumstances. The Supreme Court first addressed the issue in the abortion context in the 1988 case *Frisby v. Shultz*. In that case, the Court reviewed a local Wisconsin ordinance that prohibited picketing that focused on or took place in front of someone's home.[12]

To determine whether the law was constitutional, the Court looked at whether the government's reasons for the law justified the speech restriction. To be constitutional, a home picketing law has to "target[] and eliminate[] no more than the exact source of the evil it seeks to remedy." A complete ban on unwanted communication in residential areas could possibly be constitutional, but that would require a much more significant justification than the Wisconsin ordinance, which allowed for other forms of communication such as handbilling and solicitation.[13]

The Court found that the ordinance met this test because it was supported by a "significant government interest." The goal of the ordinance was to protect "the well-being, tranquility, and privacy of the home," which the Court found to be an interest "of the highest order in a free and civilized society." The Court justified this position by explaining that the home is where people retreat "to escape from the tribulations of their daily pursuits" and that residents deserve protection there. The Court was clear that "[t]here simply is no right to force speech into the home of an unwilling listener."[14]

Turning specifically to the picketing at issue in the case, the Court explained that the protesters' activity "inherently and offensively intrudes on residential privacy. The devastating effect of targeted picketing on the quiet enjoyment of the home is beyond doubt." Knowing that a "stranger lurks outside our home" causes psychological harm. Ultimately, the Court concluded, the ordinance was constitutional because residential picketing "figuratively, and perhaps literally, trap[s the resident] within the home, and because of the unique and subtle impact of such picketing [the resident] is left with no ready means of avoiding the unwanted speech."[15]

The Supreme Court has not otherwise addressed residential picketing ordinances, but it has heard a case about an injunction against residential picketing. In that 1994 case, the injunction included, among many other restrictions, a three hundred-foot zone around the homes of the clinic's staff where protesters could not picket, demonstrate, or use sound amplification equipment. The Court found the three hundred-foot zone unconstitutional because it was too broad and a narrower "limitation on the time, duration of picketing, and number of pickets outside a smaller zone could have accomplished the desired result."[16]

From these two Supreme Court cases that have touched on residential picketing restrictions, lower courts have engaged in detailed analyses to determine whether restrictions on residential picketing are constitutional. The lower courts have noted three key inquiries that track the reasoning in the Supreme Court decisions: (1) whether the restriction appears in a law or in an injunction, (2) how much speech the restriction limits, and (3) whether the justification for the restriction is strong enough to support the breadth of the restriction.[17]

With regard to the first inquiry, courts look more favorably at laws than injunctions, and more municipalities, counties, and even states should enact these legislative residential picketing restrictions. These laws will help limit the terror that targeted harassment causes in the lives of abortion providers, their loved ones, and their neighbors. As demonstrated throughout this book, that terror is real, especially given the murders and acts of violence committed against abortion providers in their homes. In particular, Dr. Barnett Slepian's murder in 1998 changed the landscape of anti-abortion harassment. Since Dr. Slepian's murder, many providers do not feel safe in their own homes. Providers conveyed this repeatedly as many connected their experience with residential picketing to the fact that Dr. Slepian was murdered while in his own kitchen. Residential picketing laws can help prevent this very real fear and danger.

The second and third inquiries work hand in hand: the greater the justification for the restriction, the more likely a court will accept a broader restriction on speech. The stories in this book demonstrate the harm that comes from home picketing. Home picketing does not merely cause a minor disruption in the provider's home life; rather, home protest causes many providers to fear for their safety because of the connection between personalized targeting and past violence against abortion providers. As a result, providers drastically alter their own and their families' lives to lessen the effect of home picketing.

Providers who live in areas where there are home picketing laws are grateful. One provider benefited from a home picketing ordinance that had been enacted in response to home protests that one of her neighbors faced. The neighbor had been an abortion provider at the same clinic and experienced home protests every weekend for over twenty years. Protesters spent their weekends in the provider's cul-de-sac, where they demonstrated with very large signs and brought grills and chairs for their protest, essentially camping out there every weekend.

The other provider and his wife eventually reached out to the local police about these "campout" demonstrations. Initially, the police were not receptive or concerned about the home protests, but the provider's wife persisted. She repeatedly urged the police and other local government officials to address the situation. She enlisted the help of her neighbors and, over the course of a few years, was able to convince the town to pass an ordinance to address the protesters' weekly campouts. The provider who told us about this ordinance[18] said, "She was down there constantly, and she was testifying, and this woman was amazing. She did it all on her own without help from anybody."

The provider who described this ordinance was extremely grateful that another abortion provider had succeeded in convincing the community to pass this law. While laws aimed at residential picketing do not completely solve the problem of targeted harassment, if more such laws were in place, more providers could feel safer in their homes.

## Strengthening Existing Laws Criminalizing Targeted Harassment

As detailed in the previous chapter, many existing laws already criminalize targeted harassment. However, there are several ways that these laws should be strengthened so that law treats targeted harassment of abortion providers with the seriousness it deserves.

First, the penalties that already exist under FACE should be enhanced. As FACE currently stands, a criminal conviction for a first offense is subject to a fine and up to one year in jail; for a second offense, it is up to three years. The penalty can be greater if bodily injury or death results and must be less if the violation is "nonviolent physical obstruction." In a FACE civil lawsuit, the maximum monetary award is $5,000 if a private individual brings the case or $10,000 if the attorney general does.[19]

Several providers expressed a need for FACE to have stiffer penalties to better dissuade protesters from violating the law. Stephanie McGoldrick is representative. After a protester published Stephanie's name and picture in an online newsletter he also sent to prisoners who had committed violent anti-abortion crimes, Stephanie stopped providing abortions. The government brought a FACE action against the protester and won, but Stephanie was not satisfied. "I was a little disappointed in the fine," she said. "He should have had a harder penalty." No level of penalty will stop all potential violators, but a more severe penalty under FACE could deter some from violating it.

In the same vein, state and federal law could better protect providers by creating a new penalty enhancement for committing crimes against abortion providers. Penalty enhancements exist in criminal law to increase the punishment for certain types of criminal behaviors. For instance, the federal government and nearly all states have penalty enhancements for hate crimes. These laws provide for greater punishment when a crime is committed because of the victim's race, sex, religion, and other identity characteristics.[20] In 1993, the Supreme Court approved a Wisconsin law that provided for a stiffer sentence for criminal actions motivated by hate. The Court declared the law constitutional because it did not criminalize behavior that would be protected by the First Amendment; rather, it enhanced penalties for already existing crimes.[21]

Legislators should amend their hate crime laws to include crimes directed at abortion providers because of their work. For example, the Wisconsin law states that those who select their criminal victim based "in whole or in part because of the actor's belief or perception regarding the race, religion, color, disability, sexual orientation, national origin or ancestry of that person" will have their penalty enhanced in accordance with the statute's provisions.[22] The list of factors in this statute and others like it should be expanded to include "status as an abortion provider." Adding this language would ensure that crimes targeted at abortion providers because of their work in abortion care would be punished more seriously and possibly deter some extremists from targeting abortion providers in some of the ways detailed in this book.

A third recommendation along these lines is to strengthen laws that prohibit stalking. As the National Center for Victims of Crime defines it, stalking is "a course of conduct directed at a specific person that would cause a reasonable person fear." Each state has its own specific definition with varying requirements to be considered stalking.[23]

The National Center for Victims of Crime has identified several ways that states' requirements vary, and almost all of these requirements can be strengthened by understanding how abortion providers are targeted. For instance, states vary in what types of actions satisfy the course of conduct required to be stalking. The actions described in this book, including secondary harassment and implicit threats, are geared toward causing fear in abortion providers and should be considered in a stalker's course of conduct. Separately, stalking statutes should look to whether the victim feels fear, not to whether a reasonable person would feel fear. A reasonable person standard might not incorporate the history of abortion-related violence and harassment that abortion providers live with.

Strengthening stalking laws in these and other ways could help abortion providers address anti-abortion protesters who stalk them and prevent further stalking from occurring. As Julie Burkhart's experience using her local stalking law against a protester who threatened her demonstrates, broad and effective stalking laws can be very powerful. Since the judge issued the restraining order in Julie's case, neither the protester nor his associates have demonstrated at Julie's house or clinic. Overall, Julie believes the restraining order has been effective because it sends an important signal: "We're just not going to tolerate this."

These are just three ways that existing law could be strengthened to further protect abortion providers. There are undoubtedly others, which this list is not meant to exclude.[24] In thinking about others, legislators should understand that the more they strengthen existing law by considering abortion providers' experiences, the safer abortion providers will be.

## Protecting Identity

Many abortion providers go to great lengths to protect their identity, as Chapter 6 details. They wear disguises, they take different routes to and from work, they use post office boxes for their mail, they register vehicles to a business address, they use online services to scrub the Internet of their identity, they purchase homes in their partner's name, they take their names out of government databases, they hide specifics about their work in conversation, and more. Providers do this not because they are embarrassed about their profession or because they want to avoid having conversations about the controversial topic of abortion. Rather, they do this out of a very real concern for their own and their loved ones' personal safety.

Of course, not every provider tries to protect her identity in this way. For instance, after Jennifer Moore Conrow received hate mail at home shortly before we interviewed her, she decided she could not be quiet about it. "I made the decision that I was going to be public about what happened and not just tell the very small group of people that are deeply involved in my life, not just my parents, my grandmother, and my husband." Jennifer blogged about the hate mail and posted about it on both her personal and work social media sites. Jennifer made the decision to be public so that everyone would know: "It is not okay that I get harassed at my house for work that I do."

This decision whether to disclose their identity is a common issue among abortion providers. Some providers, like Jennifer, want their identity to be part of the public record. They proudly speak about their work, advocate for reproductive justice, and expose targeted harassment. These providers educate the public about abortion and try to improve policy while helping to break down the stigma associated with abortion and abortion provision.

But, because of the extremism documented throughout this book, not all abortion providers feel comfortable having their identities public. Law should protect those who are not comfortable being public so that they are able to work in their lawful profession without living in fear. Moreover, as state legislatures are increasingly regulating abortion clinics and providers, legislators and providers should be aware of and fight against public licensure processes and systems that threaten to reveal providers' personal information.[25]

With regard to general public records, California's law that protects abortion providers' home addresses could serve as a powerful model for a national law. California's law, an amendment to a program that protects victims of domestic violence, is described in more detail in Chapter 8. The law allows abortion providers to use a substitute address instead of their home address for all public state records. The goal of the law is to "prevent future threats or acts of harassment or violence by allowing the participant to reside at an address unknown to the perpetrator(s)."[26] The provider who told us about this law said that it was "good for" abortion providers in California and that they were "lucky" to have it.

Providers in other states told us about similar protection they received from local authorities. Inez Navarro worked with her local police and the Department of Motor Vehicles to keep her license plate from being publicly discoverable. Kevin Bohannon told us that, after affirmatively requesting it, he could remove his name from the county website that lists property owners. While Inez and Kevin are grateful to have these effective solutions, these protections are not the same as nationwide (or even statewide) legislation that would allow any provider to protect personal information, not just those in sympathetic local jurisdictions.

There is federal precedent for such a law. In 1994, Congress passed the Driver's Privacy Protection Act. The act prohibits state motor vehicle departments from disclosing a driver's personal information without that person's consent. The law applies to any information that "identifies an individual, including an individual's photograph, social security number, driver identification number, name, address (but not the 5-digit zip code), telephone number, and medical or disability information."[27]

Among the goals of the law was protecting both women and reproductive healthcare providers from stalking and violence. While much of the testimony supporting the law had to do with the tragic death of actress Rebecca Schaeffer at the hands of a stalker who obtained her address through the California Department of Motor Vehicles, there was also testimony about the need to protect abortion providers.[28] When she introduced the law, California Senator Barbara Boxer specifically referred to this need by stating that "doctors and nurses shouldn't have to worry about anti-abortion activists taking down their license plate numbers and then harassing and intimidating them and their families."[29] Senator Boxer's concern mirrors the concern of many of the providers interviewed for this book. Nonetheless, almost two decades after the Driver's Privacy Protection Act became law, providers continue to worry about their personal information being discovered and used to harass them.

Because providers are still concerned about anti-abortion activists finding their personal information through public records, federal law should be expanded to protect abortion providers more broadly. As currently written, the law applies only to motor vehicle records. To protect abortion providers' information from being discovered through any government agency, the law should be amended to include all state and federal records. The law should particularly apply to state medical boards as they are often the source of information on providers. Or to protect providers in a different way than the consent-based protection already in the Driver's Privacy Protection Act, the law could be amended to do what the California law already does—require states to give abortion providers the ability to use an alternate address for all state records.[30] An expanded national information privacy law would benefit providers who want to keep their personal information from anti-abortion protesters.

## Protecting Providers from Harassment through the Legal Process

Anti-abortion protesters frequently use the legal process as a means to personally target abortion providers. Protesters have sued individual providers based on frivolous legal theories and have used the discovery process in litigation to unearth personal information about them. Protesters have also retaliated against providers who have been witnesses against them in criminal matters. This use of the legal system as a tool of harassment not only places a wasteful burden on the court system but also takes a heavy emotional toll on the providers dragged into the process.

Edwin Abrams described how emotionally distressing lawsuits can be. After Edwin pressed charges against a protester who assaulted him, the protester responded by suing him for emotional distress. The theory of the claim was that Edwin caused his assailant emotional distress because the assailant was arrested and had to spend a night in jail. Even though the clinic where Edwin worked covered the legal costs associated with the suit and the attorney assured him the case would be thrown out of court, the lawsuit deeply troubled Edwin. He explained, "It was kind of nerve-racking at first because I'm a student, I work, I don't have a whole lot of money, and if he won the case I was going to be out of money, having to work to pay him off, and I wouldn't be able to afford school." Edwin's attorney was ultimately proven correct, and the lawsuit was dismissed, but for Edwin, like Tami Madison in Chapter 7, the uncertainty of being the target of a lawsuit was very difficult emotionally.

Courts have several different tools at their disposal to protect providers from harassment in the legal process. For instance, courts have the power to impose sanctions against lawyers for bringing harassing or frivolous lawsuits and to ensure that providers' attorneys receive attorney's fees when these frivolous cases are thrown out of court. Within the context of non-frivolous litigation, courts can put a stop to legal maneuvers intended to do nothing more than harass or pry into providers' personal lives. Courts can reject requests for information, stop lawyers from asking particular questions in depositions or at trial, seal certain information from the public, or even allow providers to use pseudonyms when necessary. When providers must testify, they can do so in disguise if that is a regular part of how they protect themselves. And after a provider has testified, courts can be vigilant in warning against intimidating or retaliating against a witness and then be receptive to those charges once brought before them.

Courts are not the only entity that can protect providers from targeted harassment in the legal process. Prosecutors also play a role because they are generally responsible for bringing charges of witness retaliation or intimidation. State bar associations or ethics boards regulate lawyers and can discipline attorneys who take part in harassing providers through the legal system. All individuals involved with regulating the legal process should better understand the ways that protesters use the legal system to harass providers and protect providers by ensuring that the system is not bogged down with these frivolous and harassing claims.

## Increasing Access to Legal Services

Providers sometimes face difficulties in accessing legal services. They usually feel the need to seek counsel after being named as a defendant in a lawsuit; because they wish to initiate a legal action as a plaintiff; or they are part of the criminal process, as a witness, complainant, or defendant. Other times they have no need to be involved in a legal case, but they nonetheless need a lawyer to strategize about legal options or to help facilitate their interactions with the police or other government officials.

Some providers have ready assistance from lawyers. They have access to local or national nonprofits that have picked up their cause. Others have their own private lawyers, who either work for a fee that the providers can afford or volunteer their services. For these providers, having lawyers supporting them helps them tell their stories, strategize about appropriate responses, vindicate their claims, and defend themselves from legal attacks. For example, when she pursued trespass charges against protesters who came onto her property but wanted to remain in disguise while testifying at the hearing, Stephanie McGoldrick was fortunate enough to obtain pro bono assistance from a large law firm that was working with a women's legal nonprofit organization. She repeatedly described the legal assistance as "fabulous" and praised her attorneys for allowing her "to tell a story that needed to be told."

But not all providers have easy access to legal assistance. For many providers, nonprofit legal organizations capable of assisting them do not exist where they live or work, and these providers' experiences are not on the radar of the national organizations. While some providers are associated with clinics or offices that hire attorneys for business-related matters, these lawyers often cannot help individuals dealing with targeted harassment. Diane Dell summed up the situation: "If you don't have money to fight this kind of stuff, to pay legal costs, what do you do? You don't have much recourse."

When providers cannot afford to hire an attorney, some represent themselves. Kris Neuhaus tried this but "didn't know how to do that very well, obviously." These providers without access to legal assistance expressed frustration with the cost of representation and noted that, because of the expense, they are deterred from pursuing legal claims that might arise from the protesters' targeted harassment.

The situation is made even worse because the protesters often-times have funding to bring harassing lawsuits against the provider or the clinic, which stands in stark contrast to some providers' lack of resources to adequately defend or represent their interests. Lucy Brown expressed this frustration when she was considering taking legal action against protesters who were harassing her and her sister. After talking with a private lawyer and assessing his fees, they decided against pursuing anything. Lucy was frustrated that it seemed as though the protesters had access to free legal assistance. With these lawyers, protesters can engage in harassment through the legal system, as several of the stories in this book reveal. Without their own lawyers to fight back, providers are even more susceptible to harm.

The experiences of the providers here shed light on the depth of the need for increased and better access to legal services for providers throughout the country who are dealing with targeted harassment. As people working on the issue of access to lawyers in other contexts know, solutions to this problem are not easy.[31] Additionally, there are only a few national organizations with the expertise to provide the type of ongoing legal support needed to fill this role, and foundation support is lacking for reproductive rights work generally.

Given the nature of the problem identified here, there are at least two possible solutions that could help the situation. For both, lawyers need to be cognizant of the extent to which everyone at a clinic can experience profound issues with protesters, not just the clinic's doctors or director. As this book has made clear, everyone who is a provider can face targeted harassment.

The first possible solution is that supportive lawyers need to become better informed about the problem of targeted harassment and then be more willing to provide low-cost or pro bono assistance to providers dealing with the problem. Lawyers are part of a profession with an ethical duty to serve those who need their help. As lawyers become more aware that targeted harassment exists, understand its serious effects, and recognize that there are attainable legal remedies to this problem, they should become more likely to provide assistance.

The second possible solution is increased foundation support for the national and local nonprofit reproductive justice organizations that already do legal work on the issue of targeted harassment. With more financial support, these organizations would be able to expand their services to providers in underserved areas or possibly start a concerted nationwide provider defense strategy, such as a network of pro bono attorneys around the country who can work with providers to bring lawsuits or work with law enforcement as needed. Increased funding for these organizations could also expand their existing services within areas they already serve to include all people working at a clinic and all aspects of targeted harassment, not just the most high-profile instances. Providers who work with these nonprofits almost universally find their support extremely valuable; all providers should have access to this kind of assistance, not just those who live in a well-served area or work for an already supported clinic.

## Understanding Threats as Abortion Providers

Several providers relayed stories of law enforcement declining to take action because officials did not believe that what the protesters had done constituted an unlawful threat. For instance, even though Tamara Cocci and her colleagues routinely receive what they believe is threatening mail at home, because the police do not see the mail as a "direct threat," they tell Tamara that they cannot do anything. Likewise, protesters directed threatening comments at Inez Navarro, including telling her, "no one is going to protect you." While Inez perceived these comments as threats, the police officers told Inez that she was subject to "harassment" but not a "threat." The experiences of the providers in this book can inform legal actors so that they better understand what a threat is to people like Tamara and Inez.

Legal actors are often hesitant to label speech a threat because of First Amendment concerns. The First Amendment protects freedom of speech, but there are some circumstances when the government can restrict speech, including when the speaker issues a "true threat." The

Supreme Court has explained this in the context of abortion protest, noting that "threats to patients or their families, however communicated, are proscribable under the First Amendment." Lower courts have, without controversy, applied this principle to threats against providers.[32]

The difficulty arises when determining the precise contours of a "true threat" compared to "constitutionally protected speech."[33] In 2003 the Supreme Court provided a general definition of a true threat: "those statements where the speaker means to communicate a serious expression of an intent to commit an act of unlawful violence to a particular individual or group of individuals." Under the Court's definition, the person issuing the threat does not have to actually intend to carry out the threatened act. Rather, the person must intend to "plac[e] the victim in fear of bodily harm or death." The Court explained that the "true threat" doctrine is not concerned with protecting someone from actual injury; instead, the doctrine protects against "the fear of violence and from the disruption that fear engenders."[34]

Under this standard, lower courts have found several true threats against abortion providers. For example, as already noted in Chapter 8, federal courts found that the American Coalition of Life Activists issued true threats with its "Wanted" posters, "Deadly Dozen" list, and Nuremberg Files website.[35] A different federal appellate court found a true threat when a protester parked two Ryder trucks in front of two different abortion clinics. The court reasoned that the protester played on the then-recent Oklahoma City bombing by Timothy McVeigh, who used a Ryder truck to carry it out.[36] In yet another case, a court found that a protester issued a true threat when he repeatedly stated "Where's a pipe-bomber when you need him?" every time he saw a particular Mississippi abortion provider.[37]

From these cases, as well as many others, an important principle emerges: a threat is determined by looking at whether the person receiving it reasonably feels that the statement or conduct expresses "a determination or intent to injure presently or in the future."[38] In other words, the key inquiry is whether the person receiving the alleged threat reasonably feels fear and intimidation from it. Many factors help with this determination,[39] but an important consideration is the broader context in which the alleged threat was made—here, the context of anti-abortion harassment and violence. Historical context matters in true threat cases, as the Supreme Court made clear in the 2003 case when it evaluated whether cross burning was a true threat by looking at the historical context of the act.[40]

The historical context of anti-abortion harassment has also been relevant in lower court cases dealing with anti-abortion threats. For example, in the case involving the "Wanted" posters, "Deadly Dozen" list, and Nuremberg Files website, the court looked at the particular history of abortion-related violence and intimidation to evaluate whether the posters and websites were true threats. In making its determination, the court recounted the various murders as well as actions taken by abortion opponents leading up to the murders.[41] Likewise, in the case involving the Ryder truck parked in front of abortion clinics, the court noted that without considering the Oklahoma City bombing, the Ryder trucks would not be threatening.[42] The same contextual analysis also took place in the case of the abortion protester who repeatedly referred to needing a pipe-bomber whenever he saw a particular abortion provider, as the court noted that the pipe-bomb threat occurred "at approximately the same time" as other high-profile bombings, including the Unabomber and the Atlanta Olympics pipe bombs.[43]

The providers' experiences captured in this book speak to several of the factors courts have used in determining if a threat is a true threat and can provide a greater understanding of how and why abortion providers respond to threats. In fact, three of the factors courts have looked at—how the target reacted, whether the target reasonably believed violence could occur, and the broader context of anti-abortion harassment and violence—can be summarized as courts considering the alleged threat from the perspective of, as one federal judge described the standard, the "reasonable abortion provider."[44]

Analyzing alleged threats from the perspective of the reasonable abortion provider is an important way for both courts and law enforcement to evaluate and respond to threats because abortion providers experience threats differently than other people. Put another way, some of the conduct and speech discussed in this book might not seem threatening to people who are not a part of the abortion care community, but for abortion providers, who are almost all acutely aware of the history of abortion-related violence and harassment, it is threatening. As Alesha

Doan, a political science professor who has studied anti-abortion political harassment, has written, "[c]ontextualizing anti-abortion protest and coupling it with its intended targets . . . changes the scope and meaning of the protest altogether."[45]

Penny Santiago's story provides an example of how a better understanding of abortion providers' experiences can inform how police respond to threatening conduct. A regular protester at Penny's clinic said to Penny, "I'm going to wait for you until you get out of work, and then I'm going to give you what you deserve." Penny reported this comment to the police, but they thought Penny's concern was an overreaction. The police told her that the comment could have meant anything. For instance, Penny recalls the police saying, in reference to the protester's comment that Penny would get what she deserves, "Maybe I deserve flowers." With a better understanding of the history of targeted harassment, the police, as Penny said, "could have a context of what it really meant—it's not just a random comment, it is meaningful." After all, Penny did not feel threatened merely because of that particular comment; she felt threatened because of that comment in the context of people who share Penny's line of work being murdered, assaulted, and otherwise harmed in the ways this book describes.

Thomas Andrews shared a similar experience. Soon after Dr. Tiller was murdered, a protester told one of the staff at Thomas's clinic to "tell Dr. Andrews he can run but he can't hide." Thomas reported this comment to the FBI, but they did nothing about it because they did not consider it to be threatening. Because the comment came shortly after Dr. Tiller's murder and the protester who made the comment had publicly supported violence against abortion providers, Thomas felt threatened. If law enforcement had assessed the comment from the perspective of a reasonable abortion provider, they would have more likely understood that it was a true threat.

As the interviews and stories in this book reveal, those who are part of the abortion provider community are intimately familiar with the violence and harassment that have occurred to other abortion providers around the United States. Abortion providers share a collective memory[46] about their profession's past, and that memory is not limited to their own isolated experiences. Comments and actions directed at abortion providers almost immediately conjure this past violence and harassment, increasing the likelihood that targeted harassment is perceived as a threat. Courts, law enforcement, and other legal actors analyzing the factors that contribute to whether a statement is a true threat need to understand the way this collective memory increases almost all abortion providers' sense of fear.

## Labeling as Terrorism

Until this point in the book, we have mostly used the term "targeted harassment of abortion providers" to describe protesters' actions. However, given the context and extreme nature of targeted harassment and the serious effects it has on abortion providers' lives, these specific acts should be understood as something more: anti-abortion terrorism.

Branding targeted harassment of abortion providers as a form of terrorism has been a controversial move in the recent past.[47] In the first half of 2009, the Department of Homeland Security released two documents that took steps in this direction. First, in March, the department issued the "Domestic Extremism Lexicon." The lexicon sought to define "key terms and phrases" in the effort to combat "the threat that domestic, non-Islamic extremism poses to the United States." Among the terms was "anti-abortion extremism," which it defined as a "movement of groups or individuals who are virulently anti-abortion and advocate violence against providers of abortion-related services, their employees, and their facilities."[48]

The second document, "Rightwing Extremism: Current Economic and Political Climate Fueling Resurgence in Radicalization and Recruitment," was released two weeks later. This document was an intelligence assessment of the department's growing concern over "violent radicalization within the United States." Among the concerns were "groups and individuals that are dedicated to a single issue, such as opposition to abortion or immigration." The document compared the then-current climate to the 1990s when "social issues such as abortion, inter-racial crimes, and same-sex marriage" were exploited by extremists.[49]

Although neither document explicitly referred to anti-abortion extremists as terrorists, both did so by implication. The first document defined "terrorism," and the second document elaborated on the department's concerns about violence. In both, the department explained the extremist threat to the country with language that equated extremism with terrorism. For instance, the introduction of the second document indicated that the information it contained was provided to law enforcement officials around the country "so they may effectively deter, prevent, preempt, or respond to terrorist attacks against the United States." It also introduced its findings by saying that it had "no specific information that domestic rightwing terrorists are currently planning acts of violence." Notably, the word "rightwing" had a footnote that defined "rightwing extremism" to include single-issue opposition to abortion.[50] In other words, the Department of Homeland Security was labeling extreme abortion opponents as terrorists.[51]

The Department faced intense backlash for these two reports. Members of Congress complained that the reports were biased against rightwing groups. Supporters of the military were concerned that the reports raised the specter of military personnel returning from war and becoming dangerous. And, most relevant here, groups opposed to abortion were upset that they were being targeted as dangerous extremists and feared their free speech rights would be limited as a result.[52] Because of the public pressure, the department pulled both reports in May 2009, just weeks before Dr. Tiller was murdered. Department Secretary Janet Napolitano explained that both documents were not "authorized products" for public distribution because they had not been fully vetted.[53]

The department was wrong to backtrack on this point. While the concept of "terrorism" is multilayered and complex, federal law offers a definition of "domestic terrorism" as "acts dangerous to human life that are a violation of the criminal laws of the United States or of any State [that] appear to be intended to intimidate or coerce a civilian population; to influence the policy of a government by intimidation or coercion; or to affect the conduct of a government by mass destruction, assassination, or kidnapping."[54] The FBI, the agency charged with leading federal terrorism investigations, has articulated a shorthand definition of "domestic terrorism" as well: "Americans attacking Americans based on U.S.-based extremist ideologies."[55] Many of the providers' experiences described in this book fit these descriptions.

More broadly, terrorism scholars have long failed to agree on one uniform definition of terrorism, but some of the most common elements
in their definitions are present in the providers' experiences recounted
in this book: violence, political motivation, and fear or terror.[56] Bruce
Hoffman, a Georgetown University professor who has studied terrorism for more than three decades, offers a detailed definition that captures these elements and best addresses the types of terrorism described
throughout this book. Based on his study of the subject, terrorism is
"the deliberate creation and exploitation of fear through violence or
the threat of violence in the pursuit of political change." According
to Hoffman, it can be conducted by an organization with a terrorist
mission or by individuals who are inspired by such organizations. The
power of terrorism is that it is "designed to have far-reaching psychological repercussions beyond the immediate victim or target."[57]

This understanding of terrorism captures what providers feel is happening to them. For instance, Tami Madison explained that what the
protesters do when they target providers "goes beyond bullying. It's this
extreme bullying and intimidation and harassment." To her, protesters
create a "culture of terror" when they target her. "Most communities do
not want terrorism in their neighborhoods," she said, "and so I think
it's important to focus on that, that it's really not about abortion, it's
about extreme harassment and intimidation of people providing a legal
service and how it affects the healthcare of women."

Providers call targeted harassment terrorism because that is how they
experience it—as activity intended to threaten and scare them in an
effort to change their position on this highly political issue. Providers
know that, too often, anti-abortion protesters' activity is branded as just
another form of speech and protest protected by the First Amendment.
Yet providers feel terrorized and describe the acts they are subjected to
as terrorism. And they describe the people who commit these acts as
terrorists.

Anti-abortion protesters have also used this terminology at times.[58]
Many of them understand that they are capitalizing on the previous
murders and acts of violence to instill fear in providers in order to
try to attain one of their chief political goals, ending abortion.[59] The
anti-abortion terrorists know that a single act against a single provider
can create fear in many more providers than just the one targeted.

As Regina Dinwiddie, a longtime anti-abortion extremist and the first person to be enjoined under FACE, said about anti-abortion violence, "I hate to quote Chairman Mao, but he was right. Kill one, scare a thousand."[60]

Even less aggressive acts of terrorism play on the murders, assaults, bombings, and death threats to make providers fear for their safety.[61] Anti-abortion terrorists exploit this and have created an overwhelming sense of fear or, as terrorism scholar Martha Crenshaw explains, "emotional terror,"[62] among providers that something violent can happen to any of them, at any time. After all, if, on top of all the violence that has occurred at abortion clinics, Dr. Barnett Slepian can be murdered on a Friday night in his kitchen and Dr. George Tiller can be murdered on a Sunday morning in his church, no abortion provider is safe anywhere, anytime.

Targeted harassment of abortion providers also fits basic understandings of terrorism because the people who engage in it face the predicament that most terrorists do—how to accomplish the desired change when legitimate avenues have failed and popular opinion has not moved toward your position.[63] This is the predicament of those who target abortion providers because they want to abolish abortion entirely. Despite a succession of Republican appointees to the Supreme Court, these justices have not overturned *Roe v. Wade*.[64] Moreover, public opinion on abortion has remained relatively static, with a large majority of the American public consistently opposing criminalizing abortion in all circumstances.[65] Under these conditions, anti-abortion activists engaging in the activities highlighted in this book are resorting to the same strategy as others in their position—terrorism.

By shifting terminology to include targeted harassment within the concept of terrorism, society will further brand these actions as unacceptable, possibly reducing the burdens providers bear through a shift of societal norms. As have many of the providers we interviewed, some in government, the media, academia, and beyond have already made this shift, but based on the stories and analysis in this book, this shift deserves more widespread adoption.

Also, more concretely, with this understanding, the government will have more legitimacy when it calls anti-abortion extremism terrorism and uses appropriate law enforcement tools to combat it. Specifically,

viewing targeted harassment within the framework of domestic terrorism could enhance law enforcement investigations and prosecutions.
Doing so would not only create a more uniform way to approach issues
that providers face but also would better enable law enforcement officials and prosecutors to understand and investigate a provider's experience within the context of a potentially greater threat. It would also
allow policymakers to better track and understand the entire landscape
of potential anti-abortion terrorist threats and develop responses that
are consistent with other anti-terrorism approaches.[66]

## Conclusion

Legal reforms alone will not solve the problem of anti-abortion terrorism,[67] and the providers we spoke to understood that. To that end,
many of the nonlegal strategies discussed throughout this book could be
helpful in making providers feel safer. From personal strategies around
protecting identity and avoiding conflict to strategies around clinic
architecture and outside layout, there are many different approaches to
minimizing the harms from anti-abortion terrorism that do not require
legal reform.

Also, and this cannot be stressed enough, anti-abortion terrorism of
the kind discussed in this book is only one of many obstacles that abortion providers face in providing safe and accessible abortion care for
their patients. As many providers told us, they are very concerned with
the rash of anti-abortion legislation that has swept many parts of the
United States since 2010. According to data compiled by Bloomberg
and the Guttmacher Institute at the end of 2013, at least seventy-three
clinics have closed or stopped providing abortions since 2011,[68] with
even more closing in 2014. Some of these have closed for business reasons or because of a problem with the clinic, but most of them have
closed because of new anti-abortion legislation. This rash of legislation
is a major factor in reducing abortion access in this country.[69]

But anti-abortion terrorism is also a major problem, and a recent
study found that some of the types of targeted harassment described
in this book increase as states grow more hostile toward abortion in
their legislative policies.[70] Thus, as anti-abortion legislation is on the
upswing, targeted harassment may also increase.[71]

The reforms in this chapter are suggested ways to improve the situation for providers across the country. Law enforcement can better serve abortion providers. Legislatures can pass laws to protect providers, and the court system can more accurately understand the context of providers' experiences when addressing issues related to abortion targeting. Importantly, society can understand targeted harassment of abortion providers as anti-abortion terrorism. Taking these steps can go a long way toward making abortion providers safer.

# 10

## Why Abortion Providers Continue

I guess the normal reaction to Dr. Tiller's murder would be, "This is probably really dangerous" or "I probably shouldn't do this." But I was like, "I'm going to do this because this is really important." It didn't even enter my mind to think about not doing this work because Dr. Tiller was killed.

—TERESA SPELLMAN

I love my work. I could have been a dermatologist and nobody would care. I didn't choose this because I wanted controversy. I thought this was the right thing to do. I felt that doing abortions was the most important thing I could do in medicine. I might have been mistaken, but I still think that. I don't care what people think about this. I've had a lot of attacks in the newspapers and stuff, but I think what I'm doing matters. And if somebody asks, "Why do you do this?" Well, it matters. It matters for the health of the woman. It matters for the health of her family. It matters for the health of our society, and now it matters for freedom.

—WARREN HERN

AT THE END OF each of the interviews, after hearing all the tales of violence, home picketing, being stalked, family members being harassed, murder, and more, we asked each provider why she or he remains in this profession. The answers to this question provide an appropriate way to finish this book because the commitment, passion, resolve, and humanity that are apparent in the answers counterbalance the tales of terrorism, fear, and inadequate legal response in the preceding pages.

As many providers pointed out, no other medical care professionals face this type of risk from their jobs. Abortion providers could easily walk away from this field and live a life without harassment, threats, and fear. But, other than one provider, every person we interviewed refused to stop, despite the targeted harassment they face.

Based on these responses, this chapter recounts the reasons providers continue with this work: a commitment to patients and patient healthcare, a passion for the issue of reproductive choice, a resolve not to let the terrorists win, and a dedication to never again let women suffer like they did before *Roe v. Wade*.

## Stopped Providing Abortion

Before getting to the reasons providers continue in the face of terrorism, this section briefly discusses the providers who stopped providing abortion care because of anti-abortion protesters' tactics. Two of the eighty-seven providers we interviewed stopped, though only one stuck to that decision.[1] That one is Stephanie McGoldrick, as recounted in full in Chapter 7. Stephanie was targeted at work, followed after work, picketed at home, and explicitly threatened online and in print. She obtained a trespass conviction against two protesters and, after leaving the field, a Freedom of Access to Clinic Entrances Act (FACE) judgment against one. The FACE judgment came after a protester published Stephanie's name, address, phone number, and a photo that accompanied the message: "nothing will stop her but a bullet in the head." He published this information in a newsletter that he posted online as well as mailed to violent anti-abortion prisoners.

Despite Stephanie's legal successes against the protesters, she decided she could not continue to provide abortion care, so she found another job instead. "After the trespass and the newsletter threat, you don't sleep as well, you don't enjoy life as much. The whole family—my kids, my husband—it wasn't just me. It wasn't anything specific. It just was chronic then. It was like a chronic inflammation, a headache that won't go away."

As a result of leaving the field, Stephanie's anxiety faded, but not immediately. Stephanie did not feel relief until she heard one of the protesters speak about her in open court during her FACE trial. The protester said, "I wouldn't hurt her anymore because she's my hero because she quit." Stephanie felt conflicted when she heard that statement. "I felt like a quitter and like he won. Sort of. But that's when my anxiety level went down because he said 'I wouldn't hurt her anymore.'" After the trial, she was able to begin to live her life normally again, taking walks and leaving her drapes open at night. Shortly after the trial, when Dr. Tiller was murdered, Stephanie remembers her reaction as being, "I was glad I was out."

Reflecting on her experience, Stephanie blames not only the protesters but also the law for her decision to leave the field. "I think that if the protesters weren't allowed to come to my house, that I would not have quit. I think that's where it started. I think letting them come to your home and target you at home is key."

The only other provider we talked with who stopped providing abortion care because of targeted harassment, albeit temporarily, is Lowell Taylor. After twice being physically attacked by protesters at an airport on his way to fly to another state to work, Lowell left the field in the early 1990s. Even though his bodyguard tried to comfort him by saying that the protesters were easy to handle, Lowell knew that "these people can throw bullets." He explained, "I was scared. I was physically frightened. Emotionally frightened. It looked like violence could really break loose. And they were dedicated to that."

Lowell's retirement was short-lived. He returned to the field a year later, after he received a call from the director of a clinic where he had previously worked. The clinic director told Lowell about a young patient who had advanced AIDS and was about eighteen weeks pregnant. The director said, "I can't find a doctor who will take care of her." Lowell knew he could help this young woman, so he agreed to perform the abortion. He has not stopped since.

Approximately eight days after caring for this patient, an anti-abortion protester fired a double-barrel shotgun into Lowell's house in the middle of the night. The bullets went through the walls of his young son's playroom, which had previously been Lowell and his wife's bedroom. Thankfully, everyone was asleep on a different floor of the house, so no one was injured. Despite this incident and his prior experiences with anti-abortion terrorism, Lowell continued to provide abortion care. To this day, Lowell persists because the clinic provides him with a security service that provides him with peace of mind.

## Providers' Commitment to Their Patients

All of the other providers featured in this book persisted notwithstanding their experiences with anti-abortion terrorism. One of the reasons many gave for this persistence was that they recognize that abortion care is a crucial aspect of caring for their patients. Providers described feeling a deep connection with their patients and a responsibility to provide this necessary medical care.

For many of the providers, their patients' medical need was foremost in their mind. For example, Danielle Figueroa talked in detail about her patients' needs. "I think that when you hear the word 'abortion' you get goosebumps all over your body and you step back. But when you see someone come in with fingerprints on her throat or you see women who live in shelters, or women who already have twelve kids—they need me."

Providers know that they are the key to patients having access to the medical care they need. For example, when asked why, given everything she's been through and the extreme violence and murders that she has seen, she continues to work in abortion care, Debra Fulkerson answered that she continues escorting "because there are still women that need to get into the clinic. That's basically it." Roberta Keller talked about the same motivation: "Many times my patients haven't seen a doctor in five years, and I just feel that I provide excellent care for a group of people that are completely underrepresented and don't have good access to care."

Providers are able to help patients by taking some of the brunt of the controversy that surrounds abortion. Constance Phillips sees that as a key part of her role as a provider:

> I do feel like I'm making sure that women have access, to the best of my ability, to the services that they need, that we have a safe and secure building so that staff are comfortable coming to work there, and that clients are able to come in with the least amount of harassment possible. And if that means that I or some of our volunteers take an extra dose of harassment from protesters, then we do that. To some degree it's my job to take harassment, but it's really my job to make sure that clients can get the services that they need and that our staff are able to provide the services to them in a safe, comfortable, healthy environment.

Mathew Whitley expressed the same sentiment. "Imagine the patients having to come out of their shells, having to lose their confidentiality, lose their anonymity, coming out to be confronted by people who have never seen them." He worried about the protesters who "have these cameras taking the patients' pictures as they come into the clinics," especially because of his patients from outlying areas who fear that their communities could learn about their abortions. Mathew emphatically concluded, "Imagine that patient having to come out and confront these total strangers, as fanatical as they are. I feel more empathy for those patients than I do for myself. And that's what drove me to keep doing this. The protesters just didn't have a right to do that."

For many providers, the personal relationships they form with patients drive them to continue working through the anti-abortion terrorism they face. This connection keeps Diane Dell going:

> I like this one-on-one with individuals. I keep doing it because I do love the work. I tell my partner every day, I love my work. I love the patients that I see, even the difficult ones. Even the ones that are unhappy about being there because they're different from everybody else—they don't believe in abortion but they're special. Even when I have to deal with those folks, I still think it is a good thing to do.

Penny Santiago similarly expressed that this is the reason she continues. "To be able to share women's experiences with them and be supportive is an honor. Regardless of how many threats I get, it's not going to make me stop doing what I do." To Penny, this connection with her patients is "what's good. It's sisterhood, it's brotherhood, it's helping each other, it's supporting each other, it's peaceful, it's love, it's justice."

Several providers explained the power of patients' appreciation for their work as the reason they continue. Howard Stephens linked this feeling of gratitude and appreciation that he gets from his patients to his decision to continue. He said he has an "amazing job" notwithstanding the harassment. "Hardly a day goes by that I don't have a patient look at me and say, 'Thank you. If it wasn't for you, I wouldn't be able to do this. Thank you for being there.'" Thomas Andrews likewise told us why he continues the work in spite of the protest: "We see probably three thousand patients per year. They are all very thankful and very pleased that we're here for them."

## Commitment to the Cause

Other providers' motivation to continue stems from their commitment to a greater cause. Daniel Martin explained how this commitment shifts any perceived risk that the terrorism may pose:

> I say being a physician in general is like having a backstage pass into people's lives and then with a multifaceted issue like control of reproduction, and in particular abortion—something that's highly legalized, stigmatized, moralized—being able to meet women and families at that very critical interface and being a possibility of hope for people who otherwise don't have it, that is so essentially in accord with who I am as a person, and it is so consistent with my own sense of place in the world and my sense of spiritual understanding that it becomes even richer as I do the work.
>
> I draw lots of parallels with the civil rights movement, and I like to think that in the way that Dr. King—at some point with the very real threat of assassination and death being more real and in his face on a daily basis—reaching a point where those things dulled in comparison to realizing that you're on the right road. And so daily I get a stronger sense of that about the work that I do.
>
> I intend on living a long life. What I am absolutely determined about is not experiencing a spiritual death, a sense where I'm so vested in staying alive at the expense of my own core about what is important and what is right. And so for me to shrink back out of fear from intimidation would be a sort of spiritual death, and it would be an anxiety that I'm not well equipped to handle.

Summarizing why he will not back down in the face of protesters' terroristic acts, Daniel said, "I can handle the risk that somebody might harm me. I couldn't handle not being a person of conviction and action."

Providers had many different ways to describe the cause that motivates them. Marsha Banks sees her work as a basic aspect of human rights. In explaining why she continued despite witnessing decades of attacks, arsons, and protest, Marsha said, "It's what I was born to do really, to be a human rights advocate. It's human rights. How could anybody tell anybody what to do with their body? It's as simple as that."

Peggy Gifford also framed her commitment as one rooted in human rights, but for her that commitment is very personal. Her parents divorced when she was younger, and Peggy was raised by her mother. Because of her upbringing, Peggy explained, "I've always really identified with the need for women to be able to be autonomous and in control of their lives. If you can't control when you're going to have a baby, if you can't control when to end a pregnancy that you need to end, you're not free. That was it for me." Peggy is fearful as a result of the anti-abortion terror tactics that she and others encounter. "But my belief that abortion is a basic fundamental human right and your ability to control your reproductive life overrides that fear."

Even for someone who had a very recent, very direct, and very personal death threat, the commitment to the cause of helping women prevailed. Despite receiving a death threat at home against her and her family, Carolyn Barrick was clear: "I have a beautiful little child who I am very proud of and when my child asks what I do, I say I work for an organization that helps women. And one of the things I do is try to protect women from the mean people, as we call it."

Several providers referred to their very specific commitment to working to maintain reproductive choice and autonomy. Tracey Carter explained why she will not be deterred. "It's just a choice. It's about choice, and that's why I work here." Tracey elaborated, "I don't have to work here, but I do because it empowers, not only me, but also the other women who walk through this door, and I try to let the protesters know, even though you stand out there and you shout your ignorant, wrong information that you feed to the patients, we're still going to be here."

Chrisse France connected her refusal to back down to the morality of choice. When describing her reasons for remaining in the field, she said,

> I believe that women need to have agency over their own bodies. When you're sitting there, across from a woman, and she's telling you about her life and that she had two kids already and she's stretched to the max of her resources, I feel like this is a life-saving decision and she has the moral agency to be able to make that decision.

She explained that despite the home protests, threats, and assaults she has experienced and observed, "I feel even stronger now that I've been doing this work than I ever did probably. And I'll continue to do what I'm doing."

For Melinda Birkland, choice and reproductive health are very personal. She has four daughters and explained her commitment in terms of her hope for their future. If any of her daughters needs abortion care in the future, Melinda wants them to be able to receive the care they need. "I just want them to have access to it like they would any other healthcare. I don't want it to be a huge deal."

Several providers described their commitment to one particular aspect of abortion rights—preventing stigma. Abortion stigma is the commonly shared idea that abortion is morally wrong and/or socially unacceptable, even though abortion is a common, safe, and legal medical procedure. Many people believe that reducing abortion stigma is essential to improving women's health and access to abortion care as well as depoliticizing abortion generally.[2]

Miriam Dixon's commitment to reducing this stigma motivates her to continue through the harassment she faces. After describing working as an abortion provider as "totally my life's work," Miriam said that, in particular, the "anti-stigma thing is really a passionate thing for me. That people can be labeled and stigmatized to not execute what's their right or their human right, it makes me superpassionate." Miriam explained further, "I don't get juice out of that abortion wars kind of going toe-to-toe with the protesters. At all. It lights my fire to go toe-to-toe with a woman and help her examine her own internal self-blame stuff. That stuff makes me excited."

After talking about receiving hate mail at home for the first time, Jennifer Moore Conrow voiced a similar motivation. She said that her recent experience did not make her question her career choice, "not even for a second." In fact,

> it reinforced to me the importance of what I do and, if anything, made me feel like I have to work harder to do more to fight this stigma and negativity around abortion care and pregnancy care and women's care in general. It brought that home, literally. I always knew this was the right thing, and that just reinforced that for me. So it did the opposite of what they intended, I'm sure.

### Refusal to Let the Terrorists Win

Whereas some providers stressed their commitment to their patients or to a greater cause, other providers explained that they remain motivated out of a sense of defiance in an ongoing battle with anti-abortion terrorists. These providers explained that they would not "give in" to terrorism. Oftentimes, they even described becoming emboldened by protesters' actions.

Some of these providers described this determination and persistence as a very personal, defining aspect of their being. For example, after an anti-abortion terrorist burned down the clinic where she works, Victoria Gates explained that there was absolutely no doubt that she would return to work. "I won't give in and let someone dictate how I'm going to spend my time." Even though the work atmosphere is "very scary," she will continue because she does not "want to give them the satisfaction of walking away from something I feel so passionately about." Ellen James had a similar explanation as to why she continues in the face of increasing home picketing. "The short answer? They don't get to win. They're a blight. They are people who teach their children hatred and intolerance and meanness, and we don't need that."

For other providers, this determination is rooted in a broader belief that rights can be protected only through persistent struggle. Melinda Birkland explained, "I'm a tiny woman, but I'm kind of a firecracker. I don't like to back down to anybody, and I think that a lot of people in this world lose a lot of rights and lose a lot of privileges because they're afraid to stand their ground." Tamara Cocci likewise told us, "I strongly feel that giving in to harassment and intimidation is what allows fascists and bullies to succeed, so it really doesn't matter to me what they do."

Some providers explained that the idea of not letting the terrorists win not only prevents them from stopping but also motivates them to work harder. Olivia Armas explained:

> I get angry more than anything, and I want to keep working there because I want to show them "you're not going to intimidate me." I'm going to keep doing what I'm doing because I believe in it, just the way you believe in standing outside at ten o'clock at night preaching your sermons or whatever. I believe in helping women. It kind of fires me up more.

Along the same lines, Kevin Bohannon said that each time the protesters show up at his house, he decides to keep working longer. "So instead of retiring in a year or so, I guess I'll keep at this for a while."

### Keeping Abortion Safe and Women Alive

In addition to the reasons already described, many providers volunteered without prompting that they are motivated to remain in the field by their memory of the time prior to the Supreme Court's decision in *Roe v. Wade*,[3] when women did not have access to legal and safe abortion. These providers continue to provide abortion care despite the terrorism because they fear that if they do not provide abortion, the United States will return to a time they remember, when abortion was illegal, access to safe abortion care was difficult, and women and doctors put their lives at risk just to obtain or provide safe medical care.

From the mid-nineteenth century until the decade before *Roe*, abortion was largely illegal in the United States; thus, women risked criminal sanctions, including heavy fines and imprisonment, when seeking abortion care. Given the legal status of abortion in the century before *Roe*, many physicians across the country faced similar sanctions and risked their careers to provide safe abortions to women seeking this medical service.[4]

Stephen Tate discussed the effect of the pre-*Roe* legal climate on physicians in his state. "There was no provision for defining a lawful abortion. There were no health exceptions. For an unlawful abortion you went to jail, but the same statute didn't say what would be a lawful abortion." Providers were eventually given some guidance when, over time, case law developed in some states, including Stephen's, that allowed abortions when the woman's health was at risk. Based on that case law, some hospitals decided to provide abortions. As a result, Stephen's hospital, like many in that era, had an abortion review committee that consisted of "three or four elderly gentlemen who reviewed the cases and signed their names." Stephen initially thought this arrangement "was just awful. Why do these old guys get to decide whether this woman gets to have a safe abortion or not—and dies as a result?" However, looking back, Stephen now realizes "those guys were heroes. They were senior practitioners in the community. They had busy practices. They were making money. Being arrested for saying an abortion was okay would not have been good for their careers."

Because not every physician was willing to risk his or her career and liberty to provide or even approve safe abortions, not every woman could access qualified physicians providing safe abortion care. As a result, women went to great lengths to obtain this medical service, oftentimes risking serious illness or death from complications resulting from an unsafe abortion.[5]

Although there are limited data on abortion in the United States prior to 1973, a 1967 study estimated that 800,000 illegal abortions were performed each year.[6] Several providers we spoke with recalled entire wards of hospitals reserved for women with complications from these pre-*Roe* illegal abortions. Anthony Ward explained:

> As a resident, you rotated through the city hospital. There was a ward on it that just had patients who were post-abortion or got really sick from illegal abortions. Usually once every week, once every two weeks, somebody died. That made a tremendous impression on me. I saw some of the sickest people I have ever seen in my life. Any day you'd go in you'd see between twenty and thirty women who were super sick. And then a lot of them died.

For Anthony, "that colored how I saw abortion. That put it on my consciousness. So when I finished residency, I said, 'We've got to do something about illegal abortion.'"

Dr. P. described his residency training before *Roe* very similarly. "I went to two funerals of two women that had illegal abortions. One rolled into our emergency room with a couple feet of intestines coming out of her vagina, and the other died under our care whose sister tried to abort her with knitting needles."

In the years immediately before *Roe*, several states began to answer a building call to reform anti-abortion laws because of an increased awareness of the dangers of unsafe abortion practices throughout the country. This movement culminated in the 1973 decision in *Roe v. Wade*, in which the US Supreme Court held that the Constitution protected a woman's right to terminate her pregnancy. In *Roe* and its companion case, *Doe v. Bolton*, the Court determined that states may restrict a woman's access to abortion care at different stages of her pregnancy if the restrictions are tailored to a state's compelling interest in protecting the pregnant woman's health and potential human life; however, states could no longer ban abortion in the first two trimesters or in the third trimester if the woman's life or health is in danger.[7]

The increased availability of safe abortion throughout the United States in the years after *Roe* had a significant effect on public health and women's lives. Following *Roe*, US maternal morbidity and mortality ratios significantly decreased. History demonstrates that women seek abortion care regardless of its legal status, but whether abortion is legal, safe, and accessible is a question of life or death for women seeking this medical procedure.[8]

Unprompted by our interview questions, several providers articulated that they became abortion providers and continue in abortion practice, notwithstanding the terrorism they encounter, specifically because they remember, experienced firsthand, or heard stories of this pre-*Roe* time period in which many women suffered and died from unsafe abortions. In particular, providers' own experiences working in medicine prior to *Roe* continue to have a profound effect on their determination and persistence.

Lewis Turk's response is representative of the providers who had this pre-*Roe* connection. Lewis recalled a specific patient whose pre-*Roe* death inspired him to enter and remain in the field of abortion provision, even in the face of terrorism:

> The reason I became involved in the issue at all is because on the last day of my residency training, instead of going to the obstetrical ward, they suggested that I go to the emergency room so I wouldn't have any leftover cases. At four in the afternoon they brought in a young woman who was dead on arrival. She was a student from the local university, whose name I still remember as Deborah Little. She died in a doctor's office because he perforated her uterus and she bled internally. That was my epiphany. I said if abortion ever becomes legal, I would never allow this to happen to anyone else. And that's how I became involved in the issue.

When asked later in the interview about his concern for his personal safety because of anti-abortion violence and harassment, Lewis explicitly connected his current commitment to the pre-*Roe* history: "I just felt that it was the right thing to do, it was the right cause. As I said, that epiphany with that young woman who was brought in dead just really, really affected my life."

Providers also opened up and shared personal stories of their or their loved ones' experiences with pre-*Roe* abortion. Eva Sager's own pre-*Roe* abortion inspired her to become and remain a provider. In fact, her experience is such an important part of her identity as an abortion provider that she started her interview with this story, even though our first question to her was about what her role in abortion care has been:

My role really began in abortion when I was about eighteen years old when I had an unplanned pregnancy, many, many years ago, well before *Roe v. Wade*, and I was living here and through a clandestine network was able to locate obviously an illegal abortion provider, whom I met under the railroad tracks. We had to leave our car under the tracks. We went into the person's vehicle. I went blindfolded in the back of the car. And then we walked up and down stairs, my blindfold was taken off, and there was a three-story building, a very old building, and I walked down to what appeared to be the basement. There was a gray metal desk and a screen to change behind and college banners in a very macabre setting, all around the ceiling area.

The person used a red rubber catheter and it went right through and essentially contaminated my uterus. His only comment to me was, "I bet you haven't seen blood in a long time." I left with my roommate and then went back to our apartment. And forty-eight hours later I had a second abortion. I went to the hospital, where the obstetrician-gynecologist on call was an Irish Catholic doctor, and the comment was made to me that if I did not tell him who the abortionist was, they would tell my family. I just absolutely refused.

At that point I was very sick and septic. I had a temperature of one hundred four. I was hospitalized, put on IV antibiotics, treated in a very, very rude fashion by the nurses who considered me a woman of the night or just an immoral person, and the case was considered a dirty case.

Eva explained that she left the hospital and "vowed at some point to pursue medical training and either go to medical school or become a physician's assistant." This experience drives Eva to continue the work she does, even in the face of the extensive harassment she's experienced. "I am committed to not have women go through the experience that I had. Basically, I almost lost my life."

Similarly, when we asked her about her experiences with protesters and harassment generally, Tracey Carter recalled her mother's experience in the pre-*Roe* era:

> My mom had me when she was sixteen, and I was born when *Roe v. Wade* wasn't even in existence yet. I was born in 1970, so she had a lot of friends who had botched abortions or died from a result of a botched abortion, and back then colored folks, as they say, had to go in the backwoods to have a termination, instead of going in the back way of a doctor's office. They had to go to some old lady to have an abortion.

When Tracey had an abortion many years after *Roe*, her mother accompanied and reassured her: "Just remember, you have a choice." Recalling the pre-*Roe* era, her mother added, "It was a choice that I had you because I knew that I did not want to go somewhere where they perform abortion illegally and I probably wouldn't survive, so just remember you're going to a safe facility where you're going to have an abortion." Tracey's mother's memories of this era motivate Tracey to persist through the protesters and harassment.

Another provider also told us that a family member's memories inspire her to continue working through the harassment she faces today. Danielle Figueroa's paternal grandmother died from an unsafe abortion. That story motivates Danielle to work in abortion care, even though she has faced serious personal harassment: "My father never really talked about it. But he was very hurt that five children were without a mother. My father was the oldest. He was ten when it happened. And that hurt my father. He had a father that was mean, and he never had a mother. So that's why I'm working here. That's why I have to stay here."

Sarah Haupt draws inspiration from a close friend who died from a self-induced abortion. This memory inspired her career in abortion care and motivated her to remain in the field notwithstanding the harassment:

> I'd lost a friend in the mid-sixties to a self-induced abortion, so I knew. I knew firsthand working in doctor's offices, trying to patch women back together who had criminal abortions, and I knew the experience of my friend who was so desperate that she self-induced and died. Of course, back in those days I never dreamed that the laws would be any different or that I would ever have anything to do with it. So when the opportunity came my way, it was a really easy decision.

Sarah explained that as her career progressed and she and her clinic faced mounting harassment, "what was right was to keep going, keep the clinic open, keep providing safe abortion care. That was the best way to honor the memory of those we'd lost."

Even for providers who did not live through the pre-*Roe* era or did not have family members who told personal stories of that era, knowledge of that time serves as a powerful motivator in the face of targeted harassment. Roberta Keller explained that she continues to work as a provider because of the stories that she has heard of the pre-*Roe* era. "I've heard the stories of entire wings of hospitals, twenty beds, all devoted to women who tried to have an abortion, and at the time it was illegal." During this time, women were "suffering" because "people who didn't know how to do abortions were putting lye in their vagina, were sticking coat hangers up and perforating their uterus and their intestines. In every single hospital in the country there were twenty women at all times very, very sick, losing their fertility and dying." Roberta concluded, "So that's a reason to continue. Women deserve healthcare."

## Conclusion

We conclude with these explanations about why providers continue because we hope that the message of this book is not completely one of fear and despair. It is certainly true, as detailed throughout, that life as an abortion provider can include targeted harassment in countless ways and that this terrorism can have a serious effect on providers' everyday lives. While there are significant legal improvements that can and should be made to help providers, such as the suggestions outlined in this book, targeted harassment left unremedied by the current legal framework will not end abortion in this country. Rather, abortion providers are too committed and too passionate to allow themselves to be dissuaded.

# NOTES

## Preface

1. The Guttmacher Institute publishes some of the most widely used and respected data about abortion in the United States. See Rachel K. Jones and Jenna Jerman, "Abortion Incidence and Service Availability in the United States, 2011," *Perspectives on Sexual and Reproductive Health* 46 (2014): 3–14.

2. Elizabeth G. Raymond and David A. Grimes, "The Comparative Safety of Legal Induced Abortion and Childbirth in the United States," *Obstetrics & Gynecology* 119 (2012): 215–19. On abortion safety generally, see Ushma D. Upadhyay et al., "Incidence of Emergency Department Visits and Complications After Abortion," *Obstetrics & Gynecology* 125 (2015): 175–183; Elizabeth G. Raymond and Daniel Grossman, "Mortality of Induced Abortion, Other Outpatient Surgical Procedures and Common Activities in the United States," *Contraception* 90 (2014): 476–79.

3. Jones and Jerman, "Abortion Incidence," supra note 1; Debra Stulberg et al., "Abortion Provision Among Practicing Obstetrician-Gynecologists," *Obstetrics & Gynecology* 118 (2011): 609–14.

## Introduction

1. Stephen Singular, *The Wichita Divide: The Murder of Dr. George Tiller and the Battle over Abortion* (New York: St. Martin's Press, 2011), 207–14.

2. Ibid., 13–17.

3. Ibid., 28–36.

4.  Ibid., 105–6; Gabriel Winant, "O'Reilly's Campaign against Murdered Doctor," Salon (May 31, 2009), http://www.salon.com/2009/05/31/ tiller_2/; "O'Reilly 2006 Anti-Tiller Rant," Media Matters for America (June 1, 2009), http://mediamatters.org/video/2009/06/01/ oreilly-2006-anti-tiller-ran t-if-i-could-get-my/i 50722.

5.  We use the term "anti-abortion" throughout the book rather than other terminology sometimes associated with the same position, such as "pro-life." As sociologist Dallas Blanchard has written, the term "pro-life" can incorporate other political concerns, such as the death penalty and war. Moreover, abortion providers often believe that providing abortion care furthers life by protecting women's lives. Therefore, because this book focuses on the single issue of opposition to abortion, it uses a term that clearly conveys that. See Dallas Blanchard, *The Anti-Abortion Movement and the Rise of the Religious Right: From Polite to Fiery Protest* (New York: Twayne Publishers, 1994), 1–2.

6.  Operation Rescue continues to exist, though it split into Operation Save America (based in Dallas, Texas) and Operation Rescue (based in Wichita, Kansas), which previously operated as Operation Rescue West. "History," Operation Rescue, http://www.operationrescue.org/about-us/ history/; "Operation Rescue," Montana Human Rights Network, http:// www.mhrn.org/publications/fact%20sheets%20and%20adivsories/ OperationRescue.pdf.

7.  Singular, *The Wichita Divide,* supra note 1, at 37–57.

8.  Ibid., 71–77; W Seth Carus, *Bioterrorism and Biocrimes: The Illicit Use of Biological Agents Since 1900* (Amsterdam, The Netherlands: Fredonia Books, 2002), 144–46.

9.  The Kansas Supreme Court ultimately disbarred Kline for his unprofessional actions in relentlessly pursuing Dr. Tiller. In re *Kline,* 311 P-3d 321 (Kan. 2013).

10.  Singular, *The Wichita Divide,* supra note 1, at 99–173.

11.  "The Assassination of Dr. Tiller," Crime and Courts, NBCNews.com (broadcast October 25, 2010), http://www.nbcnews.com/id/39826191/ns/ us_news-crime_and_courts/t/assassination-dr-tiller.

12.  Singular, *The Wichita Divide,* supra note 1, at 37–39, 93–98.

13.  A comprehensive compilation of the acts of violence around abortion through 2000 appears in Patricia Baird-Windle and Eleanor J. Bader, *Targets of Hatred: Anti-Abortion Terrorism* (New York: Palgrave, 2001).

14.  For a retelling of the events of Dr. David Gunn's murder, see ibid., 206–8; for the murder of Dr. John Britton and James Barrett, see ibid., 231–35; for the murders of Shannon Lowney and Leanne Nichols, see ibid., 244–50; for the murder of Robert Sanderson, see ibid., 298–302; for the murder of Dr. Barnett Slepian, see Eyal Press, *Absolute Convictions: My Father, a City, and the Conflict that Divided America* (New York: Henry Holt, 2006); and for the murder of Dr. George Tiller, see Singular, *The Wichita Divide*, supra note 1. A great summary of the most extreme acts

of violence can be found at "Anti-Choice Violence and Intimidation," NARAL Pro-Choice America Foundation, http://www.prochoiceamerica. org/assets/files/ abortion-access-to-abortion-violence.pdf.

15. Jessica Mason Pieklo, "Hearing for Accused Planned Parenthood Shooter Overlooks His Extreme Anti-Abortion Views," Rewire (April 29, 2016), https://rewire.news/article/2016/04/29/hearing-accused-planned-parenthood-shooter-anti-abortion-views/; Richard Fausset, "For Robert Dear, Religion and Rage Before Planned Parenthood Attack," *New York Times* (Dec. 1, 2015).

16. Scott Roeder is not alone as there are links between the militia movement and the anti-abortion movement. See, e.g., Carol Mason, *Killing for Life: The Apocalyptic Narrative of Pro-Life Violence* (Ithaca, NY: Cornell University Press, 2002), 9–45; Sandi DuBowski, "Storming Wombs and Waco: How the Anti-Abortion and Militia Movements Converge," *Front Lines Research* 2 (October 1996).

17. Singular, *The Wichita Divide,* supra note 1, at 46–70.

18. Ibid., 78–81, 112–16, 151–61, 194–200.

19. Ibid., 201–344; Judy L. Thomas, "Grand Jury Weighs Evidence of Conspiracy in Tiller Murder," *Kansas City Star* (December 26, 2010). Scott Roeder appealed his conviction to the Kansas Supreme Court and lost, though the case was remanded to a lower court to correct a sentencing error. *Kansas v. Roeder,* 336 P.3d 831 (Kan. 2014).

20. The National Abortion Federation (NAF) is a North American professional association of abortion providers. Its members provide over half the abortions in North America. One of the services NAF provides for its members and the public is a compilation of clinic violence and disruption statistics. The most recent report is available at "2015 Violence and Disruption Statistics," http://5aa1b2xfmfh2e2mk03kk8rsx.wpengine. netdna-cdn.com/wp-content/uploads/2015-NAF-Violence-Disruption-Stats.pdf. This information does not reflect the actual number of incidents, which "is likely to be significantly higher, because not all providers report to NAF and not all incidents are reported." *Brief of National Abortion Federation et al. as Amici Curiae in Support of Respondents and Affirmance in McCullen v. Coakley,* 134 S. Ct. 2518 (2014), at 8 n. 3.

21. Jackie Calmes, "Planned Parenthood Videos Were Altered, Analysis Finds," *New York Times* (Aug. 27, 2015).

22. Danielle Kurtzleben, "Planned Parenthood Investigations Find No Fetal Tissue Sales," NPR (Jan. 28, 2016); Gardiner Harris, "Abortion Rights Advocates Cry Foul at New Step in Fetal Tissue Inquiry," *New York Times* (Mar. 24, 2016).

23. National Abortion Federation, "2015 Violence and Disruption Statistics," supra note 20; Fausset, "For Robert Dear," supra note 15.

24. Joshua C. Wilson, *The Street Politics of Abortion: Speech, Violence, and America's Culture Wars* (Stanford, CA: Stanford University Press, 2013).

25. There is voluminous literature in this area. See, e.g., Catherine Cozzarelli and Brenda Major, "The Impact of Antiabortion Activities on Women

Seeking Abortions," in *The New Civil War: The Psychology, Culture, and Politics of Abortion,* ed. Linda J. Beckman and S. Marie Harvey (Washington, DC: American Psychological Association, 1998), 81–104; Alesha E. Doan, *Opposition & Intimidation: The Abortion Wars and Strategies of Political Harassment* (Ann Arbor: University of Michigan Press, 2007); Diana Greene Foster et al., "Effect of Abortion Protesters on Women's Emotional Response to Abortion," *Contraception* 87 (2013): 81–87; Mireille Jacobson and Heather Royer, "Aftershocks: The Impact of Clinic Violence on Abortion Services," *American Economic Journal: Applied Economics* 3 (2011): 189–223.

26.    Feminist Majority Foundation, "2014 National Clinic Violence Survey" (November 2014), 2.

27.    Doan, *Opposition & Intimidation,* supra note 21, at 36.

28.    Other authors have similarly called for such an expansive view of the term "abortion provider." Notably, sociologist and reproductive health scholar Carole Joffe favors a broad definition of the term because all of the types of people featured in this book are "important combatants in the abortion wars." Carole Joffe, *Dispatches from the Abortion Wars: The Costs of Fanaticism to Doctors, Patients, and the Rest of Us* (Boston: Beacon Press, 2011), xv. Carol Mason, an American studies professor who has researched the rise of right-wing movements, has also lamented that others who have studied abortion providers have ignored the "experience of those clinic workers who must daily withstand death threats or harassment," Mason, *Killing for Life,* supra note 15, at 71. This is far from a universal position however. Some even take issue with the term "provider" itself, as one of our interview subjects strenuously did. To him, the word conjures the image of people who provide services or goods, not doctors who perform a medical procedure. While we respect that position, we use "provider" because it is the convention of the field, and we use the word expansively for the reasons indicated in the text.

29.    Though targeted harassment of abortion providers is a serious, current, and widespread issue, very little is known or written about it as a distinct form of anti-abortion activity. The media does not pay close attention to abortion providers' everyday lived experiences, and others who have studied anti-abortion violence and harassment tend to combine targeted harassment with general clinic protest or political activism around abortion. See generally Baird-Windle and Bader, *Targets of Hatred,* supra note 13, at 13; Dallas A. Blanchard and Terry J. Prewitt, *Religious Violence and Abortion: The Gideon Project* (Gainesville: University Press of Florida, 1993); Lori Freedman, *Willing and Unable: Doctors' Constraints in Abortion Care* (Nashville, TN: Vanderbilt University Press, 2010); Joffe, *Dispatches from the Abortion Wars,* supra note 24, at 23; James Risen and Judy L. Thomas, *Wrath of Angels: The American Abortion War* (New York: Basic Books, 1998); Center for Reproductive Rights, "Defending Human Rights: Abortion

Providers Facing Threats, Restrictions, and Harassment" (2009). Several authors have written about particular incidents of targeted harassment. Jack Fainman, *They Shoot Doctors Don't They?: A Memoir,* with Roland Penner (Winnipeg, Canada: Great Plains Publications, 2011); Emily Lyons and Jeff Lyons, *Life's Been a Blast* (Homewood, AL: I Em Books, 2005); Press, *Absolute Convictions,* supra note 14; Singular, *The Wichita Divide,* supra note 1; Bruce S. Steir, *Jailhouse Journal of an OBI GKV*(Bloomington, IN: AuthorHouse, 2008); Susan Wicklund, *This Common Secret: My Journey as an Abortion Doctor* (New York: PublicAffairs, 2008). These sources are all important works about abortion protest and politics, but none has developed a comprehensive understanding of targeted harassment of abortion providers and how law may improve providers' lives.

30.  18 U.S.C. § 248. As a result of FACE, clinics have experienced fewer blockades, an anti-abortion protest tactic common in the 1980s and early 1990s in which protesters blocked the entrance to abortion clinics with their bodies and other items, rendering the clinic inaccessible and forcing the clinic to close or never even open for the day. FACE has also been used to address targeted harassment of abortion providers. See generally US General Accountability Office, *Abortion Clinics: Information on the Effectiveness of the Freedom of Access to Clinic Entrances Act* (Washington, DC, November 1988).

31.  Freedman, *Willing and Unable,* supra note 25, at 48–49. Political scientist Alesha Doan also studied the effects of harassment on abortion providers and concluded that " [h]arassment has been an important tool used by the direct action groups of the pro-life movement. It has been an effective way of contributing to the reduction in the number of abortion providers and has had an impact on women (evidenced in the abortion rate)." Doan, *Opposition & Intimidation,* supra note 21, at 154; see also Martin Donohue, "Increase in Obstacles to Abortion: The American Perspective in 2004," *Journal of the American Medical Women's Association 60* (2005): 16–25.

32.  410 U.S. 113 (1973).

33.  For example, the Supreme Court has demonstrated its lack of awareness around these issues, as evidenced by its 2014 decision in *McCullen v. Coakley.* In that case, the Court reviewed a Massachusetts law that kept protesters from the immediate vicinity of abortion clinics. In finding the law to be an unconstitutional infringement on anti-abortion demonstrators' speech, the Court refused to label the abortion opponents as "protesters," instead portraying these individuals as docile people wanting to calmly talk with and care for the women entering the abortion clinic. Without any reference to the harassment and intimidation tactics that abortion opponents regularly engage in at clinics as well as off-site, as described throughout this book, the Court struck down the law as unconstitutional. *McCullen,* 134 S. Ct. 2518 (2014). In light of *McCullen,*

providers' experiences with targeted harassment emerge as an untold story that is important for shaping law and policy in the immediate future.

34. Guttmacher Institute, "Last Five Years Account for More Than One-quarter of All Abortion Restrictions Enacted Since Roe" (January 13, 2016), https://www.guttmacher.org/article/2016/01/last-five-years-account-more-one-quarter-all-abortion-restrictions-enacted-roe.

35. Joshua Wilson has noted this tension in his study of abortion-rights activists and anti-abortion protesters and their understanding of the law. Both sides of the debate have reason to distrust law and the state, but nonetheless both see law and the state as important to their position. Joshua C. Wilson, "Sustaining the State: Legal Consciousness and the Construction of Legality in Competing Abortion Activists' Narratives," *Law & Social Inquiry* 36 (2011): 455–83.

36. Most of the interviews took place in 2011. A handful of new interviews took place in 2012 and 2013, and we conducted a small number of follow-up interviews in those years and in 2014.

37. In order to find the people we interviewed, we engaged in a complex process of working through existing contacts and the sources they provided us. From over one hundred providers interested in participating, we narrowed the list based on our goal of obtaining a diverse group of providers along the different characteristics mentioned in the text. In the academic language of qualitative empirical research, we used a snowball approach to arrive at a statistically nonrepresentative stratified sample. See Jan E. Trost, "Statistically Nonrepresentative Stratified Sampling: A Sampling Technique for Qualitative Studies," *Qualitative Sociology)* (1986): 54–57.

38. Rachel K. Jones and Jenna Jerman, "Abortion Incidence and Service Availability in the United States, 2011," *Perspectives on Sexual and Reproductive Health* 46 (2014): 3–14.

39. Lori Freedman, Carole Joffe, and other scholars have detailed this professional marginalization of abortion care and the resulting push of abortion care out of the mainstream hospital setting and into freestanding clinics, the lack of abortion care facilities, and, importantly, the lack of abortion providers. See Freedman, *Willing and Unable,* supra note 25; Joffe, *Dispatches from the Abortion Wars,* supra note 24.

40. Providers in the book are identified with a name generated from an Internet website that creates fake names. We use these pseudonyms consistently throughout the book, so the provider identified as Kristina Romero in Chapter 1 (the first provider profiled in that chapter) is identified as Kristina Romero throughout the book. When we first describe a particular provider, we give basic employment information and the region of the country where the provider has worked. Regions are based on the US Census Bureau regions, see "Census Regions and Divisions of the United States," US Census Bureau, http://www.census.gov/geo/maps-data/maps/pdfs/reference/us_regdiv.pdf, though because it

is a more familiar term, we use "Midwest" instead of "North Central." All of the providers have agreed to how we refer to them and have reviewed their references in the book for accuracy. Anytime we do not conform a provider's description to the general practice described here, we have done so because the provider requested a greater degree of generality or, in just a few cases, more specificity. For ease of reference, we provide an index at the end of the book of references to individual abortion providers.

41. We have also very lightly edited the quotes for readability.

42. Even Troy Newman, the president of Operation Rescue, conveyed this sentiment. See Janet Reitman, "The Stealth War on Abortion," *Rolling Stone* (January 15, 2014) (noting that Newman believes that the "overt harassment" of twenty years ago is a thing of the past).

43. Audrey Hudson, "Report Citing Veteran Extremism Is Pulled," *Washington Times* (May 14, 2009). The details of the controversy are explained in full at the end of Chapter 9.

44. For an example covering the debate, see David Paul, "Why Robert Lewis Dear Is Terrifying But Not a Terrorist," *Huffington Post* (Dec. 2, 2015), http://www.huffingtonpost.com/david-paul/robert-lewis-dear-is-terr_b_8697202.html.

45. Bruce Hoffman, *Inside Terrorism*, 40–41 (New York: Columbia University Press, 2006).

46. For excellent and varied analyses of the motivations behind anti-abortion protest and extremism, see Mason, *Killing for Life*, supra note 15; Faye D. Ginsburg, *Contested Lives: The Abortion Debate in an American Community* (Berkeley and Los Angeles: University of California Press, 1989); Blanchard, *The Anti-Abortion Movement*, supra note 5; Blanchard and Prewitt, *Religious Violence and Abortion*, supra note 25; Risen and Thomas, *Wrath of Angels*, supra note 25; Celeste Michelle Condit, *Decoding Abortion Rhetoric: Communicating Social Change* (Champaign: University of Illinois Press, 1990); Jessica Stern, *Terror in the Name of God: Why Religious Militants Kill* (New York: HarperCollins, 2003); Jennifer Jefferis, *Armed for Life: The Army of God and Anti-Abortion Terror in the United States* (Santa Barbara, CA: Praeger, 2011); Faye Ginsburg, "Rescuing the Nation: Operation Rescue and the Rise of Anti-Abortion Militance," in *Abortion Wars: A Half Century of Struggle, lp$0–2000,* ed. Rickie Solinger (Berkeley and Los Angeles: University of California Press, 1998), 227–50; Doan, *Opposition & Intimidation*, supra note 21; Marian Faux, *Crusaders: Voices from the Abortion Front* (New York: Birch Lane Press, 1990); Kerry N. Jacoby, *Souls, Bodies, Spirits: The Drive to Abolish Abortion since 1973* (Westport, CT: Praeger, 1998); Frederick S. Jaffe, *Abortion Politics: Private Morality and Public Policy* (New York: McGraw-Hill, 1980); Carol J. C. Maxwell, *Pro-Life Activists in America: Meaning, Motivation, and Direct Action* (Cambridge and New York: Cambridge University Press, 2002).

47.  According to the Feminist Majority Foundation, in 2010, 2.2% of
     staff resignations at clinics were the result of anti-abortion violence and
     harassment. Feminist Majority Foundation, "2010 National Clinic
     Violence Survey," 7.

## Chapter 1

1.  Eric Rudolph is an anti-abortion extremist responsible for bombing
    abortion clinics in Georgia in 1997 and Alabama in 1998 (the latter
    killing security guard Robert Sanderson) as well as the 1996 Olympics
    in Atlanta and a lesbian nightclub in Atlanta in 1997. Patricia
    Baird-Windle and Eleanor J. Bader, *Targets of Hatred: Anti-Abortion
    Terrorism* (New York: Palgrave, 2001), 302.
2.  Several providers we talked with discussed their experiences with anti-
    abortion protesters seeking abortion care. It is common for providers
    to wrestle with the issue of caring for patients who actively seek to
    stop the provider's line of work—or worse. See generally Joyce Arthur,
    "'The Only Moral Abortion Is My Abortion': When the Anti-Choice
    Choose," Pro-Choice Action Network (September 2000), http://www.
    prochoiceactionnetwork-canada.org/articles/anti-tales.shtml.

## Chapter 2

1.  Joseph M. Scheidler, *Closed: 99 Ways to Stop Abortion* (Wheaton,
    IL: Crossway Books, 1985), 151.
2.  This chapter, like the others that follow, comprehensively summarizes
    and categorizes the stories providers told us during our interviews
    with them. The chapters do not, however, recount every relevant story
    we were told as this would be repetitive and too lengthy. Rather, the
    chapters include representative examples of each topic being analyzed.
3.  See generally Patricia Baird-Windle and Eleanor J. Bader, *Targets of
    Hatred: Anti-Abortion Terrorism* (New York: Palgrave, 2001).
4.  *Frisby v. Schultz*, 487 U.S. 474, 484 (1988).
5.  Jack Fainman, *They Shoot Doctors Don't They? A Memoir*, with Roland
    Penner (Winnipeg, Canada: Great Plains Publications, 2011).
6.  In August 1993, Dr. George Wayne Patterson was shot and killed at a
    movie theater in Mobile, Alabama. Dr. Patterson owned and was the
    doctor at four abortion clinics in Alabama and Florida. Although some
    people believe Dr. Patterson's murder is related to his profession as
    an abortion provider, his case was never solved and there was never a
    definitive link to abortion. Baird-Windle and Bader, *Targets of Hatred*,
    supra note 3, at 220–21; Ronald Smothers, "Abortion Doctor's Slaying Is
    Baffling Police in Mobile," *New York Times* (August 29, 1993).
7.  There are many reported decisions in this case, the last of which is
    *Planned Parenthood of Columbia/Willamette, Inc. v. American Coalition
    of Life Activists*, 518 F.3d 1013 (9th Cir. 2008). *Planned Parenthood of*

*Columbia/Willamette, Inc. v. American Coalition of Life Activists*, 41 F. Supp. 2d 1130 (D. Or. 1999), sets out the facts in detail. This case is discussed in more depth in Chapter 8.

## Chapter 3

1. As discussed in Chapter 2, abortion provider Dr. George Wayne Patterson was shot and killed at a movie theater in Mobile, Alabama, in August 1993. His murder was never officially linked to his profession. Patricia Baird-Windle and Eleanor J. Bader, *Targets of Hatred: Anti-Abortion Terrorism* (New York: Palgrave, 2001), 220–21.

2. Sarah also worked with Dr. Patterson and is one of the people who firmly believe that Dr. Patterson's murder was another incident of anti-abortion violence:

   It happened on a Saturday evening. He had gone downtown, there's kind of an arts district, with some good little restaurants, and he had gone down there and had supper and was heading back to his car in the parking lot behind the restaurant and was shot right there in the parking lot. Some of the buildings down there, they've renovated and they have apartments over stores or other businesses, so there were a couple of witnesses who saw it, and according to them, this slight man walked up to him and shot him in the chest, and when he fell he shot him in the neck. He assassinated him, no question about it.

   I still think this was abortion-related, even though we never saw, not that I knew of, the man who murdered Dr. Patterson protesting at my location. The protesters were, and this is hard to take, showing up on the sidewalk in front of the clinic rejoicing. Shouting "Hallelujah" and "Live by the sword, die by the sword."

3. Baird-Windle and Bader, *Targets of Hatred*, supra note 1, details all of these attacks. See also Jack Fainman, *They Shoot Doctors Don't They? A Memoir*, with Roland Penner (Winnipeg, Canada; Great Plains Publications, 2011); Emily Lyons and Jeff Lyons, *Life's Been a Blast* (Homewood, AL: I Em Books, 2005).

4. Jennifer Jefferis, *Armed for Life: The Army of God and Anti-Abortion Terror in the United States* (Santa Barbara, CA: Praeger, 2011), 23.

5. Associated Press, "Man Arrested, Charged in Fla. Abortion Clinic Fire," *USA Today* (January 5, 2012); Justin Franz, "Suspect Arrested in Kalispell Abortion Clinic Break-In," *Flathead Beacon* (March 5, 2014).

6. See Julie Palmer, "Seeing and Knowing: Ultrasound Images in the Contemporary Abortion Debate," *Feminist Theory* 10 (2009): 173–89; Rosalind Pollack Petchesky, "Fetal Images: The Power of Visual Culture in the Politics of Reproduction," *Feminist Studies* 13 (1987): 263–92.

7. See Carol Mason, *Killing for Life: The Apocalyptic Narrative of Pro-Life Violence* (Ithaca, NY: Cornell University Press, 2002) (tracing religion's

role in the anti-abortion movement); Carole Joffe and Willie J. Parker, "Race, Reproductive Politics and Reproductive Health Care in the Contemporary United States," *Contraception* 86 (2012): 1–3 (discussing the connection with race and abortion opposition); Dorothy Roberts, "Toward Common Ground on Policies Advancing Reproductive Justice," in *In Search of Common Ground on Abortion: From Culture War to Reproductive Justice*, eds. Robin West, Justin Murray, and Meredith Esser (Burlington, VT: Ashgate, 2014), 109–16 (same); Loretta J. Ross, "Fighting the Black Anti-Abortion Campaign: Trusting Black Women," *On the Issues Magazine* (Winter 2011) (same). For example, protesters yelled at Carolyn Barrick that "I'm worse than Hitler. I hate babies. I hate black people."

8. Carol Mason has detailed how stereotypes about providers' race, religion, and sexual orientation play into anti-abortion ideology. Mason, *Killing for Life*, supra note 7, at 171–79. In particular, she writes that "[b]y portraying abortion providers as shucking and jiving African Americans or greedy Jews, whose assistants are lascivious lesbians, recent pro-life writing indicts particular groups without bringing them together" (p. 176). The stories here prove that these themes also inform the targeted harassment providers face on a daily basis.

9. *Planned Parenthood of Columbia/Willamette, Inc. v. American Coalition of Life Activists*, 41 F. Supp. 2d 1130 (D. Or. 1999).

10. In early 2014, anti-abortion activists targeted three people associated with abortion, a social media contributor, a journalist, and a doctor, in an online poster and blog post reminiscent of the "Wanted"-style targeting. See David S. Cohen and Krysten Connon, "When Anti-Abortion Harassment Gets Personal," TPM (March 28, 2014), http://talkingpointsmemo.com/cafe/when-anti-abortion-harassment-gets-personal.

11. Carole Joffe, *Dispatches from the Abortion Wars: The Costs of Fanaticism to Doctors, Patients, and the Rest of Us* (Boston: Beacon Press, 2011), 48. Joffe notes that against the backdrop of technological advances in abortion care and anesthesia starting in the late 1960s, which eliminated the need for hospital surgical procedures for abortion care, the freestanding clinic model emerged as the site for abortion care, in part because "clinic directors were (and still are) free to hire staff members, such as nurses, counselors, and receptionists, supportive of abortion and abortion patients. In contrast, hospitals back then did not have the flexibility to assign only supportive staff members to abortion work, a situation that continues in many hospitals today."

12. This effect of professional harassment and the stigma surrounding abortion care is explored extensively in Chapter 5 of Lori Freedman, *Willing and Unable: Doctors' Constraints in Abortion Care* (Nashville, TN: Vanderbilt University Press, 2010).

13. Ibid., 93–94.

14. Ibid., 102–03.

15. An increasing number of states are requiring abortion doctors to have hospital privileges. As a result, an emerging anti-abortion protest tactic

is to picket hospitals to pressure them to refuse privileges to providers. See Robin Marty, "Anti-Abortion Protesters Are Coming to a Hospital Near You," Think Progress (May 30, 2014), http://thinkprogress.org/health/2014/05/30/3442899/hospitals-abortion-access/.

16. These laws greatly concern many providers. Marietta Spring said that these laws are "much bigger" and "much scarier" to her than "the idiot on the corner with the sign." Albert Tall characterized these anti-abortion laws as "disruptive," just like the targeted harassment he has faced. For an excellent discussion of this new wave of anti-abortion legislation, see Robin Marty and Jessica Mason Pieklo, *Crow After Roe: How "Separate but Equal" Has Become the New Standard in Women's Health and How We Can Change That* (New York: Ig Publishing, 2013).

17. The authors of the study differentiated between violence (bombings, arson, gunfire, chemical attacks, anthrax hoax letters, bomb threats, arson threats), vandalism (clinic invasion, robbery, break-in, and other building/site damage), and harassment (blockades, noise disturbances, videotaping or photographing, threats, approaching cars, lawsuits, Internet harassment, and other harassing behavior). Jennefer A. Russo, Kristin L. Schumacher, and Mitchell D. Creinin, "Antiabortion Violence in the United States," *Contraception* 86 (2012): 562–66.

18. Rickie Solinger, "Pregnancy and Power Before *Roe v. Wade*, 1950–1970," in *Abortion Wars: A Half Century of Struggle, 1950–2000*, ed. Rickie Solinger (Berkeley and Los Angeles: University of California Press, 1998), 17–20; Rickie Solinger, *The Abortionist: A Woman Against the Law* (Berkeley and Los Angeles: University of California Press, 1994), 195–218.

## Chapter 4

1. Susan Wicklund, *This Common Secret: My Journey as an Abortion Doctor* (New York: Public Affairs, 2007), 80.

## Chapter 5

1. Carol Mason, *Killing for Life: The Apocalyptic Narrative of Pro-Life Politics* (Ithaca, NY: Cornell University Press, 2002), 57–58.

2. Ibid.

3. Lisa Harris et al., "Physicians, Abortion Provision and the Legitimacy Paradox," *Contraception* 87 (2013): 11–16.

4. "48% said that the protesters did not upset them at all, 25% said they were a little bit upset, 12% reported being moderately upset, 9% reported being quite a bit upset, and 7% were extremely upset." Diana Greene Foster et al., "Effect of Abortion Protesters on Women's Emotional Response to Abortion," *Contraception* 87 (2013): 81–87.

5. Katrina Kimport, Kate Cockrill, and Tracy A. Weitz, "Analyzing the Impacts of Abortion Clinic Structures and Processes: A Qualitative Analysis of Women's Negative Experience of Abortion Clinics," *Contraception* 85 (2012): 204–10.

## Chapter 6

1. Lisa Harris calls this difficult decision that many providers face "disclosure management." Lisa Hope Harris et al., "Dynamics of Stigma in Abortion Work: Findings from a Pilot Study of the Providers Share Workshop," *Social Science & Medicine* 73 (2011): 1062–70.

2. Lori A. Brown, *Contested Spaces: Abortion Clinics, Women's Shelters and Hospitals* (Farnham, UK: Ashgate, 2013), 95–187.

3. These security considerations stand in stark contrast to the growing trend among states to impose burdensome design and architectural requirements on abortion clinics that are not medically necessary. For an overview of these laws, see Guttmacher Institute, "Targeted Regulation of Abortion Providers," State Policies in Brief, http://www.guttmacher.org/statecenter/spibs/spib_TRAP.pdf; Rachel Benson Gold and Elizabeth Nash, "TRAP Laws Gain Political Traction While Abortion Clinics—and the Women They Serve—Pay the Price," *Guttmacher Policy Review* 16 (2013): 7.

4. Katrina Kimport, Kate Cockrill, and Tracy A. Weitz, "Analyzing the Impacts of Abortion Clinic Structures and Processes: A Qualitative Analysis of Women's Negative Experience of Abortion Clinics," *Contraception* 85 (2012): 204–10.

## Chapter 7

1. International law can be another source of law. The Center for Reproductive Rights has been doing important work attempting to use international law to protect abortion providers. The Center's work has focused on abortion providers as human-rights defenders. See Center for Reproductive Rights, "Recognizing Abortion Providers as Human Rights Defenders," http://reproductiverights.org/en/project/recognizing-abortion-providers-as-human-rights-defenders. Although this is an important legal theory that may provide protection for providers, the providers we talked with did not have experience using international law to address their problems with targeted harassment.

2. In order to avoid identifying Calvin, we do not use the actual language from the ordinance. Calvin's description of the ordinance here comports with the ordinance's language.

3. 18 U.S.C § 248. FACE is described in more detail in Chapter 8.

4. In opt-out training programs, medical training is provided to all residents except those who affirmatively choose not to participate. See Carole Joffe, *Dispatches From the Abortion Wars: The Costs of Fanaticism to Doctors, Patients, and the Rest of Us* (Boston: Beacon Press, 2009), 25–27.

## Chapter 8

1. Michael Wines, "Senate Approves Bill to Protect Abortion Clinics," *New York Times* (May 13, 1994).

2. Organizations working on issues of clinic violence and provider harassment have compiled some of these laws. See National Abortion

Federation, "Legal Remedies to Address Clinic Violence and Harassment: A Handbook for NAF Members" (2014), http://prochoice. org/wp-content/uploads/Legal_Remedies.pdf; NOW Legal Defense and Education Fund and The Feminist Majority Foundation, "Drawing the Line Against Anti-Abortion Violence and Harassment" (1996 with revisions), http://www.feminist.org/rrights/pdf/DrawingtheLine.pdf.

3.  *Abortion Clinic Violence: Hearings Before the Subcomm. on Crime and Criminal Justice of the H. Comm. on the Judiciary*, 103d Cong. 213–36 (June 10, 1993) (statement of Janet Reno, US Attorney General). Two briefs filed in the 1993 Supreme Court case of *Bray v. Alexandria Women's Health Clinic* give excellent descriptions of the clinic violence and blockades of that era. See *Brief of 29 Organizations Committed to Women's Health and Women's Equality as Amici Curiae in Support of Respondents, Bray v. Alexandria Women's Health Clinic*, 506 U.S. 263 (1993); *Brief for the National Abortion Federation and Planned Parenthood Federation of America, Inc. as Amici Curiae in Support of Respondents, Bray v. Alexandria Women's Health Clinic*, 506 U.S. 263 (1993).

4.  *Abortion Clinic Violence*, supra note 3.

5.  Wines, "Senate Approves Bill," supra note 1.

6.  18 U.S.C. § 248.

7.  Robert Pear, "After New Law, Abortion-Clinic Protests Fall," *New York Times* (September 24, 1996).

8.  National Abortion Federation, "NAF Violence and Disruption Statistics," http://prochoice.org/wp-content/uploads/Stats_Table2. pdf. NAF statistics do not separate out events in 1994, when FACE was passed in May. The most recent data from the Feminist Majority Foundation show similar trends. Feminist Majority Foundation, "2014 National Clinic Violence Survey" (November 2014).

9.  Several states have their own version of FACE with similar protections as the federal law. See, e.g., *Cal. Penal Code* § 423. None of the providers we interviewed mentioned these state laws. The National Abortion Federation includes these laws in its compilation of legal remedies for abortion providers. See National Abortion Federation, "Legal Remedies," supra note 2.

10.  In 2000, the Supreme Court upheld a Colorado law that created a floating eight-foot bubble zone within a one hundred-foot buffer zone outside of Colorado abortion clinics after determining that the content and viewpoint-neutral buffer zone law was narrowly tailored to serve Colorado's legitimate interest in protecting the area surrounding abortion clinics and patients. *Hill v. Colorado*, 530 U.S. 703 (2000). In June 2014, the Supreme Court affirmed that, in general, the constitutionality of buffer zone laws is determined by looking at whether the law is narrowly tailored to serve the government interest that it seeks to advance—in other words, that the law does not burden more speech than is necessary to further the government's interests. *McCullen v. Coakley*, 134 S. Ct. 2518 (2014). While the *McCullen* Court found that the Massachusetts buffer zone law at issue

served the state's legitimate interest in "ensuring public safety and order, promoting the free flow of traffic on streets and sidewalks, protecting property rights, and protecting a woman's freedom to seek pregnancy-related services," the Court ultimately concluded that the Massachusetts buffer zone did not pass constitutional muster because the specific buffer zone was too burdensome on the plaintiffs' speech (p. 2535 (quoting *Schenck v. Pro-Choice Network of Western N.Y.*, 519 U.S. 357, 376 (1997))). As of the writing of this book, it appears as though narrowly tailored buffer zone laws remain a viable option for localities as the Supreme Court did not explicitly overturn *Hill* or otherwise state that buffer zones are automatically unconstitutional. Nonetheless, some states and localities have refused to enforce their buffer zones in light of *McCullen*, and other places that continue to enforce theirs are being threatened with litigation.

11.  Cynthia Kendrick voiced the opinion of many of the providers we interviewed when she said that these types of laws made "a huge, huge difference" with general clinic protest. Cynthia cautioned, though, that these laws are "only as good as the police who enforce them."

12.  A 2013 member survey by the National Abortion Federation supports this position. The survey found that 92% of the 112 responding clinics were "concerned about the safety of their patients and employees in the areas approaching the facility" and that 57% of the facilities reported in the past two years that "facility employees have expressed concerns for their personal safety." On buffer zones in particular, 76% of surveyed clinics that had buffer zones in place thought that the buffer zone changed safety and access around the clinic in a positive or even strongly positive manner, while none of the responding clinics believed that it had a negative or strongly negative effect. *Brief of National Abortion Federation et al. as Amici Curiae in Support of Respondents and Affirmance, McCullen v. Coakley*, 134 S. Ct. 2518 (2014), at 16 & Appx. C.

13.  California Safe at Home, "Enrolling Agency Guide: Reproductive Health Care Services," http://www.sos.ca.gov/safeathome/forms/reproductive-guide-bowen.pdf.

14.  *Cal. Gov. Code* § 6215.2(1).

15.  Ibid., §§ 6215, 6215.5, 6215.7.

16.  This provider is not identified here, even with a pseudonym, so as to not link the provider to a specific state.

17.  The National Center for Victims of Crime has an excellent website that gives an overview of stalking laws and details the specifics for each state with links to each state's laws. See National Center for Victims of Crime, Stalking Resource Center, "Stalking Laws," http://www.victimsofcrime.org/our-programs/stalking-resource-center/stalking-laws; see also Amy M. Sneirson, "No Place to Hide: Why State and Federal Enforcement of Stalking Laws May Be the Best Way to Protect Abortion Providers," *Washington University Law Quarterly* 73 (1995): 635–64.

18. Several commentators have written about civil remedies in this regard. See Alice Clapman, "Privacy Rights and Abortion Outing: A Proposal for Using Common-Law Torts to Protect Abortion Patients and Staff," *Yale Law Journal* 112 (2003): 1545–76; Rachel L. Braunstein, "A Remedy for Abortion Seekers Under the Invasion of Privacy Tort," *Brooklyn Law Review* 68 (2002): 309–50; Angela Christina Couch, "Wanted: Privacy Protection for Doctors Who Perform Abortions," *American University Journal of Gender and the Law* 4 (1996): 361–414.

19. 28 U.S.C. § 566. Federal regulation spells out these duties in more detail. 28 C.F.R. § 0.111.

20. The National Task Force on Violence Against Health Care Providers, also sometimes referred to as the National Task Force on Violence Against Reproductive Health Care Workers, is discussed in more depth in Chapter 9. See US Department of Justice, "National Task Force on Violence Against Health Care Providers: Overview," http://www.justice.gov/crt/about/crm/faceweb.php.

21. The last reported decision is *Planned Parenthood of Columbia/Willamette, Inc. v. American Coalition of Life Activists*, 518 F.3d 1013 (9th Cir. 2008). Other key opinions can be found at *Planned Parenthood of Columbia/Willamette, Inc. v. American Coalition of Life Activists*, 290 F.3d 1058 (9th Cir. 2002) (en banc decision upholding verdict against defendants), and *Planned Parenthood of Columbia/Willamette, Inc. v. American Coalition of Life Activists*, 41 F. Supp. 2d 1130 (D. Or. 1999) (final trial court decision against defendants).

22. See, e.g., *Tompkins v. Cyr*, 202 F.3d 770 (5th Cir. 2000) (affirming verdict against anti-abortion protesters for intentional infliction of emotional distress, invasion of privacy, and civil conspiracy against an abortion doctor and his wife).

23. However, the number of civil FACE cases brought by the federal government varied under the different presidents. From 1999 through 2007, only one civil FACE case was filed, whereas from 2009 to 2012, the Department of Justice opened twenty investigations and filed eight complaints. See US Department of Justice Civil Rights Division, "Protecting Women's Rights" (2012), 3, http://www.justice.gov/crt/publications/wmnrights.pdf.

## Chapter 9

1. A small number of providers leave the field because of targeting. The Feminist Majority Foundation has estimated that 2.2% of staff resignations at clinics are because of harassment. See Feminist Majority Foundation, "2010 National Clinic Violence Survey" (September 2010), 7. Moreover, others never enter the field in the first place out of fear. For instance, Anthony Ward's daughter was so affected by the harassment Anthony faced that, even though she's now a pro-choice gynecologist, she does not provide abortions, out of fear of protesters. Medical

sociologist Lori Freedman has studied people, like Anthony's daughter, who avoid the field of abortion care out of fear. See Lori Freedman, *Willing and Unable: Doctors' Constraints in Abortion Care* (Nashville, TN: Vanderbilt University Press, 2010), 48–49.

2.  On the history in the United States, see Leslie J. Reagan, *When Abortion Was a Crime: Women, Medicine, and Law in the United States 1867–1973* (Berkeley and Los Angeles: University of California Press, 1997); Carole Joffe, *Doctors of Conscience: The Struggle to Provide Abortion Before and After* Roe v. Wade (Boston: Beacon Press, 1996). On the current situation internationally, see World Health Organization, *Unsafe Abortion: Global and Regional Estimates of the Incidence of Unsafe Abortion and Associated Mortality in 2008*, 6th ed. (2011), http://whqlibdoc.who.int/publications/2011/9789241501118_eng.pdf; David A. Grimes et al., "Unsafe Abortion: The Preventable Pandemic," *Lancet* 368 (2006): 1908–19. On the current situation in the United States and in Texas, where abortion has been seriously restricted since 2013, see Daniel Grossman et al., "The Public Health Threat of Anti-Abortion Legislation," *Contraception* 89 (2014): 73–74; Laura Bassett, "The Return of the Back-Alley Abortion," Huffington Post (April 3, 2014), http://www.huffingtonpost.com/2014/04/03/back-alley-abortions_n_5065301.html; Amanda Robb, "An Interview with a Texas Abortion Doctor Who Can No Longer Do His Job," The Investigative Fund (December 16, 2013), http://www.theinvestigativefund.org/blog/1898/an_interview_with_a_texas_abortion_doctor_who_can_no_longer_do_his_job/. For an accessible look at all of these issues together, see David A. Grimes and Linda G. Brandon, *Every Third Woman in America: How Legal Abortion Transformed Our Nation* (Carolina Beach, NC: Daymark Publishing, 2014).

3.  A 2003 special report to the California legislature also includes other suggestions for law enforcement in dealing with anti-abortion crimes. See Robert Richard Springborn, "Special Report to the Legislature on Senate Bill 780: California Freedom of Access to Clinic and Church Entrances Act and Reproductive Rights Law Enforcement Act" (2003), http://oag.ca.gov/sites/all/files/agweb/pdfs/cjsc/publications/misc/net780/rpt.pdf.

4.  James Risen and Judy L. Thomas, *Wrath of Angels: The American Abortion War* (New York: Basic Books, 1998), 361–64. After the murders, the clinic director "called the Justice Department back and said, 'Now is it the time to make an arrest? Now?'" (p. 365).

5.  Susan Saulny and Monica Davey, "Suspect in Doctor's Killing Tied to Vandalism Case," *New York Times* (June 2, 2009); Democracy Now, "Abortion Clinic Manager Reveals He Warned FBI of Suspect in Murder of Dr. George Tiller, Says Killing Could Have Been Avoided" (June 3, 2009), http://www.democracynow.org/2009/6/3/jeff.

6.  *McCullen v. Coakley*, 134 S. Ct. 2518 (2014). When the Supreme Court reviewed a First Amendment challenge to a fixed buffer zone law in

Massachusetts, it expressed concern that the state had not shown there were past violations of the law necessitating the buffer zone. The Court expressly noted that, before the law, the police department "made 'no more than five or so arrests' at the Planned Parenthood in Boston and that what few prosecutions had been brought were unsuccessful" (p. 2526). The Court ultimately found that while Massachusetts had a legitimate interest in protecting the space outside of reproductive health facilities in the state, the fixed buffer zone law placed too great a burden on the protesters' speech (pp. 2534–41). While the ultimate effect of *McCullen* has yet to be determined, the Court's opinion in this case demonstrates the importance of no tolerance policing and maintaining records of all violations around abortion clinics.

7.  Feminist Majority Foundation, "2014 National Clinic Violence Survey" (November 2014), 8.

8.  *See* generally *Dennis v. Sparks*, 449 U.S. 24 (1980); *Adickes v. S.H. Kress & Co.*, 398 U.S. 144 (1970).

9.  In striking down the Massachusetts fixed buffer zone law in *McCullen v. Coakley*, supra note 6, the Supreme Court rejected as inconsequential a police officer's testimony that a fixed buffer zone law would "make our job so much easier" and suggested other means for law enforcement to police the area around abortion clinics, none involving such bright-line guidelines as a fixed buffer zone. The Court concluded that other means of policing are available and not "nearly so difficult" as the police and Massachusetts suggested (*McCullen*, p. 2540). Notwithstanding the Court's opinion in this case, the experiences of the providers we interviewed echo the officer's testimony and demonstrate that police are more responsive and better able to maintain a safe environment when they have a clear law to enforce. Based on the experiences of the providers interviewed for this book, it appears that jettisoning a fixed buffer zone law, such as the now unconstitutional law in Massachusetts, will likely create more confusion for law enforcement officers seeking to maintain order and safety around abortion clinics.

10. See US Department of Justice Civil Rights Division, "Protecting Women's Rights" (2012), 3, http://www.justice.gov/crt/publications/wmnrights.pdf.

11. US Department of Justice, "National Task Force on Violence Against Health Care Providers: Overview," http://www.justice.gov/crt/about/crm/faceweb.php.

12. *Frisby v. Shultz*, 487 U.S. 474 (1988).

13. Ibid., 485–88.

14. Ibid., 484–85.

15. Ibid., 487–88.

16. *Madsen v. Women's Health Center, Inc.*, 512 U.S. 753, 775 (1994).

17. See, e.g., *Klein v. San Diego County*, 463 F.3d 1029 (9th Cir. 2006); *Veneklase v. City of Fargo*, 248 F.3d 738 (8th Cir. 2001); *Douglas v. Brownell*, 88 F.3d 1511 (8th Cir. 1996); *Murray v. Lawson*, 138 N.J. 206

(1994). The United States Court of Appeals for the Eleventh Circuit recently upheld the residential picketing provision of a municipal ordinance, passed by the city of Winter Park, Florida, which creates a fifty-foot buffer area around residential properties and prohibits picketing targeted at a person, group of people, or type of person living at the property. *Bell v. City of Winter Park*, 745 F.3d 1318 (11th Cir. 2014). Despite protesters' challenge to the ordinance, the Eleventh Circuit analogized the Winter Park ordinance to the law at issue in *Frisby* and similarly found that "the type of picketers banned by the Winter Park ordinance generally do not seek to disseminate a message to the general public, but to intrude upon the targeted resident, and to do so in an especially offensive way" (at 1323, quoting *Frisby*, at 486).

18. For confidentiality purposes, this provider did not want even her pseudonym connected with this story.

19. 18 U.S.C. § 248(b) (criminal penalties); § 248(c) (civil penalties).

20. Alison M. Smith and Cassandra L. Foley, "Congressional Research Service: State Statutes Governing Hate Crimes" (September 28, 2010), http://www.fas.org/sgp/crs/misc/RL33099.pdf.

21. *Wisconsin v. Mitchell*, 508 U.S. 476 (1993).

22. *Wis. Stat.* § 939.645.

23. National Center for Victims of Crime, Stalking Resource Center, "Analyzing Stalking Laws," http://www.victimsofcrime.org/docs/src/analyzing-stalking-statute.pdf?sfvrsn=2.

24. For instance, as of the editing of this book, San Francisco law enforcement officials are vigorously enforcing a provision of the city code that prohibits "aggressive pursuit of another" as a way to protect abortion clinics. Jonah Owen Lamb, "SFPD Keeps Abortion Clinics Safe and Gives First Amendment Rights to Protesters," *San Francisco Examiner* (September 5, 2014). Other jurisdictions may consider similar laws as a way to prevent abortion providers from being followed and harassed.

25. Two recent efforts, in Tennessee and Indiana, highlight this concern. In 2012, the Tennessee legislature proposed a bill that would require the online publication of the names of all doctors who perform abortions. See Richard Fausset, "Tennessee Abortion Bill Would Require Publishing Names of Doctors," *Los Angeles Times* (March 19, 2012). The reporting provisions were ultimately removed from the version of the bill that passed. See HB3808 Amendment No. 1, HA 0954 (March 21, 2012). In Indiana, legislators proposed making certain abortion clinic licensure agreements publicly available and thereby exposing the identities of the clinic workers and hospital staff involved in the agreements. While the legislation was pending, we and several others contacted the Indiana legislative committees involved and highlighted the issue of targeted harassment and the problems that could stem from such publicly available information. In the end, the particular provision at issue was removed from the final version of the legislation. See Brandon Smith, "Abortion Bill

Changes Address Privacy Concerns," Indiana Public Media (February 25, 2014), http://indianapublicmedia.org/news/abortion-bill-address-privacy-concerns-63519/.

26. *Cal. Gov't Code* § 6215; California Safe at Home, "Enrolling Agency Guide: Reproductive Health Care Services," http://www.sos.ca.gov/safeathome/forms/reproductive-guide-bowen.pdf.

27. 18 U.S.C. § 2725(3). The Supreme Court has upheld the law as constitutional. *Reno v. Condon*, 528 U.S. 141 (2000).

28. *Protecting Driver's Privacy, Hearings, Subcommittee on Civil and Constitutional Rights of House Judiciary Committee* (1994); Cong. Rec. S15761-65 (November 16, 1993); Cong. Rec. H2522-24 (April 20, 1994).

29. *Brief of Feminist Majority Foundation et al. Amici Curiae in Support of Petitioner United States, Reno v. Condon*, 528 U.S. 141 (2000) (No. 98-1464).

30. The law would have to be carefully crafted to avoid constitutionality issues that the consent-based law avoided in *Reno*, such as by tying it to federal spending. If it cannot be crafted to avoid these issues, the California law should become a model for other states.

31. There is a voluminous literature around what is commonly called "civil Gideon." *Gideon v. Wainwright*, 372 U.S. 335 (1963), guarantees criminal defendants a lawyer if they cannot afford one. There is no such constitutional right for civil cases, though there are efforts throughout the country to increase access to legal representation in civil cases. See generally National Coalition for a Civil Right to Counsel, http://www.civilrighttocounsel.org/.

32. *Madsen*, supra note 16, at 773. Representative lower court cases that have applied this principle from *Madsen* are *Planned Parenthood of the Columbia/Willamette, Inc. v. American Coalition of Life Activists*, 290 F.3d 1058 (9th Cir. 2002); *United States v. Hart*, 212 F.3d 1067 (8th Cir. 2000); *United States v. Dinwiddie*, 76 F.3d 913 (8th Cir. 1996); *United States v. McMillan*, 53 F. Supp. 2d 895 (S.D. Miss. 1999).

33. *Watts v. United States*, 394 U.S. 705, 707 (1969) ("What is a threat must be distinguished from what is constitutionally protected speech"); see also Kenneth L. Karst, "Threats and Meanings: How the Facts Govern First Amendment Doctrine," *Stanford Law Review* 58 (2006): 1337–1412.

34. *Virginia v. Black*, 538 U.S. 343, 359–60 (2003).

35. *Planned Parenthood*, supra note 32.

36. *United States v. Hart*, supra note 32.

37. *United States v. McMillan*, supra note 32.

38. *Planned Parenthood*, supra note 32, at 1077; *United States v. Dinwiddie*, supra note 32, at 924–25.

39. Factors can include whether the alleged threat was conditional, whether it was directed at and communicated to the listener, how many times the alleged threat happened, how the listener and others reacted, and whether the listener reasonably believed that violence could occur. This list is not exhaustive, nor is any one factor required or determinative. *Planned Parenthood*, supra note 32, at 1078; *United States v. Dinwiddie*, supra note 32, at 925.

40.  *Virginia v. Black*, supra note 34, at 352–57.

41.  *Planned Parenthood*, supra note 32, at 1078–80.

42.  *United States v. Hart*, supra note 32, at 1072.

43.  *United States v. McMillan*, supra note 32, at 905.

44.  *United States v. Smith*, No. 4:95 CV 25, at 34–35 ¶ 17 (E.D. Ohio, 1995).

45.  Alesha E. Doan, *Opposition & Intimidation: The Abortion Wars and Strategies of Political Harassment* (Ann Arbor: University of Michigan Press, 2007), 3.

46.  Celia B. Harris et al., "Collaborative Recall and Collective Memory: What Happens When We Remember Together?" in *From Individual to Collective Memory: Theoretical and Empirical Perspectives*, eds. Amanda J. Barnier and John Sutton (New York: Psychology Press, 2008), 213–30.

47.  It is controversial, but it is not unprecedented, as we are far from the first commentators to use this term to describe targeted harassment of abortion providers. See, e.g., Carole Joffe, "Terrorizing Abortion Providers: The 'Other Abortion War' Quietly Continues," RH Reality Check (April 5, 2011), http://rhrealitycheck.org/article/2011/04/05/terrorizing-abortion-providers-other-abortion-warquietly-continues/ ("[G]iven the totality of the record of violence against providers since the 1970s—[targeted harassment tactics should be seen] as one element of a larger campaign of genuine terrorism"); Carol Mason, "Who's Afraid of Virginia Dare? Confronting Anti-Abortion Terrorism After 9/11," *University of Pennsylvania Journal of Constitutional Law* 6 (2004): 796–817; Frederick Clarkson, *Eternal Hostility: The Struggle Between Theocracy and Democracy* (Monroe, ME: Common Courage Press, 1997), 139–85; Anne Bower, "Shelley Shannon: A Soldier in the Army of God—Part I," *Body Politic* 5 (1995): 14 ("These people easily classify as domestic terrorists who should be taken seriously"); Michele Wilson and John Lynxwiler, "Abortion Clinic Violence as Terrorism," *Terrorism* 11 (1988): 263–73.

48.  US Department of Homeland Security, "Domestic Extremism Lexicon" (March 26, 2009), http://www.webcitation.org/5gYPnOstE.

49.  US Department of Homeland Security, "Assessment: Rightwing Extremism: Current Economic and Political Climate Fueling Resurgence in Radicalization and Recruitment" (April 7, 2009), http://www.fas.org/irp/eprint/rightwing.pdf.

50.  Ibid., 2.

51.  This was not an entirely unprecedented move by the federal government. For example, in 2006 the Department of Justice released the "Counterterrorism White Paper," which recognized "anti-abortion extremists" as a current domestic terrorism threat. The white paper described domestic terrorism as including "acts that are dangerous to human life, violate federal or state criminal laws, and appear to be intended to intimidate or coerce a civilian population, influence government policy through intimidation or coercion, or effect the conduct of government by mass destruction, assassination or kidnapping." US Department of Justice, "Counterterrorism White Paper" (June 22, 2006), 59, http://trac.syr.edu/tracreports/terrorism/169/include/terrorism.whitepaper.pdf.

52.  See, e.g., Steven Ertelt, "Obama Admin Terrorism Dictionary Calls Pro-Life Advocates Violent, Racist," LifeNews.com (May 5, 2009), http://www.lifenews.com/2009/05/05/nat-5019/.

53.  Audrey Hudson, "Report Citing Veteran Extremism Is Pulled," *Washington Times* (May 14, 2009). This rush to pull the government's labeling abortion providers and other right-wing extremists as terrorists stands in contrast to the government's labeling environmental activism as terrorism. See Will Potter, *Green Is the New Red: An Insider's Account of a Social Movement Under Siege* (San Francisco: City Light Books, 2011), 46–52. In contrast to the violence that has been a part of anti-abortion terrorism, there has been no violence associated with environmental activism (although there have been crimes like arsons and bombings that could have resulted in violence but did not).

54.  18 U.S.C. § 2331; see also 28 C.F.R. § 0.85(l) (providing that "terrorism" includes "the unlawful use of force and violence against persons or property to intimidate or coerce a government, the civilian population, or any segment thereof, in furtherance of political or social objectives"); Jerome P. Bjelopera, Congressional Research Service, "The Domestic Terrorist Threat: Background and Issues for Congress" (January 17, 2013), http://www.fas.org/sgp/crs/terror/R42536.pdf (in the "Summary" section, defining domestic terrorists as "people who commit crimes within the homeland and draw inspiration from U.S.-based extremist ideologies and movements").

55.  Bjelopera, "The Domestic Terrorist Threat," supra note 54, at 4 (citing Federal Bureau of Investigation, "Domestic Terrorism in the Post-9/11 Era" (September 7, 2009), http://www.fbi.gov/news/stories/2009/september/domterror_090709). Additionally, Jerome P. Bjelopera has explained that the statutory definitions are "too broad to capture what the FBI specifically investigates as 'domestic terrorism'" and that the Bureau has "historically emphasized particular qualities inherent to the actors who engage in domestic terrorism," such as lacking direction from a foreign group. Bjelopera, "The Domestic Terrorist Threat," supra note 54.

56.  Alex P. Schmid, *Political Terrorism: A Research Guide to Concepts, Theories, Data Bases and Literature* (Piscataway, NJ: Transaction Publishers, 1983), 76–77, 111.

57.  Bruce Hoffman, *Inside Terrorism* (New York: Columbia University Press, 2006), 40–41. In his look at the government's efforts to target environmental activism under the guise of eradicating terrorism, journalist Will Potter discusses three common principles of scholarly definitions of terrorism, principles that are similar to Hoffman's definition: "1) Terrorism is associated with the unlawful use of violence, or threats of violence, by non-state agents. 2) Terrorism is intended to instill widespread fear in a civilian population beyond those targeted. 3) Terrorism is used to force a change in government policy." Potter, *Green Is the New Red*, supra note 53, at 36–44.

58.  In April 2004, Clayton Waagner, an anti-abortion activist convicted of sending hoax anthrax letters to clinics in the wake of the September 11 attacks, said, "It's been clearly demonstrated that I am the anti-abortion extremist, a terrorist to the abortion industry. There's no question

there that I terrorized these people any way I could." Elliot Grossman, "Prosecutors Want Life Term for Waagner," *Allentown Morning Call* (June 26, 2004).

59.   "Perhaps the failure of the anti-choice movement to contain its violent wing can be explained, in part, because confrontational, coercive, and violent tactics have reduced the availability of abortion." Marcy J. Wilder, "The Rule of Law, The Rise of Violence, and the Role of Morality: Reframing America's Abortion Debate," in *Abortion Wars: A Half Century of Struggle, 1950–2000*, ed. Rickie Solinger (Berkeley and Los Angeles: University of California Press, 1998), 84.

60.   See *Soldiers in the Army of God* at 1:15 (HBO Home Video, 2006), https://www.youtube.com/watch?v=5d1n0zDngPI; Risen and Thomas, *Wrath of Angels*, supra note 4, at 362–67; Press Release, US Department of Justice, "Federal Court in Missouri Issues First Permanent Injunction Under FACE Against Kansas City Woman" (March 22, 1995), http://www.justice.gov/opa/pr/Pre_96/March95/155.txt.html.

61.   Anthropologist Faye Ginsburg explains that "it is not altogether clear where or whether the line between violence and rescue tactics should be drawn." Faye Ginsburg, "Rescuing the Nation: Operation Rescue and the Rise of Anti-Abortion Militance," in Solinger, ed., *Abortion Wars*, supra note 59, at 233.

62.   Martha Crenshaw, *Explaining Terrorism: Causes, Processes, and Consequences* (London and New York: Routledge, 2011), 25.

63.   Ibid., 113.

64.   "Safety Valve Closed: The Removal of Nonviolent Outlets for Dissent and the Onset of Anti-Abortion Violence," *Harvard Law Review* 113 (2000): 1210–1227; Joshua C. Wilson, *The Street Politics of Abortion: Speech, Violence, and America's Culture Wars* (Stanford, CA: Stanford University Press, 2013); Celeste Michelle Condit, *Decoding Abortion Rhetoric: Communicating Social Change* (Champaign: University of Illinois Press, 1990), 151 ("In fact, the more the mass consensus accepting abortion seemed to solidify, the more frustrated and active became the minority of those who accepted the unalloyed pro-Life discourse"); Sarah Erdreich, *Generation* Roe: *Inside the Future of the Pro-Choice Movement* (Seven Stories, 2013), 46.

65.   Although roughly half of the population considers itself "pro-choice" and the other half considers itself "pro-life," specific questioning about the legality of abortion reveals more complexity, though much stability. Ever since *Roe v. Wade*, Gallup's polling shows that just over half of the population believes that abortion should be legal only under certain circumstances, just under 30% of the population believes it should be legal in all circumstances, and around 20% believes it should be illegal in all circumstances. Thus, about 80% of the population is against the abolitionist position. See Gallup, "Abortion," http://www.gallup.com/poll/1576/abortion.aspx.

66.   Crenshaw, *Explaining Terrorism*, supra note 62, at 216–19 (discussing the "high costs" of terrorism based on the enhanced government response);

Bjelopera, "The Domestic Terrorist Threat," supra note 54, at 61–62 (describing the impact of the terrorist designation on federal law enforcement efforts). For example, as Jerome P. Bjelopera has articulated, many incidents of "domestic terrorism" involve other types of criminal activity, such as a firearm or arson; and, as a result, an individual act may be prosecuted under one of those other criminal laws and not as "terrorism." As such, even known domestic terrorist suspects may not be charged as terrorists (pp. 5–6). This is further complicated by the government's use of the word "extremism" interchangeably with the word "terrorism." While this interchange has its advantages, particularly for prosecutors not wanting to publicly charge someone with "terrorism," it can produce troublesome results. As it currently stands, three individuals can commit the same act of trespassing but be separately labeled a "trespasser," "extremist," and "terrorist" (pp. 7–8). For these and many additional reasons, it is currently difficult for law enforcement agencies to accurately track all relevant cases and determine the actual scope of a potential domestic terror threat (pp. 4–11).

67. For instance, criminologists William Alex Pridemore and Joshua D. Freilich employed a complex statistical analysis and concluded that "laws protecting abortion clinics and personnel have no effect on crime." William Alex Pridemore and Joshua D. Freilich, "The Impact of State Laws Protecting Abortion Clinics and Reproductive Rights on Crimes Against Abortion Providers: Deterrence, Backlash, or Neither?" *Law and Human Behavior* 31 (2007): 611–27. They did, however, conclude that there may be other reasons for these laws, such as protecting a woman's right to choose (p. 623); see also Lori A. Brown, *Contested Spaces: Abortion Clinics, Women's Shelters and Hospitals* (Farnham, UK: Ashgate, 2013), 55–57 (discussing the complexities involved in enforcing bubble zones).

68. Esmé E. Deprez, "The Vanishing Abortion Clinic," *Business Week* (November 27, 2013).

69. Although the numbers of legislative efforts have increased recently, they are not new. See generally Dawn Johnsen, "'Trap'ing *Roe* in Indiana and a Common-Ground Alternative," *Yale Law Journal* 118 (2009): 1356–93; Melody Rose, *Safe, Legal, and Unavailable? Abortion Politics in the United States* (Washington, DC: CQ Press, 2007).

70. Jennefer A. Russo, Kristin L. Schumacher, and Mitchell D. Creinin, "Antiabortion Violence in the United States," *Contraception* 86 (2012): 562–66.

71. The Feminist Majority Foundation has already observed that increase. In the organization's 2014 study, it found that clinics are "reporting significantly higher levels of threats and targeted intimidation of doctors and staff than in prior years." Feminist Majority Foundation, "2014 National Clinic Violence Survey," 2.

**Chapter 10**

1. This count does not include Elizabeth Moll, who was profiled in Chapter 7. To this point, she has not started providing abortion care, but it is not because of protesters. Although protesters thwarted her efforts to expand her practice in her current location and intimidated a potential landlord at a different location, she ultimately decided not to look for other locations for two separate reasons: (1) her state changed its regulations of abortion clinics, and Elizabeth did not believe she could conform a clinic to those new requirements and (2) another provider moved into the area and began to provide services. It is also important to note once again that our research methodology does not involve a randomized, statistically representative sample, so the fact that only one out of eighty-seven of the providers we interviewed permanently stopped providing abortion care because of targeted harassment may not be indicative of all providers.

2. This definition of "abortion stigma" comes from the Sea Change Program, which is an organization working toward a societal shift around abortion through research and advocacy. Sea Change, "What We Do," http:// seachangeprogram.org/what-we-do/the-problem-stigma/. For more on abortion stigma, see a special issue of *Women & Health* completely devoted to the topic. *Women & Health* 54 (2014): 593–671 (featuring seven original articles about abortion stigma); see also Rebecca J. Cook and Bernard M. Dickens, "Reducing Stigma in Reproductive Health," *International Journal of Gynecology and Obstetrics* 125 (2014): 89–92.

3. 410 U.S. 113 (1973).

4. See generally Leslie J. Reagan, *When Abortion Was a Crime: Women, Medicine, and Law in the United States 1867–1973* (Berkeley and Los Angeles: University of California Press, 1997); Carole Joffe, *Doctors of Conscience: The Struggle to Provide Abortion Before and After* Roe v. Wade (Boston: Beacon Press, 1996).

5. See generally Ellen Messer and Kathryn E. May, *Back Rooms: Voices From the Illegal Abortion Era* (Buffalo, NY: Prometheus Books, 1994); *Motherless: A Legacy of Loss From Illegal Abortion* (Philadelphia: Attie & Goldwater Productions, 1992) (DVD).

6. See Willard Cates, Jr., David A. Grimes, and Kenneth F. Schulz, "The Public Health Impact of Legal Abortion: 30 Years Later," *Perspectives on Sexual and Reproductive Health* 35 (2003): 25–28.

7. See Reagan, *When Abortion Was a Crime*, supra note 3, at 218–22; *Roe v. Wade*, 410 U.S. 113 (1973); *Doe v. Bolton*, 410 U.S. 179 (1973).

8. Lori Freedman, *Willing and Unable: Doctors' Constraints in Abortion Care* (Nashville, TN: Vanderbilt University Press, 2010), 12; Cates et al., "The Public Health Impact," supra note 6. International experience, including modern-day experience, also demonstrates this fact. *See* World Health Organization, *Unsafe Abortion: Global and Regional Estimates of the Incidence of Unsafe Abortion and Associated Mortality in 2008*, 6th ed. (2011), http://whqlibdoc.who.int/publications/2011/9789241501118_eng.pdf.

# ACKNOWLEDGMENTS

⸺⸳◈⸳⸺

THE AUTHORS OF ANY book rely on the help of so many people who have been selfless and generous with their time, thoughts, and assistance. This is even more true for a book like this. First and foremost, we would like to thank the eighty-seven abortion providers that we interviewed. This book would not exist without their assistance. They went above and beyond our wildest dreams in terms of welcoming us into their world, opening up to us about some of the worst moments in their lives, and allowing us to use their experiences to try to make the world a more just place. With almost every interaction we had with the providers, they expressed heartfelt gratitude for our efforts with this book. We left those interactions so confused because *we* were the ones who were grateful—not only for how they helped with this project but also for everything they do every day as abortion providers.

There are two people who are directly responsible for this book. Jennifer Boulanger is the inspiration for this entire project. Working on her case, which both of us did, was an honor. It was from Jen's struggles that Krysten first conceived this entire project. As we conducted our research, Jen's continued support opened almost every door we knocked on. For all of the reasons in the book, providers may not have trusted us to talk about this subject if we were unknown. Because of Jen, they did; and this book is what it is because of her.

Jenifer Groves also provided excellent support from the beginning of this project. Most importantly, it was her brilliant idea to attend a national conference as a way to find interview subjects. Without Jenifer, this research would have likely resulted in a short article; because of Jenifer, we have this book.

Our colleagues at Drexel University were essential to this book in every imaginable way. Deans Roger Dennis and Daniel Filler were enthusiastic supporters of this project from the first moment we discussed it with them. Both supported our research in ways we could have never imagined. From the outset, when we realized that we had so much to learn about how to conduct this type of research, and continuing to the end of the writing process, Tabatha Abu El-Haj, Rose Corrigan, Daniel Filler, Donald Tibbs, Kevin Woodson, and Emily Zimmerman guided our way. We received overwhelming support in coordinating every aspect of the research process from Zhiying Feng, Bernadette McCloskey, and Donna Strunk. The people behind the Drexel Institutional Review Board, in particular Lois Carpenter, Danyelle Greene, and Jack Medendorp, were kind, patient, and helpful. Heather Rose, Alexis Duecker, and Suraji Wagage provided thorough and incredibly useful research and editing assistance, and Tracy Tripp gave us early insight into the world of abortion providers. Sarah Greenblatt and Alex McKechnie helped publicize our work both on and off campus. Jerry Arrison's stunning design expertise made all of our visual work pop. Everyone in the law school library was eager and gracious to assist. In particular, Sunita Balija made obtaining sources seamless and Peter Egler, Stephanie Huffnagle, and Lindsay Steussy provided great research.

Through this project, we were welcomed into the cadre of people who research abortion-related issues, qualitative empirical research, or both. In particular, Carole Joffe's work and dedication to the field is unequaled. We quickly found that the same is true of her generosity and mentorship. Eleanor Bader, whose excellent book from over a decade ago chronicled early anti-abortion violence in detail, graciously helped us conceptualize our book and offered pearls of wisdom from her similar experiences. Jessica Silbey gave us detailed advice early on when we were thinking about how to structure our research.

The world of abortion provision opened for us thanks to the incredible generosity of so many. The National Abortion Federation welcomed us at their annual meeting. Everyone at the National Abortion Federation has been incredibly helpful, particularly Rob Borger, Lisa Brown, Michelle Davidson, Sharon Levin, and Chris Quinn. Planned Parenthood Federation of America has also been immensely helpful. Lisa Stern facilitated our access to Planned Parenthood clinics for this research and has been a staunch supporter of ours since. Probably our biggest ally was Ellen Gertzog. Ellen linked us with providers with speed, ease, and good humor. She was our lifeline to the world of Planned Parenthood. Charlotte Taft of the Abortion Care Network was also helpful in connecting us with independent providers and talking with us about the landscape of abortion provision. Everyone at our local clinics, such as the Philadelphia Women's Center and the Allentown Women's Center, made us feel welcome when we visited their warm and caring facilities early in the research process to learn about the day-to-day operations of abortion clinics. Several others whom we do not want to name for fear of compromising confidentiality generously connected us with particular providers.

David comes from the world of abortion advocacy and already knew how wonderful the people within that world were, but they once again proved it with their help on this research. In particular, Sue Frietsche, Carol Tracy, Terry Fromson, Dabney Miller, Barbara DiTullio, Amal Bass, Tara Pfeifer, Tara Murtha, Tom Zemaitis, Kathy Eisenberg, and everyone else at the Women's Law Project were constant sources of advice, wisdom, and support. Susan Schewel, Judy Walker, and everyone on the board of the Women's Medical Fund helped conceptualize the research and then disseminate it to a wider audience. Bonnie Scott Jones, Jordan Goldberg, Karen Leiter, Katrina Anderson, Diana Hortsh, and Nicole Tuszynski from the Center for Reproductive Rights opened up their offices and research to us while going out of their way to connect us with providers.

Our writing process was immeasurably helped by others. Sherry Sly expertly and quickly transcribed all of the hours of interviews. The people behind Dedoose provide a brilliantly simple yet powerful online research platform that made our work easy. When it came time to share our work and receive comments about it, we were met with an overwhelming eagerness from so many people. We received invaluable feedback from several of the people already mentioned, some of the providers we interviewed, as well as Caitlin Borgmann, Liz Sepper, Steph Herold, and Jessica Mason Pieklo. Cecelia Cancellaro has been an expert resource throughout the publication process, including connecting us with the incredible people at Oxford University Press. In particular, David McBride, Sarah Rosenthal, and Suvesh Subramanian have provided enthusiastic assistance that has immensely improved the final product.

*From Krysten*: I am incredibly thankful and humbled to have been involved with this book and would like to thank the many people whose support made my efforts possible.

I would like to thank David for his enthusiasm about this project and his dedication to its success. I am constantly inspired by David's wealth of knowledge, commitment to women's rights and reproductive justice, and his kindness. I am immensely thankful for the initial opportunity to work with and learn from David when providing research assistance for Jennifer Boulanger's case, and I am grateful for all of his subsequent guidance and mentorship.

I would also like to thank my teachers—from grade school to law school. My teachers have challenged me, sharpened my critical thinking, and provided countless hours of mentorship. With the help of these incredibly selfless people, I developed the passion and curiosity that led to this project.

I am similarly grateful for the support of my friends and family and for all of their wonderful feedback and guidance. In particular, I would like to thank my mother, Debby Connon—my greatest teacher—for her unwavering love and encouragement. I am constantly inspired by my mother's patience and kindness, and it is through her support that my efforts in this book were possible.

*From David*: The idea for this book came from one sentence in an e-mail that Krysten sent me in December 2010, after she met Jennifer Boulanger for the first time. From that one sentence grew this entire book. I am so thankful for Krysten's stroke of creative genius and her willingness to share her brilliant idea with me. Working with her has been a true pleasure.

I am endlessly grateful for everything that Carol Tracy, Terry Fromson, and Sue Frietsche at the Women's Law Project have given me.

Not only would this book not have been possible without them, but my career would not be either. They taught me how to be a passionate feminist lawyer, and I will always owe my professional accomplishments to them. I am in constant awe of what they do.

I also could not have done this without the loving support of my family. My parents, Marcia and Arnold Cohen, are, respectively, a teacher and an obstetrician-gynecologist. So it is only natural that I am a professor working on advancing women's health. Their commitment to learning and healthcare for all has guided my path. My in-laws, John and Kathleen Ehrenberg, have also inspired my commitment to social justice. All four of them helped in innumerable ways by talking through this research as well as supporting the behind-the-scenes logistics that go into an endeavor like this. My siblings, Rachel Goldstein and Seth Cohen, have also been hugely supportive of everything related to this project, as have my might-as-well-be-family-member friends Matt and Brooke Salzman.

Finally, no amount of words can convey how thankful I am for everything Josh, Leo, Cassie, and Bella bring to my life. In many ways, I do what I do to make the world that Josh and Leo will grow up in a better place. In every way, Cassie has taught me what that better world is. Her unflagging commitment to women's rights and reproductive justice from an almost laughably early age has inspired me. Her support has enabled me. And her love has empowered me.

To her in particular, and to everyone else, thank you.

# PROVIDER INDEX

*For an explanation of this index, see page 13 and note 36 on page 290.*

# INDEX